Tomorrow's Global Executive

Tomorrow's Global Executive

Henry Ferguson

Dow Jones-Irwin
Homewood, Illinois 60430

© DOW JONES-IRWIN, 1988

This publication is designed to provide accurate and
authoritative information in regard to the subject matter
covered. It is sold with the understanding that the
publisher is not engaged in rendering legal, accounting, or
other professional service. If legal advice or other expert
assistance is required, the services of a competent
professional person should be sought.

*From a Declaration of Principles jointly adopted by a Committee
of the American Bar Association and a Committee of Publishers.*

This book was set in Times Roman by TC Systems.
The editors were Mary Lou Murphy and Jane Lightell.
The production manager was Irene H. Sotiroff.
The drawings were done by Benoit Design.
Arcata Graphics/Kingsport was the printer and binder.

ISBN 11-55623-057-5

Library of Congress Catalog Card No. 87–71259

Printed in the United States of America

1 2 3 4 5 6 7 8 9 0 K 5 4 3 2 1 0 9 8

For Sam
Whose surname is Sanity

Preface

This book is for tomorrow's *global* executive. In particular, it is for that person who is already in an executive or managerial position. Persons at the entry level may want to model their career development on this profile, but our focus is on the in-service executive or senior manager facing a new world of global competition.

The American who intends to remain or to become a business executive over the next 10 to 20 years will have to practice *global* management. Corporations, even small and medium-sized manufacturing and service companies, will become geocorporations—a new phenomenon that may take the place of the multinational corporation. It is entirely possible that our political leaders may try to disassemble the global marketplace by fighting trade wars and erecting protective barricades in the late 1980s. But they cannot destroy the global interdependence that modern industry, communications, information, transportation, and society have created. Interdependence is simply a fact of economic life.

Thus the American executive who is not self-consciously global may well find his or her company gradually wilting until it faces bankruptcy. If executive success is not elusive, the young person just entering a business career might well consider becoming tomorrow's global executive.

We have tried to put tomorrow's global management in a historical and cultural context, and there should be plenty of substance here for the executive seeking an understanding of the globalization of the marketplace and what it means for the American manufacturing or service corporation. Therefore, our comments on global trends and current trade policies may serve as a counter-point theme that defines the context and makes the how-to aspects of the book more practical and less abstract.

We are convinced that there is nothing firmly fixed and universal in business or in society. Thus, the advice offered to any executive should be taken from an American perspective in the later 1980s, not as universals valid everywhere or forever. If time changes the context, the reader should be prepared to adapt the advice and the structure of what is offered here. At the time these words were written, however, America was stumbling without much clear direction in a marketplace savaged by the entrepreneurship and national policies of the Japanese.

While the Japanese (Korean, Taiwanese, etc.) incursion into the American marketplace surely is a threat to American business, it is just one face of the phenomenon now known as the "globalization of markets" (Levitt, 1986). The challenge is for an American corporation to respond not by trying to keep the Asians out, but by constructing a clearly global strategy to meet the competition. Its executives should respond by developing the perspectives and the skills of tomorrow's global executive.

We call the company that adopts this strategy a global corporation. In a more restrictive sense, the term can define those companies that have already established both marketing and sourcing operations around the world and are moving rapidly toward the standardization of product and quality to achieve the lowest possible price. However, in this book global corporation means a company that has done or has started to do what we advocate.

Although unusual, we use the terms *international* and *global* interchangeably. At the same time, we believe that *international* carries an unnecessary, but historic meaning. *International* tends to imply bilateral trade and connotes trade between one nation and other nations—or trade as it has existed since the Industrial Revolution began. *Multinational* has acquired a restricted meaning from the 20-year ascendency of corporations that operate in many lands and employ management from different nations.

Global, on the other hand, implies transcending nations, nationalities, and national boundaries when conducting business. It seeks more meaning in a larger vision, and acts transnationally between many nations. The global executive is a person who recognizes the reality of global economic interdependence and senses the profound threats and implications that interdependence bears for national economies. Global vision leads to strategies that are comprehensive and not related to one or another specific market or source. We hope to convince you that global strategy is the most indispensible first step toward making the newly interdependent world work for your company.

Planning a global strategy and acquiring the attitudes and skills needed to execute it are the principal themes of this book. These themes are market-related. We are firmly committed to the old proposition that a company that is not market-oriented is already in deep trouble. Marketing, in our view, stands at the very center of the corporate purpose and is a central theme around which business revolves. This is *not* a book about marketing, but marketing perspective informs the entire text.

There are no easy answers to complex problems, especially marketing problems, for this is a world characterized more by confusion, ambiguity, and paradox than by logic and simple formulas. Even the suggested use of export growth as a foundation for globalization of the corporation (Chapter Two) is far too simple.

We have laid out the book to follow the general format of the training programs and seminars we have designed and administered for a number of trade associations. These seminars and speeches have been attended mostly by Chief Executive Officers (CEOs), Chief Financial Officers (CFOs) and the principal marketing vice presidents. The audience for this book is the same group of senior managers, with particular reference to those from medium-sized and small corporations. Some of the forms, charts, and checklists we use in seminars have been adapted for use either by the individual manager reading the book for self-improvement or by the corporate trainer preparing a program for managers.

Many of the examples and illustrations given of offshore management relate to India. That is because I have spent 25 years doing business with that country, including several years managing a binational office in New Delhi and 15 years managing the American side of binational business arrangements. From that experience, I have acquired many examples of how to conduct business in other parts of the world—and how not to. India is *not* typical of any country except India, but the illustrations could have been drawn from other lands—it just so happens that I know these illustrations from first-hand experience or from talking with colleagues. If the illustration is something I have experienced, the first person singular is used, but in the text, I take the editorial "we" for granted.

A how-to book in business management deserves all the feedback it can get. We ask the reader to provide comments, suggestions, criticisms, anecdotes, aŕld fresh information. Each reply will be acknowledged and, if the material ends up in the next edition, acknowledgment of the source will be made. We thank you in advance.

I owe much to a host of persons who have influenced my thinking about international management over several decades. Friends encouraged me to proceed and provided inspiration for many of the illustrations given in the text. Associates in the Indian publishing industry, Michiko Kaya in Japan, and John Gay in Africa reminded me of many incidents that would make my points come alive. Many others, over the years, have made great contributions to the perspectives that inform this book. More recently several trade association executives have pressed me to reconsider the impact of global interdependence on corporate management. The thoughts and expressions are mine exclusively.

Jenny M. Ahlin, my research associate, has been invaluable, not only in masterminding that enormous clipping files, but in pursuing intelligent research independent of close supervision. She has identified a number of sectors that I had overlooked. She has been an ideal associate and employee in many other respects as well. We wish her good luck on her return to her native Sweden.

My children and their spouses, a noisy but brilliant lot, kept up the pressure to get it done and out. My long-time personal, business, and intellectual associate, Joan Ferguson, continues to exercise a creative influence over everything I do or say, far beyond what she recognizes. There are times when we fight over every word, but those fights invariably make the paragraph read better. I need them. To this book she has been a sounding board, auditor, editor, and constant (but benevolent) critic. To her, thanks for that and for much, much more.

Henry Ferguson

Contents

sion. Recruitment of American Managers. Recruiting Non-American Partners, Associates, and Employees. Redundancy. Drawing in Managers: *Dangers of Offshore Employee Specialization.* Summary.

CHAPTER ONE

The Global Executive

An Introduction to Tomorrow's Global Management

Joyful for its opportunities or bleeding from its effects, American executives agree that the globalization of markets is approaching, if it hasn't already arrived. But, just as their responses are still uncertain, their idea of the global executive—the executive in the global marketplace—is still very vague. This book is aimed at tomorrow's global manager.

Our mission is to draw up an agenda to guide today's corporate executive in seeking a place in tomorrow's highly competitive, global marketplace. We want to show how to organize and staff your corporation to succeed in this new business world. Even if you are an established hitter on the team, your success will be shaped by how well you and your company are able to capitalize on the opportunities and openings the globalization of markets offers, whether you work in manufacturing or in an industry that sells tradeable services. Continuing to manage and market as if nothing has changed or to pretend you can reverse the momentum toward global interdependence is the road to ruin.

This book is about running tomorrow's global company. If you believe that you and your company have enough business in the domestic market, are independent of world markets, are unaffected by imports, and are not planning to be part of market globalization, this book is not for you.

The person who wants to be tomorrow's global executive, by exercising tomorrow's global management today, should understand some of the forces that are sweeping the world economy. First, Japanese imports are not a domestic American problem, but part of a larger picture. The Japanese success is proof positive that national boundaries no longer present impossible obstacles to the marketing ingenuity of managers. If *they* can do it here, then why can't *we* do it in other parts of the world? Even if Japan is partially closed to us right now, it won't be forever. Besides, there are plenty of other places to practice tomorrow's global management. That's what competitiveness is all about in an interdependent world.

For a couple of decades, we've heard a lot about the multinational corporation. The petro-giants and some of the larger firms in heavy industries became so gigantic—and so political—that they decentralized management and drew in both foreign capital and foreign executives. At present, the multinational corporation is either changing into a global corporation (the more restrictive definition: seeking common product in all markets at the lowest price) or is retreating into a purely national identity. The larger U.S. manufacturers are resorting to offshore sourcing for part or all of their products. Foreign corporations have invaded the U.S. market, backed by supportive government policies and restrictions on others' penetration of their home markets, but armed with determination to succeed over the long haul in the United States.

Peter Drucker in *The Wall Street Journal* (April 20, 1985) says that currency exchange rate fluctuations have become such a part of economic reality that business will simply have to learn to consider them as just one more cost item, more volatile and less predictable than other costs, but not so different. This means that a business should separate into two distinct parts; the core business that is permanently domiciled in one country, and the peripheral functions capable of being moved very fast according to differentials in major costs (labor, capital, and exchange rates). This is merely one evidence of a more general phenomenon—there are no longer businesses that can be labeled by country ("American business"). Now there are world businesses managed by nationals of one country or another.

The global executive sees these trends as offering *opportunities*. Tomorrow's global executive respects these changes, but prefers not to see them as threats. The global executive regards today's threats, problems, and challenges as learning experiences from which the individual manager and his or her corporation may capitalize in the global marketplace.

Admittedly, dozens of U.S. industries are reeling from the onslaught, caught with technology and equipment that is outdated, and wedded to marketing practices that have been shredded by the Japanese incursion. A recent high-priced study for one trade association surveyed the market for the industry's product and measured the foreign competition. It then warned somberly that the industry must act politically to stem the foreign tide or the domestic industry would be overwhelmed by the Asians. No room was made in the study for a positive, global response.

At the same time, another trade association programmed its annual convention around three themes: globalization, technological change, and (among the principal responses to these) restructuring of the industry. It doesn't take much intelligence or foresight to see which of these responses makes the most long-term sense. Historically, protection by government policies has never saved an industry from its own short-sighted management or its lack of competitiveness in the marketplace. Protection offers temporary relief at most—and, most of the time, not even that.

> One automaker, barred by quotas from importing steel for car doors, simply began to have complete car doors fabricated offshore. The supposed protection of the steel companies and steel workers resulted in a loss of jobs in *both* the auto industry and the steel industry!
>
> One steel distributor buys Brazilian and Korean steel in spite of import quotas. For him, it is not a question of cost. He buys foreign steel because he knows it is of higher quality, so he finds ways around the quota system, protection be damned.

Tomorrow's global executive should be concerned with present problems, but should look at them from a global perspective. A historical perspective should not be a vision narrowly shaped by a history in which America presented such an enormous domestic market that her own manufacturers and service industries hardly needed any other market. When we have finished the profile of the global executive, today's agenda for him or her should be more obvious.

More important, while the dust is settling on trade policies and their fairness, what can the executive (with his or her own aspirations) do to assure the future?

First, tomorrow's global executive should be pursuing a new profession in management that will bear a superficial resemblance to today's picture, but with important, advanced skills and with shifted emphasis. Second, tomorrow's global executive, whether in a service industry (with a tradeable service) or in manufacturing, should be informing today's management that survival lies in exporting. Third, the global executive should be seeking the best possible source for product, even if that means taking manufacturing or service work offshore. We might like to turn the clock back to see business locked away in convenient compartments of nationality, but the present world does not permit us that luxury. Attitudes that consider offshore sourcing or importing subversive to the national economic security are from an age that has passed. We do not presume that national identity is unreal or an unimportant part of our lives. Rather, we presume that taking advantage of the opportunities global interdependence offers us, whether by exporting or offshore sourcing, is a surer means to protect the national economy than by trying unrealistically to lock out the rest of the world.

Exporting is the one part of foreign trade over which we, the business managers of America, can have some control. Sure, there are unfair barriers to our exports overseas, a strong dollar does hurt, and there are many cultural barriers as well, but we can be much more the master of our destinies if we manage our export marketing with skill and intelligence. It is the one thing we can do right now, irrespective of how government policies shake out.

Export management, especially marketing management, offers something more to today's corporate executive and to tomorrow's global corporation. It is important beyond its obvious benefits to the U.S. economy. Its real importance to the global executive is that it suggests the management shape of the future. The professional demands of today's exporting suggest the kinds of skills and knowledge that tomorrow's global executive—the manager for the globalized marketplace—will have to possess. Developing an export presence requires many of the skills and much of the knowledge we believe tomorrow's manager will have to display. Chapter Two argues that export development is a logical, even inevitable, first corporate step toward going global.

American managers need to develop skills in managing exporting, and they need to see that export marketing is not just a happy addition to lush domestic markets. The next chapter tries to persuade the American executive that export marketing is both an immediately available key to revive American economic strength and also a program for building an executive career. The manager of the mid-80s who wants to be CEO within the next decade or two had better see exports as something more than an add-on, just as he or she should not embark on offshore manufacture or purchase of product as a panic response to Asian competition. Exports and offshore production are matters that any manager will simply have to master to get ahead, because markets are becoming more truly global.

This is a how-to manual for the executive of the next two or three decades who is determined to succeed, both for the company and for his or her professional career. Our message is positive; our purpose is to control what we can control and to do it well so we may broaden our span of control. If we can do that, then we will be assured that this country will respond creatively and positively to the global marketplace.

It is a sorry sight when business and labor plead for protection from competition. Preying on vulnerable Congressmen and Senators (especially in election years), these predators may very well succeed in protecting themselves from the healthy exercise of competition. This protection is obtained at a colossal cost to the American economy.

The Federal Reserve estimated that protective barriers cost the American consumer $14 billion in additional costs in 1985 alone. To protect a job paying about $8,000 a year in shoe manufacturing, quotas add $70,000 to the prices U.S. consumers must pay for shoes.

Most authorities acknowledge that some countries aren't playing fair, and government *should* act like an umpire and try to do something about it. But the traditional American answer to unfair competition lies not in being unfair ourselves, but in playing a better game. "They play rough," it is said. Well, we can play rough, too, while still competing fairly. Competition is the way American business acquired its awesome reputation. Global management means competing at your very best. Global management views foreign competition here as only one side of a much larger issue, a challenge to creativity and constructive activity. So, instead of pleading for protection, we wish our colleagues were pleading for removal of any U.S. restraints on export of goods. There are many federal restrictions on exports, from timber harvested on federal lands to North Slope oil, and to high-tech hardware and software that the Soviets might use against us.

We believe that resistance to globalization and the pressure for protection is the effect of fear of the unknown. It is the fear of working in areas where people don't run businesses as we do, or speak in other languages, or have different political attitudes, or eat odd foods. This fear keeps many 100 percent American businesspersons from entering global competition. Add a dash of chauvinism to justify such fear, and the attitude breeds protectionism.

What are the alternatives to protection? One of the most worrisome alternatives is the Ostrich Syndrome. At its best, the ostrich business sees only what it wants to—mostly a golden age in the past when workers did what the boss told them to do and when Americans bought any product that had an innovative character and inherent quality. A business any bigger than the corner dry cleaner can only hurt itself by denying the new reality of an interdependent economy. Yet this is the most popular alternative to becoming global: default. Do nothing. Pretend. And hope.

The more positive response lies in learning a lot more about how our new, interdependent world works and how to sell our products in the new global marketplace. Instead of crying out for protection by government, here's a simple plan for finding strength within ourselves: *go global.* This we may do in a coherent, methodical fashion while asking government for legitimate support.

Theodore Levitt believes that the globalized marketplace has arrived (Levitt, 1986). The global executive should consider the validity of the Levitt thesis in the offshore markets he or she must face. We have some reservations about it. Global economic interdependence is clearly a fact of life; the separate national and regional economies are becoming more inextricably intertwined in resources, markets, and fiscal policies. The full globalization of markets has still not been fully realized. Globalization of markets is a process clearly under way in *some* product lines and *some* market segments. Anecdotal evidence has demonstrated the reality of global market homogenization. Some dispute this view. John M. Culbertson sees globalization as just one more fad among economists (in the *Harvard Business Review* [which Levitt himself edits]

v. 64, 5, September–October 1986). We think that Culbertson argues an outdated economic nationalism, but it is risky to assume that globalization has already occurred and that there is a single global marketplace—that seems to be rushing reality.

At the present time there are still distinct and, in some cases, monumental differences between markets. Our argument is that those differences are principally cultural in nature, arising from the historical development of the values, beliefs, and attitudes of each particular culture. Cultures in most major geographic regions share a kinship of values, and most market regions have a number of strong similarities despite religious, economic, and political disparities. Europe approaches being a single market, though clear differences are apparent between Northern, Southern, and Eastern European areas in terms of market and culture. Levitt's thesis on globalization of markets works best when you look at Europe and perhaps lump Japan in with it. It does not work so well when you try to include the Third World countries as well.

The globalization of markets means simply that there is no market that is not interdependent on other markets. It implies that, as time goes on, national markets will become more homogeneous and merge with regional and global markets in which quality and price will drive the marketplace.

The other side of globalization is offshore sourcing and captive manufacture. No company is free of dependence on other markets—even if it doesn't export anything. To seize a small slice of the new global marketplace, a company has to have the vision of increasing globalization of markets and increasing interdependence of nations and economies. This kind of guiding vision will form the earlier stages of the export marketing development process. It will make it possible to see domestic export sales, indirect export sales, offshore distributorships, joint ventures, and offshore partnerships in a growth perspective (see Chapter Two). That perspective, in turn, feeds back into the corporate culture and makes it more global in its outlook.

Not every executive or business is a potential exporter, but almost everyone has a stake in building exports, such as the stockholder in the corporation, the banker, the civil servant, or the small businessman or woman whose trade depends on regional and national economic strength. Some service industries neglect exports because they haven't had offshore experience. It hasn't occurred to them that their services are exportable. Architecture, engineering, consulting, insurance, and information industries could join banking and transportation as major exporters of tradeable services.

There's an even greater benefit, if we look at the long haul. If we undertake export of goods and services as a *learning experience* (and see each stage of it as a separate lesson), we will begin to comprehend our opportunities in the globalized marketplace. In our view, it is a wiser policy to acquire offshore experience from the management of exports than from producing goods offshore. The rationale for offshore sourcing tends to be largely negative and reactive to world forces, while exporting is positive and proactive and largely within our control. Mind-set among executives goes a long way toward achieving corporate goals.

If the United States uses globalization for its own purposes, the American executive is going to have to be conversant with exports. It works vice versa, too. For the career of the 80s and 90s to succeed, it will have to have a global marketing dimension. For the American in the late 1980s, that means a learning experience in exports and particularly in export marketing *management*. Note that in the last sentence the word management was emphasized, not marketing. The two activities do belong together as *marketing management*.

This message is not just for executives of manufacturing firms already exporting or for managers in the multinationals. It applies to small firms, middle-sized firms, and large firms. It applies to service firms that sell tradeable services, such as hotel rooms, insurance policies, and real estate, as well as banking and transportation. Let's all nail this message to the office, washroom, or coffee-room wall where it can be seen by every manager who aspires to corporate or individual success in an age of globalization.

THE FOUR BASIC TRUTHS OF GLOBAL BUSINESS

Management is the necessary framework to successful global business, especially marketing management. Yet this seems to be the weakest suit of the medium-sized and small business in America. Let's examine some truths about global marketing.

As a way of emphasizing the importance of a new approach

to management and at the risk of seeming too cute, we offer *Theory Q.*

Theory Q sees management as a cultural phenomenon which is therefore responsive to changes in the cultural surroundings in which business is conducted. To manage in a globalized market-place, therefore, requires (1) that the culture of the company's origin be understood, (2) that the corporate culture of the company be understood, and (3) that the corporate culture be manipulated and altered to fit changed or different cultural contexts in which the company must operate, without yielding ground on the company's basic mission.

Let's put this in more vivid form. The form we use here is borrowed from the Four Noble Truths of the Buddha. Categories like this can help get a point across, and the Buddha said something that is a rare universal truth about a globalized marketplace. His idea was that the only feature of life that is unchanging is change itself. The only permanent face of reality is impermanence. In a book that purports to give how-tos for upwardly mobile executives and managers, eternal change and impermanence may seem to be a paradox. Tomorrow's global executive will, if anything, have to be able to live and work with paradox and ambiguity. Borrowing a style from the Buddha reminds the reader that a globalized market-place is a changing, paradoxical, confusing, and ambiguous arena in which to operate. But how much more challenging and fun!

Here are the Four Truths of Global Marketing on which general global business success will be founded:

The First Truth—global marketing means exporting the company's marketing management, not just its products.
The Second Truth—exporting the company's marketing management requires that executives understand their own corporate culture.
The Third Truth—knowing the corporate culture means knowing the company's mission and how to maintain it by rites
and rituals, hierarchies and titles, heroes and heroines.
The Fourth Truth—the corporate culture (including marketing
management) must be manipulated and adapted to fit into
cultures overseas where it doesn't fit naturally, without fundamentally compromising the company's integrity (accomplished by following the *Eightfold Path to Global Success*).

Responding to Globalization

The Eightfold Path forms eight chapters of this book. To support the Eight Rights of that path, we should explore each of the Four Truths.

A word of warning: while we survey exporting and export marketing, keep in mind that our long-term goal is to understand and respond aggressively to globalization. The one worry we have about what has been written about globalization of markets (Levitt, 1986) is that the American executive will run off half-cocked into foreign markets without the necessary changes in his or her management practices. That, global market homogeneity notwithstanding, would be folly.

Export Marketing Management

The First Truth for the global executive of tomorrow, then, is that a commitment to export marketing development means more than selling overseas. It means establishing a solid and thorough corporate commitment to offshore marketing and recognizing that export marketing is more than the selling of a product or products overseas. The export of the company's own existing marketing management must be directed consciously—and conscientiously—toward exploiting opportunities in a globalized marketplace.

The Corporate Culture

The Second Truth is that corporate executives have to know the company from top to bottom especially when an operation as crucial as marketing is going to be exported. After all the shouting about strategic planning in recent years (and more recently about corporate culture) few executives take the time to find out what the company really is and how it really operates (Deal and Kennedy, 1982; Davis, 1985).

The corporate culture literature implies that we should recast strategic planning as *strategic history*. How little care we take of corporate history! The current company mission and its direction in the marketplace are the products of historical developments, many reaching back to the company's origins or the families that nursed it in its early days. Even more recent and rapidly accelerating shifts of direction are historical, for after all they have already happened. Giving little heed to how the company got to where it is is like driving drunk.

The person who fails to learn the lessons of history is doomed to repeat them, and the executive who fails to see a new marketing departure in the light of corporate history is likely to misapply the corporate culture and do serious damage to the company. The executive who is a student of history must also remember that historical perspective itself changes as the company of the present changes. Don't wed yourself to today's view of the corporate history, for even the view must change.

The Corporate Mission

The Third Truth is that for the new global executives to know their corporate culture a program is required that is much like strategic planning. They must look backward into history as well as forward to goals, objectives, and strategies. The global executives must understand more than the corporate mission statement—they must understand the fragile web that is the corporation, its networks, its communications, its values, and the attitudes its managers and employees share toward the rest of the world. They will need to know its rites and rituals, its heroes and villains, who eats with whom, who parks where—the very stuff of everyday life that makes the company tick. And, of course, the company's accumulated export or trade history is also part of the corporate culture.

This stuff can be found first in looking at the company's real history (generally not found in the slick book published for the centennial or the silver anniversary). Then move to what the company says about itself in its current mission statement. How did that mission statement evolve? How does headquarters speak of the corporate mission? Go further: look at how the receptionist greets people, how employees spend their time, how advancements are accomplished, how long people stay in their jobs, what people talk about in meetings, what jokes, stories, and anecdotes they tell about themselves and their company.

Understanding corporate culture also means understanding how the corporation, meaning its board of directors, chief executive officer, and senior executive staff, regard the company *in its present historical context*. If the leadership sees the company backed up against the wall by Asian competition with its salvation either an act of God or Congress, it is reflecting a vision of its own corporate culture which is seriously ill. If it sees its company as adrift in a lifeboat with others in the American industry, at least it recognizes some of the true dimensions of global interdependence. If it sees itself as seizing the rapid globalization of economies and recognizes that globalization will give it fresh life and renewal, then it has a good chance of realizing a global marketing role. The global executive who is concerned about career success should seriously seek to identify how the company sees its own culture within the current historical and cultural context.

The New Global Mission

Once management knows its own corporate culture, it should evolve a new corporate mission statement. If the company is planning to go global, to build up export marketing, then the new corporate mission statement must be one that will apply not only in the United States, but wherever the company does business. To do this implies a kind of high-wire act for which few American executives are prepared. The balance between the company's historic roots and achievements and the need to mold, adapt, and manipulate the corporate mission to fit into other environments and contexts demands a great deal of the company and its management. Yet global interdependence forces that challenge upon us.

The corporate mission should rise above the concept of the multinational. The multinational is a company that is structured to do business in a world made up of different and often competing markets and producing sources, managed by nationals drawn from the countries in which the company operates. Its corporate national origins are indicated by the location of its headquarters and its chief financial support. Peter Drucker and Ted Levitt argue that the multinational is dead (Drucker, 1986; Levitt, 1986).

A new corporate mission statement will almost certainly say something new about the company, if not in the mission statement itself, at least in the company literature that elaborates on or explains the mission statement. And, most importantly, it should be saying something new about itself and its global role in its orders to today's export marketing managers and for the global executive.

Marketing management is very close to the heart of the corporate culture. We have a theory that if marketing management is not at the core of the corporate culture, the company is already in the last stages of bureaucratic decay and there is little hope of redemption. On the other hand, if the corporate culture is not embodied or embedded in the marketing management already, then something else is seriously wrong with the corporation's communication system. Marketing management *must* express the corporate culture or it won't be able to market in any real sense of the term.

Adapting Corporate Culture to Global Interdependence

This leads to the final Truth: when a company exports its corporate culture—management, marketing management, fulfillment management, distribution, credit, and collections—the countries where it lands have their own context. Although it is essential for corporate leadership to understand corporate culture within the cultural environment in which it was created and prospered, leadership must also recognize that new markets demand adaptation of the corporate culture. Bring a corporate culture, raw and brashly American, into a new market that (1) doesn't expect it, (2) doesn't care whether it succeeds or fails, or (3) wants it to go away and be left alone and it will not have much chance of survival unless this culture can be manipulated to settle into the host culture. This is the greatest challenge to global management—set the corporate culture down into other cultural contexts and *make it work.*

One reaction to globalization may see the developing homogenization of markets as the same as Americanizing global markets. That is not what is meant, and the time-frame is inaccurate.

Globalization is a process that has been going on throughout the 20th century, but has accelerated in recent years. There probably never will be total global homogenization, but the principal market thrusts will certainly be global. This has not already happened in all industries and in all parts of the world. Globalized markets are not identical with the domestic American market that has dominated U.S. corporate life up until now. Marketing is spelled with a capital M in U.S. business textbooks, but marketing offers different faces in other parts of the world. The American executive who thinks all that is necessary is the expansion of American marketing to other world markets fails to recognize the differences among markets, nations, cultures, and peoples.

One of the more surprising experiences for many U.S. business-persons, especially in the developing countries, is to be told: "We don't need you." Maybe they do—maybe they don't, but the fact that the statement is made should be a warning that not all nations are happy to see us come.

> Take the case of my friend, Jim, who managed a major U.S. farm equipment manufacturer's operations in India. India totally frustrated Jim. He knew that it critically needed his equipment for its economic development, but India didn't want American equipment on just any terms—especially not American terms. In effect, India said: "Jim, we need your product, but we need it only on our own terms, even if that takes us much longer." Jim, frustrated and angry, found it diffi-cult to tell headquarters what the problem was, and the company felt resentful at realizing such modest short-term profits from so much effort.

David Ricks gives many amusing examples of American corpo-rate blunders abroad. Many come from failure to recognize the adaptation demanded of marketing when moving into a new cul-tural environment (Ricks, 1983).

> Otis Elevator has taken an unusual approach in China. It has entered into a 30-year joint venture agreement with a factory in Tienjin, but the agreement is not much more than a marriage contract. Otis oper-ated so long in the old China that it knew how to use the China connection to its greatest advantage: make a bond and stick to it over a long term. In fact, it adapted its corporate culture to the Chinese environment. Otis understood that it had to manipulate its own corpo-rate culture to operate in the culture of the People's Republic of China in the first instance by a rare sense of corporate patience. (Though I learned this from talking with an Otis executive, see Pye, 1986; Hen-dryx, 1986).

The corporate culture has to be fine-tuned not only to Ameri-can demands, but to the surprising perspectives and unexpected dimensions of life overseas—even if the goal sought is a global marketplace characterized by profound homogenization and driven largely by price and quality.

THE EIGHTFOLD PATH TO GLOBAL SUCCESS

Conforming the corporate culture to the environments in which marketing has to take place is the real challenge. It cannot happen and be ultimately successful unless there is a firm and long-term commitment on the part of the board and the senior executive staff.

It also won't happen unless some very special management changes take place within the entire operation, specifically in the export marketing operation. Let's call those changes the Eightfold Path which is composed of Eight Rights. Those Rights are:

Right Planning
Right Involving
Right Operating
Right Timing
Right Communicating
Right Researching
Right Networking
Right Negotiating

Note that they are all expressed in the present continuous tense to show that they are ongoing and must be on the agenda at all times.

Right Planning makes global marketing an integral part of the whole corporate strategic plan, leading to a self-consciously global market presence.

Right Involving embraces all employees, especially U.S. staff, into the global marketing operation so it becomes important to everyone, and no one ever forgets it.

Right Operating makes the global strategy and the global involvement of employees operational—especially the work of offshore employees who must deliver product on time, on appropriate terms, and at the right price while maintaining open communications with offshore staff and distributors.

Right Timing commits the firm for the long haul and doesn't expect quick results. It makes a safe estimate and then doubles it or triples it, not just for ultimate globalization, but for each offshore market targetted.

Right Communicating puts effective communicating close to the top of global management priorities. If the executive doesn't know the language, he or she learns it; if she or he can't do that, then interpreters are hired and trained in advance.

Right Researching solicits input from the target countries—even if the executive has to go get it in person—and tests the "loyalties" of those who provide the input. The executive questions all research he or she has commissioned abroad to a much greater extent than domestic research, whether it relates to production or marketing. Tomorrow's global executive learns that politics and social priorities in different countries will affect operations in different and often surprising ways, and while seeking some general rules for managing these differences will always act in the appropriate political and social context.

Right Networking takes special pains to find out how decision-makers are identified in the target market, then goes on to identify the *real* decision-makers there, not just the person who looks important. Having identified the decision-makers, the manager consciously builds their network and his or her own network into a new, global network.

Right Negotiating assures that negotiations offshore lead to long-term, profitable relationships and won't become the company's Achilles Heel in global operations.

SUMMARY

Tomorrow's global executive starts out by seeing America's present economic circumstances as part of a worldwide phenomenon, a step that helps to frame a world view that will be suitable to the global marketplace. The global executive then systematically acquires the skills and knowledge necessary to manage in a global marketplace, using export marketing management as a learning process. Export marketing management demands that the marketing manager possess most of the skills outlined for the global executive. Experience is the best teacher, so marketing management is not a bad place to start.

The global executive will be a global planner, manager of people, communicator, researcher, networker and negotiator.

CHAPTER TWO

Entry Strategies

The Four Truths and the Eightfold Path are not a substitute for effective lobbying for fairer trade with the U.S. government in Washington and foreign governments in their capitals. Government policies, statutes, and regulations do make a big difference, but they are not always amenable to change, and rarely subject to control. Likewise, they are not a substitute for technological and production modernization. Reformed corporate management and updated technologies and production facilities go hand-in-hand with enlightened national policies and up-to-date operations.

The best response to the onslaught of foreign competition among American corporations is to seek foreign markets through systematic exploitation of the learning opportunities and sales openings available to them. Manufacturing and service companies must become exporters or expand their existing export operations while continuing to work for freer and fairer trade. The long-range goal is to build up their own capacity for effective operations in a globalized market.

The global executive must focus on using exports for expansion into global markets, in order to globalize the corporation and acquire important personal and professional experience.

We emphasize export development over offshore sourcing because we believe that the executive's perspective influences how well he or she produces. If an executive is reactive, responds to every pressure, and seeks short-term solutions to immediate problems, we believe this executive has a limited perspective. The rush to open factories in Asia in order to acquire cheap labor reflects a current conviction that America isn't "competitive." Through technology and both improved production and improved management, we can compete with any nation in most (but obviously not all) product lines. That's what we advocate in developing exports. To do this, the global executive needs a long-range perspective and must be motivated positively toward a constructive, proactive response. Because attitude is so important, we emphasize the proactive over the reactive, the constructive long-term development of exports over the somewhat negative, short-term recourse to offshore production or sourcing.

Export marketing in the 1980s should mean something very special to the American company: the most positive opening into a new era of global marketing. An effective global entrance requires the *systematic* development, over a number of years, of a significant market position in one or more other countries. "Special" implies a complete home-office commitment and it means a major, long-term, enthusiastic global commitment. If the company views exporting as the export of its marketing management and not just the sales of a product or products, this special quality will come to life. That perspective implies a reform of management practices and probably a restructuring of the corporation. That's a lot more than filling orders from Lagos or Bombay or Edinburgh.

Remember, the ultimate goal is to globalize the company in order to capitalize on the global marketplace. That cannot be done unless the marketing management is exportable. So a fresh mindset is needed to see exports as more than product sales, but as a new framework for the company as a whole. It starts with a special commitment to go global. The special commitment will put export marketing into the perspective needed for it to succeed as an essential part of the entire corporate strategy.

EXPORTING: A STEP TOWARD GEOCOMPETITION

Exporting American goods into offshore markets, no matter how small the scale, offers the global executive important insights into what will be required of managers in the future. Even if your job has nothing to do with exports, it might pay to be familiar with some of the most basic details. These basics are offered as part of the learning experience.

A second purpose, however, is to provide a context in which we may dissect the challenge of *global strategic planning*. Export marketing management demands a clearcut strategic plan with sufficient corporate patience built into it to allow waiting for the results that are several years away.

Isn't it curious that there are at least 18,000 companies in the United States that *could* export, but don't? These figures from the U.S. Department of Commerce are startling enough, but become even more unsettling when stacked against the fact that 28 percent of all the U.S. exports in 1983 were made by only 50 exporters. A more general figure on imports and exports from the early 80s is that only 250 corporations conduct 80 percent of U.S. foreign trade.

And we wonder why the Japanese are nipping at our heels? Add a third purpose to this chapter: to stir some executives to seriously consider exports as an expression of their determination to keep U.S. industry alive and well in a globalized marketplace. It is too easy to ask for a display of American economic patriotism. Economic nationalism is a perspective that hides realities from corporate leaders in today's global market. But that doesn't mean that we can't put some life back into U.S. industry in foreign trade of goods and services.

Most U.S. companies that consider exporting will retreat before seemingly formidable obstacles. Lack of knowledge is the first, and most serious, problem. Fear of uncertainty is the second. The first can be cured by training and information, the second will remain but may be reduced. What fazes the intrepid American business? Business practices abroad, U.S. and foreign documentation, shipping requirements and regulations, export financing, offshore credit information. These obstacles can stifle all but the most determined executives. (See Czinkota, 1982, for a fuller analysis.)

First, exporting a product is relatively easy, as my own experience demonstrates.

How I remember our first export! The order arrived in the morning mail, that pleasure-pain time of day when the small entrepreneur prays that the orders and checks will outnumber the bills. It came from Australia. Unsolicited, we hadn't the faintest notion of how people in Perth had heard about our little firm and its oddball products.

We delighted in filling that order, even the complex task of making out the customs documents. But what we did about it in a marketing sense is pretty typical of the small business: we put the Australian customer on our mailing list. Then, each time we cranked out a mailing piece, we threw the Australian address aside because it couldn't go bulk mail, surface mail would delay its delivery until our product was out-of-date (we were in publishing where the product has about the same shelf life as fresh fish), and it would cost $1.76 or so to Perth by air. So we never kept in touch. We never made another sale.

Later, when the domestic market softened underneath us, how we could have used those Australian and Canadian and African orders we had taken so for granted and had never pursued with any marketing skill! For all intents and purposes, we had treated those orders like domestic orders, with little regard for the global opportunities that even a small firm could realize.

Therein lies an important truth: export sales help ease the downside of the domestic business cycle. Any executive who has lived through a recession or two (or three) will allow that any moderation of the American cycle is beneficial. Because international cycles either precede or (more likely) follow U.S. cycles, this is very important insurance. Whether this will continue to be true as the marketplace becomes more thoroughly globalized is open to question, but that will take years to mature. For that reason, it is reasonable to expect present differentials to continue at least for the foreseeable future.

We will expand this later when we discuss Right Planning, for the same principle applies to offshore sourcing for the manufacturer. Flexibility allows elbow room during downturns in the business cycle.

Another point needs to be made here. Exports have historically tended to yield higher operating profits than domestic sales. This fact is the result of a large number of interactive factors, but the truth has been proven again and again. Exports spread up-front cost (R&D, pre-production costs, etc.) over a larger number of sales and over a vastly larger market, which makes them attractive. It shouldn't escape notice that mark-ups are much less dependent on domestic competition and other local factors, so margins generally tend to be more favorable.

In short, exports should be at the top of the marketing priorities of any foresighted corporation, especially one that sees the trend toward globalization presenting threats to its survival. We will show here that, although vastly different from domestic marketing, export marketing *can* be known and it can be mastered—for exceptional profit opportunities. This may not be a book about marketing, but marketing must be central to any managerial process.

Justification for exporting products is, therefore, relatively easy to argue. Exporting products is a step in the right direction on the road to globalization of markets, but it must be supplemented by both a restructuring of the company and a revision of its perspective of its own marketing management.

What follows in this chapter relates to the export of products. The export of services follows different routes for each specific field, but the same principle of the learning process applies to service exports. Here we relate using the export of products as a way of learning how to export marketing management with the long-range goal of becoming global. To become global you must learn everything there is to know about the various stages of export involvement and turn that learning into a coherent commitment to a global strategy. Marketing management will be the principal export in that strategy and, through its export, product will follow. Export of marketing *management* is a feature of globalization, just as offshore production or sourcing is a feature. For the global executive, it is the most immediately important feature.

For today's export marketing manager and for the corporate executives in the global marketplace, the great advantage to any of the export channels outlined later—domestic, indirect, or outside distribution arrangements—is that they represent a very serious level in the learning process. Both the corporation as a whole and the managers who steer it can gain valuable experience in exporting, especially in the tedious details and paperwork aspects, if they start with one of these options. Experience, as always, is the best teacher, and is especially worthwhile when the risks are kept under control.

This is an important lesson (see Figure 2-1). Any serious analysis of the phenomenal success of the Japanese in penetrating American markets will reveal that the Japanese introduced their products through *American* distributors in almost every instance (see Kotler, 1985). Our image of major Japanese firms crashing in our doors full-blown in their present mature form is not historically accurate. They initially retained American distributors and used them as a way of learning about the American marketing environment. Once the Japanese exporter was certain of how business was done here, especially marketing, the tie with the American distrib-

FIGURE 2–1
Entry Strategies toward Global Markets

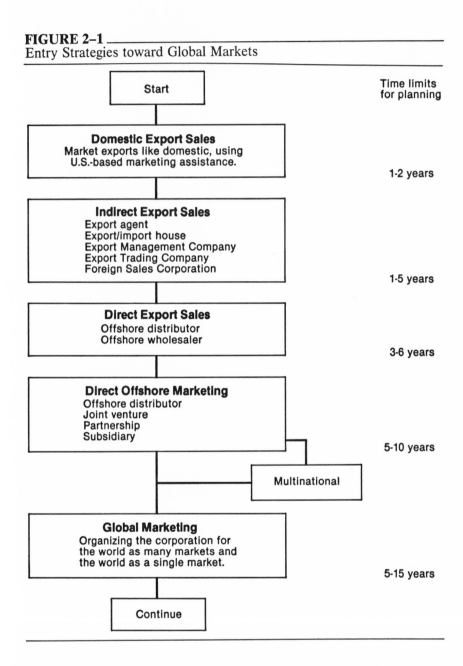

utor was broken and the Japanese established their own wholly-owned U.S. subsidiaries. There are many distributors who learned that the Japanese were not to be their friendly allies forever.

A major question for the global executive is: if the Japanese could do it in the United States, why can't we do it elsewhere? More important, what can we lose trying?

With that thought, let's turn to some learning opportunities in export management by reviewing the main export entry strategies and their follow-up toward a global plan.

Domestic Export Sales

Sadly, most small businesses that engage in export selling treat their export markets as if they were domestic ones. They see global markets as homogeneous, approachable by the same time-honored marketing ideas taught in college and business school for the last 50 years.

There is justification for this attitude. Our own experience is a case in point: our first export sales resembled domestic sales in virtually every respect except the destination on the shipment. These are called "domestic export sales" because the marketing that yielded these sales was identical to the marketing of goods and services in the domestic market, and the nature of the sales transaction is almost identical with a domestic sale.

There are commission agents in the United States who are given buying orders by foreign governments and corporations. They look for the lowest possible price and are given a commission by their foreign clients. There are also some governmental or quasi-governmental agents who execute orders on behalf of their governments, including orders for goods that are not for government use but for resale in the home country. Add to these the U.S. agencies that buy for offshore delivery to governmental clients and the direct but domestic export market is substantial—and relatively easy to spot.

So far, so good. It's a good place to start. But if you want your global sales to grow into a central part of the business, you cannot linger here. Yet, in our consulting experience, the greatest hurdle for an American business to clear is to transform "domestic export sales" into true export or even global marketing. There are a number of clear steps progressing from domestic export sales to global marketing.

It is, after all, easiest just to fill those over-the-transom orders that come in from outside the United States. All of a sudden, you're an exporter!

Most businesspersons know that over-the-transom order-filling is *not* marketing. So their minds are already searching for the next best thing. "Domestic Export Sales," to speak a bit more positively, shows that marketing managers do seek opportunities with the United States to sell to overseas customers. They scan the Department of Commerce's export opportunities listings, they contact commercial counsellors at foreign embassies, they look at the bids published in U.S. trade journals, they look at World Bank and U.S. AID requests for proposals or bids, and they may even go to trade shows abroad. In short, they do their offshore marketing in much the same way and in much the same places as they usually perform their domestic marketing operations.

There is absolutely nothing wrong with this. But the attitude that regards this as export marketing tends to limit the executive's perspective of both the company's export potential and the extent of global markets. We need a new view of both the company and the world.

Knowing that domestic export sales are better than waiting for the phone to ring, managers also understand that they can see only a small fraction of the market, one that is both highly restricted by its information sources and highly competitive because everyone else can see the same opportunities.

Domestic export sales, however, have a real place even in the global marketplace: they are a lesson on the learning curve of global marketing.

Indirect Export Sales

One must discover some step toward a more aggressive posture in exporting. The next logical step from seeking exports through a domestic sales plan is to explore indirect export sales. This means that the company exports through someone else. Indirect exports may be made through an American export/import agent, a combination export management firm, or an export trading corporation that will handle the product. Like domestic export sales, indirect export sales are positive, but only if they are seen as a step in the learning process or a stage in a strategy to convert the company into a global marketing firm.

The export broker will not serve a permanent role or as a company's export department, and often export brokers overlap with the commission agents mentioned earlier. But a firm may be lucky enough to find a broker whose business allows for continuing relationships. The export agent generally rewards the manufacturer by handling the frustratingly complex details of shipping and insuring, and sometimes pays on domestic terms, relieving the producing company of having to go to the banks for financing. But the agent is weak in *marketing* in the full sense of the term. In short, the broker offers an excellent service, especially to small companies, but with serious limitations on continuity and on marketing.

> One of our favorite images is of an Armenian friend, John, who knows everyone who is anyone in the Middle East. John can sell almost any product in the Arab world because he has cousins living all over West Asia and each one knows how to sell the Middle Eastern buyer. But don't look to John for marketing: it's not within his grasp. Because he can sense an immediate need, he can sell, but because he lacks staying power, he cannot market.

An export management company is a different creature. The export management company effectively serves as the company's export department. It specializes in certain fields or regions, but represents noncompetitive products. Usually, it has its own marketing function overseas. Here, the company may take title to the goods and pay on domestic terms. Because the typical export management company has clear-cut access to particular locations or has distributors who handle product lines in certain territories, it can be of immense help to the small exporter.

With an export/import house, the manufacturer leaves the export and physical distribution of the product up to the house, but still has to control and manage the market. In an export management company, much of the marketing function is assumed by the export management company. The manufacturer supplies only basic marketing expertise with respect to the product and has no responsibility for market research, positioning, segmentation and other strategic marketing elements. These companies can sometimes supply spare parts and technical assistance to customers.

An export management company ordinarily will specialize in a particular industry, for instance, abrasive products of all kinds, or insulating products of all kinds. Here, the channels of distribution are sufficiently clear that a distributor abroad does the marketing, relying on close and enduring contacts with the management company to assure ready supply of product, spare parts, and technical assistance. But the distributor is in this instance more clearly a marketing representative.

The U.S. Department of Commerce makes a pamphlet available, *The EMC—Your Export Department*, and also publishes a directory of over 1,000 EMCs, *U.S. Export Management Companies Directory*. For solid information, contact your district office of the Department of Commerce, International Trade Administration, for the name of the trade specialist assigned to your region. The Department is enormously helpful—especially to small and beginning exporters, and the trade specialists are at your service.

The management company has years of experience, and experience is an important source of learning. The client corporation can learn by skillful tapping of the management company's offshore experience. What is learned can then enable the producing corporation to break free of the export management company and fly on its own. Most management companies recognize that this is going to happen, and they know that they must generate new client corporations to stay in business.

Export management companies relieve some of the strain of exporting. They assume full or qualified responsibility for marketing and promotion, take full charge of the physical handling of the goods, provide limited market research and relevant information on foreign financial, patent, and licensing arrangements. They live off commissions, generally. There are great advantages to using an EMC: only a minimal investment is required to open foreign markets, and company employees do not have to be assigned to the offshore operation (Cateora, 1985 is good on this point).

The first of these advantages is also a disadvantage, for the EMC cannot be expected to make a serious capital investment on the manufacturer's behalf, and a serious financial commitment may be needed to make the product really roll overseas. The second of these advantages looms as a potentially serious disadvantage. *Not* involving employees in the global mission implies that the company has not made the kind of global commitment we believe is necessary for it to succeed in the face of foreign competition. Without that involvement, the plan may not work.

A new confusion has been added to the picture. Export Trading Companies (ETCs) are a recent invention of the U.S. government to help stimulate exports, but the term is one that has been in general use elsewhere, especially with respect to Japanese companies. The generic export trading company may be a European or Japanese company with offices in the United States. Generally the generic company buys and takes title to goods for resale in international markets. It has highly elaborate and often very old distribution networks in other parts of the world. It is largely through Japanese ETCs that U.S. companies have been able to break into the difficult Japanese market at all. A disadvantage is that they may concentrate their efforts for particular suppliers rather than for all suppliers.

There are advantages to the ETCs authorized by recent U.S. statute. First, some major U.S. companies, including money-center banks, have formed ETCs, giving substantial presence to the ETCs. Second, competing U.S. companies can join together in an ETC without liability under the anti-trust laws, if authorized by the Department of Commerce. The authorization process has been awkward, restricting participation, but recent improvements in procedure may help. And ETCs have not yet fulfilled their potential.

To work with an export trading company is, in effect, to turn over the company's exports to a special corporation established specifically for export trading. If that company is well established abroad—such as the ETCs established by General Electric or Sears or one of the money-center banks—there are distinct advantages. The drawback is that the other company really may not understand the particular manufacturer's product line or its particular market segment. And it may put its own product lines in a higher priority position, either deliberately or inadvertently. Now we have to face the shakiness of the existing ETCs, as demonstrated by Sears' dismantling of its ETC in late 1986.

Direct Export Sales: Offshore Distribution

There is a more aggressive approach than these domestic ones: an American marketing manager seeks an offshore distributing channel. Once again, this *must* be regarded not as a final goal, but as one more step in the learning process, one more stage of the movement toward globalization of marketing.

Further, offshore distribution more directly and deeply involves the producer's marketing management in offshore marketing. Here, we begin to see the need to export the *management* of marketing if the sale of goods is to take place at a volume and price deemed necessary. To manage relations with an offshore distributor calls for many of the skills and attitudes advocated for tomorrow's global executive, outlined later in detail. The marketing manager must manage relations with a distributor of another nationality with other loyalties, and often with limited facility in American business English and American business practices. The export marketing manager must conduct and assess research of a foreign market, using research of unknown reliability, and he or she must go out there alone to explore the potentials. The export marketing manager must be able to recommend a schedule for building distribution in that market, must identify and use local networks for marketing purposes, and must be able to communicate effectively and negotiate satisfactory terms with distributor, financial sources, and others. Complex? You bet! That's why we emphasize the export of marketing management above the export of product.

There are several forms of offshore distribution. At base level, there is the sales representative or agent, much like the familiar manufacturer's representative in the United States, working on a commission basis for a term.

> The Harris Corporation has had remarkable success with its sales representatives. These reps felt that the company's short-wave radios were among the highest quality available around the world. Harris also paid very generous commissions, said to be considerably higher than those paid by any other competitor, and put substantial resources into a marketing effort to back up these sales representatives. Certainly these factors account for some of their success. (For an analysis of this example, see Keegan, 1984.)

The most common form of offshore distribution, however, is the licensee or the distributor who handles the company's products within a given offshore market, usually a distributor with experience in that product line or a closely allied group of products. Two other, less common forms are worth noting. One is the FSC— Foreign Sales Corporation. FSCs were established several years ago to provide tax incentives to replace the faltering Domestic International Sales Corporations (DISCs) which were under heavy political pressure from the GATT countries and even domestically. FSCs are subsidiaries of U.S. parent corporations incorporated outside the United States, but only in certain specified countries. An exporter would be able to avoid U.S. income tax on a portion of the earnings from such exports. Like many gimmicky Federal tax-related incentives, the FSCs have not been generally successful, and have tended to appeal to older, established industries. Then there is the third party entrepreneur who handles *ad hoc* deals, direct sale to the end-user, and sale to a state trading corporation for resale in its home country.

If the marketer chooses the easiest of these, the offshore, lo-cally-based distributor, he or she then must rely on that firm to generate all sales in that market, with help from the firm's friendly banker (certainly one who knows how to finance international trade). For a mom-and-pop firm with a limited product line, this level may make sense even over the long term. Surely, that kind of casual, add-on export is better than nothing. But it is not very far up the export growth curve, and it has serious management problems.

> A friend of ours has a high-tech business that produces a product useful in hospital operating rooms where heart surgery is performed. His approach to exports—which won him his Governor's Export Promotion Award—was to find a local distributor in Germany who had experience in health industry sales and then turn Europe over to him. The distributor is doing very well indeed, not only in Germany but elsewhere. His German product lines help our friend's product because in other European nations German goods have a reputation for high technical quality.
>
> There is a problem; our friend is now totally dependent on a for-eigner for his offshore marketing, a person over whom he has no real managerial or marketing control. If there is ever a crunch between the German distributor's loyalty to Germany or to our friend's company, how do you suppose his decision will come down? (See Chapter Four.)

A further problem is more fundamental. Selling *ad hoc* through these channels does not lead to the development of a marketing plan outside the United States. At best, it stretches out the cost of developing and producing the product over a higher volume of goods. Our export marketer will do very well to use one of these channels if the company is very small, if export potential is limited to a small part of the product line, if there is only a small potential for its products in isolated parts of the world, or if it is just embarking on an export development program.

Licensing has advantages, but also has serious disadvantages in these chaotic times. When U.S. companies were not looking to expand globally, a long-term license to market a product or service represented the same benefits as a franchise arrangement at home: steady income, a surrogate presence overseas, and lack of financial risk. In times as rapidly changing as our own, licenses often backfire, leaving a company panting for the freedom to seize an opportunity that a licensee might be ignoring or, worse, capitalizing on for itself. As a temporary expedient, and, again as part of the learning process, licensing has its values.

> Ricks tells of one U.S. firm that licensed an English firm to manufacture and sell its products in the United Kingdom, but agreed to give the English firm an exclusive right to sublicense the U.S. expertise in other countries, for it then had no marketing commitment to exports. ("We've always had enough business right here in the States" may become America's most famous last words!) Within a few years, global markets developed for the company's products, and it was stuck with another party getting the benefits. Had the penthouse suite cared enough, it might have taken the time to work out a better, more profitable agreement.
>
> Another U.S. firm, a drug manufacturer, gave an Asian company a manufacturing license. The Asian market, which up to then had been nothing at all, boomed, leaving the U.S. firm as almost an outsider. Had it committed itself to a more direct form of involvement, it could have earned greater profits. (Ricks, 1983, 104)

We should use our first venture into offshore distribution as an educational phase in a concerted, planned drive to offshore marketing independence. In recent years, sales by agents or offshore distributors accounted for better than three quarters of export sales by the vast majority of the companies Czinkota (1982) surveyed, the larger companies marketing through their own subsidiaries or joint ventures.

Direct Export Sales: Toward Global Marketing

A firm commitment to develop exports should allow a few years' initial joint venture experiment with an offshore partner, before taking the final two steps: establishment of an offshore sales subsidiary and establishment of an offshore production subsidiary. Such experimenting helps the company gear up for the ultimate challenge of becoming a real presence in the global marketplace. Experimenting should precede establishment of a direct, on-site presence in the target markets. Through a subsidiary or other direct corporate operation designed to handle sales in the target country, the experience gained in using a distributor-intermediary may be expanded and improved on. The export of the company's culture takes on the sharpest edge in establishing an offshore subsidiary.

In our scheme, offshore production becomes the final step in a process toward globalization. This kind of investment represents a very substantial commitment. We worry about those hastily-established, quickly abandoned production facilities in Singapore and Mexico, for they represent serious capital investment made on quicksand. Build the offshore presence first for marketing, second for production. Here's where the new marketing managers—and global executives—come into their own. Having learned from domestic export sales and indirect export sales, the marketing manager with global ambitions will be viewing the total involvement of the company in offshore marketing operations as the last preliminary before it is effectively global. To the executive whose mind is focused on offshore sourcing as the first step in globalizing the company, we have a reminder. Remember that the phenomenon is the *globalization of markets*. If the mind is still set on that vast and precious U.S. market, perhaps the global perspective is still missing. Offshore sourcing and producing is a feature of globalization, but if the marketing imagination is still set on Peoria and Albany, then it is scarcely global in concept (see, in particular, the next chapter).

There will be skills and broad economic and political knowledge required for establishment of serious joint ventures and subsidiaries in other countries. We'll consider the special management qualities needed later on. It would be a mistake to imply that all nations welcome joint ventures or subsidiaries of American companies. After all, nationalism and domestic market perspective affects other nations as well as the United States. (The trick is to go global before all of them catch on to the power of the idea.)

In sum, while joint ventures, partnerships, and offshore subsidiaries are the key to major success, each of these steps is open to serious pitfalls and therefore requires a much more solid front-office commitment than domestic export sales or indirect export sales. The corporate commitment must visualize export marketing as more than product sales. It must visualize exports as first and foremost the export of the company's own entire marketing management, adapted for implementation in different climates, cultures, and contexts. This is the theme of Chapter Three.

> Coca-Cola has for some time practiced a form of global marketing (described in Quelch and Hoff, 1986), but ran into the shoals of national pride, even chauvinism, in India. India demanded that all companies with foreign ownership make available their special formulas to the government. Coke had never revealed the secrets of its syrup, and chose to withdraw from India. An attempt to approach the world as a single market is faced with a lot of surprising traps—as Coca-Cola discovered.

SUMMARY

For the global executive the key is that a commitment to export marketing development means more than a determination to begin selling overseas. It means the establishment of a solid and thorough corporate commitment to offshore—nay, *global*—marketing in the firm knowledge that export marketing is more than selling a product or products overseas. It means the export of the company's own existing marketing management, directed consciously—and conscientiously—toward exploiting opportunities in a globalized marketplace.

Export marketing requires some special steps on the part of the top management, then it requires some very special skills on the part of the individual export manager. All else is secondary to making the key corporate decisions that make exports a company priority and to equipping the marketing manager with the special skills for managing export marketing.

Exporting today is a first step toward meeting the challenge of globalized markets. Today's export marketing manager must become tomorrow's CEO of the global corporation or the learning process and the rich experience will have been wasted (see Chapter Four).

We have put the company's decisions into the Four Noble Truths categories. We have put the executive's skills into the Eight

Rights. The Four Truths overlap in the first of the Eightfold Path, Right Planning, for there the corporate mission and the executive's marketing plans must integrate to form a single company strategic plan. No one can assure success, but there will be no success if these fundamental principles that are unique to export market development are not followed.

TOMORROW'S EXECUTIVE IS A GLOBAL PLANNER

An Inventory of Skills and Attitudes

- A global vision of his or her own career.
- A global vision for the corporation.
- Skill to identify and use global sources of information without being distracted by U.S. preconceptions, values, or attitudes.
- A keen historical perspective and ability to use it to shape future direction.
- A sense of balance between past and future: What has been done versus what can be done.
- Skill to build theoretical constructs from generalizations, from hard fact, and from experience into successful global strategy.
- Skill to drive a planning process to conclusion.
- Skill to retool a plan from feedback.
- Skill to constructively, understandingly, and effectively manipulate people in processes.
- Skill to create and then give substance to a new corporate mission without undermining the corporate culture.

The Global Planner

Do U.S. corporations practice global strategic planning? There may be a few. If by global planning is meant strategic planning with an international character, matching the corporate mission to global realities through an internal review process, the number doing it will be very small.

As tomorrow's global executive uses experience in export development to prepare for a professional career in an interdependent world, so tomorrow's global corporation uses exports as part of a coherent strategy to exploit the opportunities of a globalized marketplace. A global strategy emerges from a process of planning that prepares the company for the future and reorients managers and employees to a new, more global mission.

Strategic planning generally fails to incorporate or integrate global perspectives. Most companies approach exports, offshore sourcing, joint ventures, overseas subsidiaries, as add-ons to the company's goals and objectives which remain overwhelmingly domestic. This is not true of the multinationals, but their plans have been characterized by multinational thinking rather than a truly global perspective—a fine distinction, but a real one.

Then too, strategic planning has been more notable for the exercise given to managerial thought-muscles than for its achievements in corporate practice. As we know now, domestic mind-set blinds a corporate executive to the new realities of globalized markets and encourages thinking that finds its inspiration in such statements as "That's the way we've always done it" or "If only it weren't for the Japanese. . . ." Global strategic planning today is noted chiefly for its absence from the American executive suite.

The global executive must be a global planner, and tomorrow's global management starts with a carefully-organized global strategy.

The global planner has studied and digested the Four Truths, including the reality of change here and around the world. He or she knows that the company simply has to have a new mission statement that covers more than the United States. Even if the old statement is *generally* true, he or she must convince the board of directors that a freshly-wrought statement will make clear the company's determination to make a global marketing commitment really work. The global executive is working today to convince his or her colleagues that a new mission statement that includes the wider world will transmit an essential message to employees, shareholders, security analysts, union leaders, bankers, and customers.

One American company changed nothing in its approach to global operations. However, it did change the name of its Spanish subsidiary to its own American name. When the American name went on the front, and the American flag went up the flagpole, the company introduced a new technology, and management boasted that it was revitalizing Spanish operations.

The Spaniards were both wounded and furious. The Spanish name had been highly prestigious in Spain, and they felt the company was belittling their previous achievements. Spanish pride was hurt, the Spanish press attacked, the workers staged a slowdown, and local authorities dogged the normal work of the company by stringent enforcement of petty regulations. (Ricks, 1983, 123)

"Business as usual," like this illustration, is prescription for disaster in a globalized marketplace. Existing strategic plans must be revised and, some good, hard thinking applied to the possibilities that might be offered by major restructuring of the corporation. This issue transcends the individual company.

The real issue facing the U.S. economy today is not just government spending and our enormous deficit, but whether American manufacturing and service industries can become competitive in today's rapidly changing and increasingly interdependent world. A great many national leaders are worried about this issue. The real issue is long-range and far more crucial to the health and security of the American economy than the sudden spate of imports or the monthly merchandise trade deficit, troubling as those both are. We must be able to see the woods from the trees. We must turn our talents to competitively seeking global markets.

That issue has two important corollaries:

1. To meet global conditions, are there structural changes needed in American business?
2. Do the new circumstances require management shifts, especially in recruiting, training, developing, supervising, and communicating with managers?

Japanese management techniques have attracted much attention in the past few years, though application here has shown only spotty success. At the same time, the current rash of corporate restructuring appears to be more a response to takeover threats and other last-minute pressures than to broader business strategy, and does not represent the execution of a global strategy. Any recasting of management strategies has been driven by short-term profit-and-loss considerations, not by long-range survival and growth. At the company level, there has not been much concern for the global changes that are so striking in today's world.

It is time for *global strategic planning* to go to the top of the corporate agenda. This is especially true for medium-sized corporations and small that don't think they need it—or choose to ignore the new world as incomprehensible. Fancy the small-town Chrysler dealer trying to explain his manufacturer's bail-out by the federal government. The local E. F. Hutton manager when the kiting scandal broke, the GE manager who has to explain his new corporate ally, Kidder Peabody, being tarnished with an insider's scandal—they really want to *ignore* the inexplicable. (For a real-life case study, see Bellah, 1985.) That is what many companies, especially smaller ones, prefer to do with respect to the often unpleasant reality of global interdependence.

We are not talking simple, small-scale problems like Chrysler's $1.2 billion government guarantee. We are talking about the very survival of American free enterprise. Much of American business has not accepted either the reality of global interdependence or the need to evolve new strategies to meet its new challenges.

Each and every business—whether or not it is currently involved in international trade, services, or finance—should be working at the top level to plot its global strategy over at least the next five to ten years. The Japanese plan ahead in 30-year spans.

Yet the global strategies we read about are either purely marketing strategies aimed at specific offshore markets or production economies. Either the company examines how to sell its product in other countries or it examines the potential for producing its goods in cheap labor nations. These are great, as far as they go. But overseas marketing and offshore manufacturing plans do not add up to a global strategy any more than an army's field tactics add up to a comprehensive strategy.

At the heart of planning a global strategy is the fundamental change in management that is this book's theme. There is no such thing as purely domestic industry any more. Every business is, to some degree, an international business. Any corporate leader who thinks his or her business is apart from the global economy is tomorrow's bad corporate news. The good news will be a new, global corporate mission.

The corporate mission statement of each and every American company should be reviewed and revised to encompass the global dimensions of present economic realities. Not only should potential markets and economical manufacturing locations drive corporate planning, but the broader economic and political issues must be included. Global strategies without consideration of international flows of capital, the remarkable development of the "new" nations of the South, the political realities of North-South and East-West—even politics within the blocs—are not global strategies. That's Point One.

Point Two is that American management has to reflect global strategies at every level—both with respect to managing people and managing processes. Fundamental shifts in management recruitment, training, supervision, organization, and communications have to be undertaken so that each executive and manager is personally and professionally committed to the corporation's new, global mission and equipped with the skills to carry out the mission.

The change of corporate mission statement from one aimed at an American market to one that is global in character may in the long run be the easier of these two steps. Global strategic planning, like normal strategic planning, involves management at all levels, but if management has not already acquired the attitudes and skills necessary to think and act internationally the new mission statement will end up as inappropriate as a cherry in a martini. What is needed is a bottom-up, top-down change in management perspective and concentration.

Global strategic planning must therefore go hand-in-hand with management reform. It recognizes, first, that there is a management culture and knows the dimensions and traditions of that culture. Second, it recognizes management as culture-bound. To build and to execute global strategies requires intensive corporate introspection and a new capacity to operate in contexts where management is not understood the same way, where negotiations are conducted in strangely different ways, and where binding ties between partners in business are defined quite differently.

Global strategic planning starts here. If we are to survive the trade wars of the 80s, it has to start now. To succeed, it must reach all managers at all levels. Tomorrow's global executive is needed today. Tomorrow's global executive is a global planner.

Management organization and practices are the foundation on which global strategies can and must be built. But until management attitudes and skills change so that both the management culture and the culture in which business is conducted are fully understood, it is unlikely that effective global strategies can be wrought. The danger is that American management will see global interdependence more as a threat than as the opportunity for a really creative, wholly American cultural response to a stirring challenge.

MISSION OF THE GLOBAL EXECUTIVE

What role should the global executive play in redesigning corporate strategy? What particular reshaping of his or her own talents would help convert today's eager manager into an executive for the globalized marketplace?

At the beginning of this chapter is an inventory of the skills and attitudes we feel define the global planner. Each later chapter begins with such an inventory of the global executive's skills and attitudes. These inventories won't stand alone, of course, because skills and attitudes only stand on observation, knowledge, information, and action. However, they do help us distinguish tomorrow's global executive from the domestic market-bound American manager of the past.

Start out with a couple of attitudes. The usual personal and professional ambition and enthusiasm are expected of today's and tomorrow's global executive. What characterizes the global executive is a perspective that sees a changing world as demanding changing perceptions, changing operating procedures, and changing attitudes. A global vision of one's own career doesn't mean selling out American identity or any less determination to make American business successful in global competition. It means seeing where opportunities lie even if they defy "common knowledge." It means, above all, not being fearful of the world beyond our borders. It means learning as much as possible about how other people view the world and how they behave in business.

A global vision recognizes the interdependency that has gripped economic aspects of humanity in recent decades, especially since World War II. Will this vision ultimately lead to a new view of political identity? This is not clear today, though it is hard to see how the nationalistic identity of the past 200 years is a helpful construct in a world characterized by global markets. A global perspective and recognizing interdependency as a fact rather than a positive or a negative force may lead to decisions that appear hard-hearted or even "disloyal." Decisions that close plant doors in towns where the company grew up or lead to layoffs of loyal workers are always difficult. But such decisions appear differently when seen in a global perspective.

A community impacted by a plant closing and its layoffs will be hurt by a decision based on globalized markets. But the end good strengthens the company and therefore the entire economy—indeed the economic health of the world—and both the community and the workers will ultimately benefit. Short-term agony versus long-term welfare is always a tough shot to call. Having lived in an area that was devastated when the textile industry moved South, we have seen the localized impact of such decisions. Still, folks in that textile mill valley drive Toyotas, watch television on their SONY's, record the NFL games on their Japanese VCRs, fuel their cars with Arab and African petroleum distillates, and eat bananas from Honduras. If we followed the logical consequences of keeping those plants open and jobs going, would that quality of life be present in the valley?

The national figures show, too, that during those same years when we have suffered our greatest deficits in the balance of trade, the U.S. economy has generated more jobs than ever before in its history. Yes, many middle-aged steel workers have lost their jobs and are finding it virtually impossible to find work that pays as well. That is an agonizing human tragedy, but it is a tragedy offset by a more general growth of work and a more general prosperity. So, while we should bend every effort to relieve the suffering of displaced workers, we should also take stock of the many jobs created in importing and distributing goods produced elsewhere. Global interdependence is a hard reality to swallow, but it is a reality that cannot be denied—one with both pluses and minuses.

In developing a global vision for one's corporation and for one's executive career, there is no reason why human-heartedness and altruism cannot inform decisions. In fact, in Chapter Four we will make a strong argument for understanding and empathy in the management of persons associated with the global business. A global vision is not hard-hearted, but it is hard-headed. A global vision rejects as irrelevant business attitudes and practices that are leftovers from a day when American business had a monopoly hold over an enormous, captive continental market. A global vision looks at the remarkable success of the Japanese in going global. At the same time this vision remains critical of the Japanese inability to reconcile themselves with the consequence of global success. Their borders will be much more open to the commerce of others than they have been historically.

Thus the global executive must be able to identify and use sources of information from outside the United States without judging them on the basis of U.S. business history, values, or attitudes. In the present context of global planning, we must not make marketing decisions based on our expectations of how American buyers will respond. We must not base marketing strategies on the characteristics and peculiarities of an American marketplace. We must not base our distribution arrangements on the past behavior of American distributors in an American market. First, we must understand what values, beliefs, and attitudes color the offshore marketplace and the principal actors in it. While there will be more on market research later on, suffice it to say here that the global executive will be able to use knowledge and information gained from abroad without prejudging it according to purely American management or marketing criteria.

At the same time, tomorrow's global executive will have a keen historical sense—understanding both where we, the Americans, have come from and where they, the offshore producers or customers, have come from. A historical sense will make it possible to shape future direction without doing injustice to the kinds of values and attitudes alluded to earlier. It will prevent the false premise that globalized markets are merely Americanized markets located somewhere else from pervading the corporate decision-making apparatus.

This intuitive sense of the historical dimension of both the world and the corporation should yield a sense of balance between past and present, allowing for sensible alternatives to be worked out between what has been done and what can be done.

> The absence of historical and global perspective is illustrated in one industry we have been examining recently. Imports of finished automobiles, fabricated automobile components, and the direct import of the particular parts manufactured in this industry has led to an industrywide crisis. The response to the triple threat has been to see only the external dimension, ignoring the domestic industry's domestic focus, its obsolescent plants, and its unimaginative management. In a report by a leading research firm, there was no regard for competitiveness in global markets or the historic decline of American manufacture. This short-sightedness is leading to demands that the industry be protected against imports through federal legislation. What has always been done in this Rust Belt industry is, however, ruling vision of what can be done, a singularly restrictive historical vision.

The manager with broad historical sense will seize the opportunity to create productive capacity in ways that will compete with the imports and will aggressively seek to meet the competition in markets outside the United States. The global executive is able to tell the difference between rusty thinking and creative approaches.

The corporation and its managers have to be able to react fast. I believe it was Peter Drucker who suggested that the "instant factory" may become as characteristically American as instant coffee or instant soup. Factories built offshore to take advantage of today's low labor costs or advantageous rates of exchange may be closed tomorrow as those factors change. Offshore production and offshore marketing will help to moderate the business swings we have become so accustomed to. Short-term to-and-fro swings are less a problem than immediate and rapid changes that become enduring, forcing the manager into surprising decision crises. The permanent shifts in the global economy put more pressure on the executive than following the business cycle.

The world is changing very fast, and it is impossible for any single individual to know everything. The span of managerial knowledge has been much foreshortened by the explosion of information and the narrowing of technical specializations. Yet the generalist is the only person who can command the corporate world of the future. Thus it is critically important for tomorrow's global executive to possess the finely-honed skills of moving from personal and professional and corporate experience, from factual knowledge and data, and from generalizations to theoretical formulations. The global executive will not only be a person equipped to cope with change, complexity, paradox, and ambiguity, but will be a person able to make sense of it all in order to make wise and far-reaching corporate decisions.

Today's executive who wants the company to be counted among tomorrow's global managements would be well advised to sharpen the "synthetic" skills. This doesn't mean learning to fake it, but being able to put things together that don't come together. It means being able to create your own generalizations from facts and from experience, and being able to draw up a theory from generalizations. It means being able to create a "synthesis"—your own construct of what you have learned—out of a confusing mass of competing forces and contradictory facts. This skill can serve as an expert guide to decision making, especially in the preparation of corporate global strategies.

We add to our inventory several skills that any manager ought to possess, but reinforcing them here is important. First, tomorrow's global executive will sense the managerial tools needed to drive a planning process toward a conclusion. He or she will know that planning is just as important for the involvement of the people it inspires as for the concrete plan that emerges. Being able to assure employees and other managers that planning is not just a time-busting exercise, but a way of giving them ownership in both the process and the plan will go a long way to assuring that any plan emerging will be implemented in practice. So driving a global strategy to a conclusion—seeing it appear in a new corporate mission statement and in the annual report—is at the same time the skill to make a strategic plan operational.

Manipulating people has earned a bad name in recent years, and justifiably so. We have a hard time finding an appropriate synonym for manipulation, however. It means, of course, to handle, and carries the connotation of dextrous handling. Dextrous management of both American and non-American employees engaged in a planning process is an essential ingredient in involving people and driving toward a consensus that endows "ownership" in what has been accomplished. Note, however, that we have qualified "manipulate" by the adverbs "understandingly," "constructively," and "effectively." Later on, when we discuss loyalties in managing other people, we will discuss at greater length the necessity for emphathetic understanding. When you are crossing cultural lines in management, understanding how other people behave is essential, but it is not very useful to understand if it is not in turn informed by empathy. Empathy, a much misinterpreted word, means to project oneself into someone else's mind to see how he or she perceives an issue, you, the corporation, the mission, or even the world. Empathetic understanding is a key to manipulating people without invoking the worst sense of the term *manipulating*.

Business International (1985) identified some characteristics of tomorrow's international manager. Their characteristics mirror our own independent ideas about the global executive, incorporated in this book, but one of them stands out: an ability to detect weak signals. Tomorrow's global executive will not only have a strong sense of intuition (to which we will refer repeatedly), but will have such a sharply tuned set of perceptions that he or she will be able to sense trends before others. Whether these trends are economic, social, political, or attitudinal, it is important for the global executive to be able to sense them in order to build them into the new global strategy for the corporation, as well as to make operational decisions. The American business tradition makes hash of intuitive sensitivity. It is particularly harsh on the manager who believes he or she has heard weak signals from the marketplace, from the workforce, or from the government. We believe that this is expensive arrogance in a globalized marketplace. Those weak signals are as important as the bomb-blasts that we have traditionally waited to hear. For global strategies, this is a high-order skill.

Finally, the global executive will have to possess the skill to be able to create and give substance to the new corporate mission— the new global strategy—without undermining the corporate culture.

One familiar U.S. company, caught in an advanced technology it couldn't bring off, had grand plans to be at the heart of the American office equipment revolution and broadcast the new strategy throughout the corporation. When general recession, lack of capital resources, and a temporary downturn in the office equipment market led to a revision of the strategy and general retrenchment, the new management found that the corporate culture, focused around an old-line company loyalty, had been shredded and carried out with the trash.

A look at A&P suggests something of the same experience: A&P has survived the trauma of a new strategy, but at the cost of lost loyalty from employees and customers that is only now coming back.

The global executive, whose task is to help the corporation enter the global age through a coherent and fully-committed global strategy, must understand the strength that corporate culture gives to the company and be sensitive to how it may be manipulated to yield the globalized results intended—without destroying the company's culture in the process.

GLOBAL STRATEGIC PLANNING: A PROCESS

Tomorrow's global executive should play a role in today's global strategic planning. Because present rank and power in the corporation will vary, we'll concentrate here on what the corporation's role might be in going global rather than on the role of the global executive.

In the course of our seminars on export marketing management and international management we have found it useful to run through an exercise on the present strategic plan of the company. Form A reproduces the format we have used to kick off. Note that we start with the company's present mission statement. This should be more than a slogan. If the company hasn't boiled it down into one sentence, than you should try to get it into one or two.

This mission statement is a nifty target for strategic planning. The revision and reform of grand, corporate strategy should concentrate on a powerful, focused statement like a mission statement. So much is normally true, but, if the change of direction toward globalization cannot be pressed into a mission statement for the whole company, then it is unlikely that strategic planning will work. Strategic planning aims to place effectively into corporate operations the results of a thorough review of the company's goals and objectives. The process should look something like Figure 3–1: it starts with today's mission statement and ends up with a new, global mission statement.

FIGURE 3–1
Global Planning Process

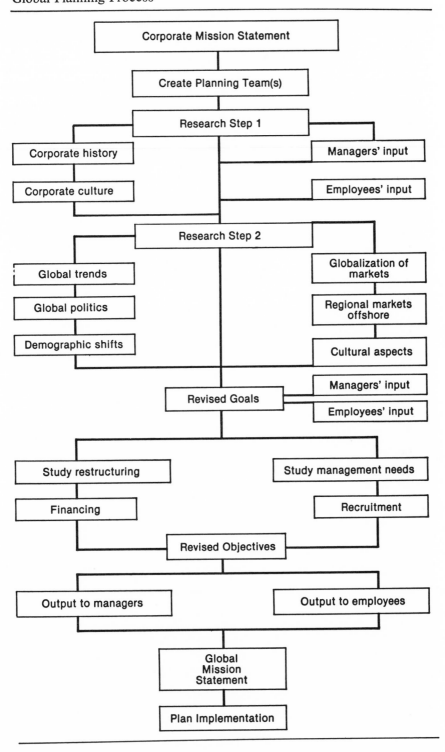

**FORM A. STRATEGIC PLANNING
FOR INTERNATIONAL BUSINESS**

If your present corporation has a *Mission Statement,* spell it out in these spaces:

_____

_____

Summarize the four or five most salient goals and objectives sought by your company's strategic plan:

1. _____

2. _____

3. _____

4. _____

5. _____

List the markets which *historically* your management has set as its highest priorities:

1. _____ 2. _____ 3. _____
         4. _____ 5. _____

List in the order of priority to your management, the five most important target markets for development:

6. _____ 7. _____ 8. _____
         9. _____ 10. _____

Where do *international* sales and *global* sales fit in these markets? (Circle all numbers from above, add any comment you wish.)

1   2   3   4   5   6   7   8   9   10

You may wish to work through Form A before going on. The central part of Form A asks for a summary of the main aspects of the existing strategic plan for the corporation. Many companies went through exercises in strategic planning in the last decade, but have filed them away where they will do the least harm. Before you begin a fresh look toward globalization, you have to review the previous plan. As a way of analyzing it, we ask that management's *historically* important market priorities be listed, then compared with management's priorities for market *development.* The differences between these indicate where management believes it is go-

---

FORM B. AIMS OF STRATEGIC PLANNING

A. In the left hand Column, rank *management's* goals in order of importance:

____ Return on Investment ____

____ Earnings on Sales ____

____ Customer Satisfaction ____

____ Image of the Company ____

____ Employee Satisfaction and Morale ____

____ Market Position ____

____ Innovative Character of Products ____

____ Quality of Product ____

____ Quarterly Financial Results ____

____ Stock Value ____

____ Future Prospect of the Company ____

Add other goals you believe management has *established.*

____

____

____

____

B. In the right hand Column, rank these in an order needed for your company to move into a global strategy, adding such other goals as *you* think will be necessary.

C. One of the first tasks of a global strategic planner is to reconcile these two sets of priorities.

---

ing (which is not the same thing as a strategy, but offers shape to planning). Finally, we ask the global executive to assess these according to their international or global dimensions.

Form B follows this with directions to examine management's overall priorities and then rate the same priorities according to your own independent, professional judgment. This exercise is designed to give a point of departure for an exercise in global strategic planning, although it is clearly much too sketchy to fairly represent a corporation's overall goals.

A fresh, major, company-wide strategic planning project should be undertaken if a global plan is to work. Though success with strategic planning has varied, disenchanting a large number of senior and middle managers, the planning process has an important place in the globalization of a company.

First, globalization of markets by a single company will not work unless the commitment to globalization is made at the very top. Second, it will not work unless the commitment is pervasive throughout senior and middle management. Third, it will not work unless the commitment is understood and acted on throughout the support and production staff.

Europeans already know that their economic and corporate survival depends on operating and marketing across national boundaries. Here in America, our first and most difficult obstacle is to break an American-market-first mind-set. It is an understandable perspective, arising from two or more centuries exploiting the world's wealthiest market and from the isolation of American management and labor from direct experience in other markets. The American market perspective must be changed if globalization is to take place.

This limited, continental perspective affects how executives, managers, and employees react to global matters. In our experience, we get one of two responses: the "Ho-Hum Syndrome" and the "Yuk Syndrome." Ho-Hum is sheer apathy: we couldn't care less because "We have a satisfactory market right here already" (or, worse, "Go away, problems enough I've got already"). Yuk! is rejection of dealing with the unknown, the unfamiliar, the unclean, the un-American, the nonwhite.

Either of these attitudes will stifle the movement toward globalization. Either attitude will leave it to the Japanese, Koreans, and others to seize the opportunities globalization offers. Both must be the first targets of a concentrated effort on the part of management to globalize.

For this reason, the usual practices of strategic planning make good sense here. Normally, strategic planning involves large numbers of persons reaching in rank all the way from the executive suite to the production floor. A pyramid could be drawn of personnel involvement, but to draw planning as a structure immediately misapprehends its purpose. Planning is not a structure, it is a process. And any process is a people process. What is important is how people interact with one another, not the product of the process. That's why a lot of strategic plans are best left in the files when the design is completed, for the dynamic part of planning has been the drawing in of people who are not ordinarily consulted, their involvement in the process, and their acquisition of ownership in the results.

Once more, we see a management process as offering a learning experience. If nothing else comes out of global strategic planning, it is a learning experience that will destroy the Ho-Hum and Yuk syndromes. We need to learn to open the eyes of American management and labor to a larger world of opportunity and challenge. We will return to this point time and time again.

The first and overriding responsibility of the global executive is to convince everyone connected with the company that the corporation means business by globalization—that it is totally and irrevocably committed to participation in the globalized marketplace. All employees, shareholders, financiers, distributors, and suppliers must know of the company's shift of focus and begin to contribute to its success. Without proclaiming the new, global mission, the support of these interests will be difficult to attract. Without involvement of a wide spectrum of employees in the process of planning the new mission, why should shareholders, financiers, distributors, and suppliers believe the company is serious about going global?

Planning is a people process. It is a way to help executives, managers, and other employees learn about the globalization of markets and the company's opportunities. The global executive will drive the planning process toward a globalized mission statement because it is a way of indoctrinating, training, and implicating personnel in the global mission. In the process, the concept of exports as an ''add-on'' to the top of a lush American market will be totally destroyed.

GLOBAL STRATEGY AND THE CORPORATE CULTURE

Globalizing the strategic plan of a company, finally expressed in a new corporate mission statement that includes the whole world, touches very close to the heart of the corporation. Like any therapy or surgery, it is dangerous, for it cuts close to the essential organs that give the company identity and dynamic movement.

Strategic planning has earned its tarnished image because, like many health fads, it failed to take the whole body into account. Just as many doctors are now seeking to treat the whole person, strategy revision should consider the corporate whole. That means very close attention to the corporate culture, for the corporate culture is the people-centered lifeblood that gives the company its identity and keeps it working through the human beings who are employed in it. Corporate culture is the sum of all the practices, rules, traditions, communications, and power structures that give it form. Tampering with the corporate culture without understanding what makes it work is like performing by-pass surgery with a kitchen knife.

Corporate culture is rooted in history but sustained by what the company practices today. The global planner, therefore, must apply his or her sense of history and the tools of historical analysis to understand how the company emerged, what were the positive forces in its growth and success, and what are the principles, practices, and behaviors that sustain it now.

This means looking beyond the power centered in the penthouse suite. It means looking at how power is communicated and exercised, how power is respected or defied. It requires finding out how the mission and traditions of the company are sustained by rites and rituals, by rewards and punishments, by the creation of heroes and the vilification of villains. It implies understanding both the formal structure of management authority and the informal, often hidden, actual structure. It means tapping into the informal communications patterns to find out who is actually reporting to whom. It even means digging into the meaning to employees of such things as parking privileges, executive dining suite, and vacation associations among managers. It becomes relatively personal at times. (We are still waiting for "the" book on corporate culture. Davis, 1985, is excellent, but short of seminal. Schein, 1985, does not focus on business. A breezy view is Deal and Kennedy, 1982—perhaps a bit too breezy.)

Because the corporate culture is the force that keeps the corporation alive, disturbing it can kill it. In the formulation of a global strategy, therefore, caution must be exercised that the dynamism of the corporate culture is enhanced and sustained, not endangered. The corporate culture thus becomes a foundation for globalization, even though aspects of the culture may present obstacles to globalization. The global strategy builds on the pre-existing culture of the company in order to export that culture to other parts of the world. Understanding culture comes first; change comes as a consequence of understanding.

While the real challenge is in operations—after the global strategy is set—planning should continually ask whether the corporate culture is exportable, and whether some aspect of it ought to be carefully molded to make it more universally dynamic around the world. The main purpose of considering corporate culture, however, is to understand it so that when the time comes to fit it into a broader cultural context than the context of U.S. business, the appropriate adaptations and relevant communications can be undertaken.

If the new global corporate mission statement is not respectful of the existing corporate culture, then it is unlikely that the export of marketing management—the key to globalization—can be successfully accomplished. Either the export of marketing management to a globalized marketplace will fail or the company will disintegrate.

RESTRUCTURING FOR A GLOBAL ROLE

It is difficult to generalize about corporate structure with respect to the global marketplace. Many different approaches to globalized markets can be found, as illustrated by Quelch and Hoff's article (1986) on Nestlé and Coca-Cola. So far, there is little evidence which structure is most suitable, arguments being made for matrix management and for centralized management. Clearly, the structure of the corporation must relate to the corporate culture and vice versa, and the structure that is adopted or perpetuated should be responsive to clear-headed global strategic planning.

Restructuring is going to be required of many American companies if they are to seize global opportunities that are now falling to the Japanese. In planning a global strategy, nothing structural should be sacrosanct: deal delicately with the corporate culture, but deal effectively with corporate structure. In Chapter Six, we will examine the effect of financing on corporate timing. The Japanese and German freedom from the hourly vagaries of the stock market due to their much larger proportion of debt to equity, coupled with their cozy banking relationships, gives them much more flexibility and corporate patience than is true of most American companies. Leaf forward to that section to put it into the planning context. Japanese and German companies (the Koreans and Taiwanese, too) are much more highly leveraged than are American companies, giving them freedom from the short-term perspectives of the stock market (For a penetrating analysis, see Ellsworth,

1985). This kind of restructuring is only part of the thorough analysis that ought to be conducted during the construction of a global strategy.

GLOBAL STRATEGY: SOME SPECIAL CONCERNS

The global strategy must, at every step of the process, ask and re-ask some questions that are unique to global business. (We would argue that they should concern *every* business manager right now.) We have put these in the form of a list. These questions barely scratch the surface and many more specific concerns will face the global planners in almost any corporation as they proceed with the global strategy formulation. They are suggestive, however, of some of the unusual problems that face global strategy-building.

Some of these questions are unanswerable. However, they should be faced and an approach made to resolving them. The challenge of global planning is to grapple with major issues like these. Fear doesn't go very far toward grappling with them.

Is our definition of the problem sufficiently global?

Is our response to the problem sufficiently global?

Have we identified appropriate information from outside the United States that will help us answer this question?

Have we interpreted offshore information without prejudging it from an American marketing point of view, without imposing our viewpoint on it?

Have we involved employees who have offshore experience in ways that will help the planning process?

Have we involved our offshore employees and colleagues in ways that will help the planning process?

Have we considered macro economic and political processes in our planning (such as shifts and potential shifts in economic strength between the industrial and developing nations, between the free world and the Soviet bloc)?

Have we considered the role of regional shifts in our planning (such as the potential shift in industrial strength to the Asian rim, as China, India, and other populous nations develop semi-skilled and skilled labor)?

Have we considered both the export of goods to global markets *and* the production of goods (or services) outside the United States as part of the same phenomenon and therefore equally part of the global challenge?

Have we assessed accurately the nature and strength of the potential *global* competition we may meet as we enter a globalized marketplace?

Have we built in enough flexibility to react to rapid market development (and deterioration) in different parts of the world, and to rapid changes in production costs (up and down) in different sourcing areas?

Have we created a managerial structure and process that will be able to do *more* than cope with rapid changes, that will respond constructively and profitably to changes?

Have we created a way of balancing our regional strengths against our regional weaknesses?

Have we taken into account relevant, current U.S. trade policies and potential changes in them over the next few years, including possible changes of administration?

Have we taken into account possible foreign retaliation to new U.S. trade policies?

Powerful as these questions are—and there are some real rockers in there—these are obviously only generalized starters. The difficult questions lie within the corporation for solution by those who are most familiar with them. We suggest that the strategic planning process proceed according to formulas with which the company and its management are familiar. There are no special or secret procedures for global strategic planning as compared with the more familiar domestic plans. The central feature of global strategy is to break mind-sets and to introduce information and perspectives from outside the usual, domestic sources.

Breaking mind-set, we repeat, must be company-wide and at all levels. Global strategic planning must be conceived of and executed as a learning process for all levels. It can become a learning process only if a broad group of employees participate in the planning experience and can convert what they learn into new approaches to their jobs.

Tomorrow's global executive should be right at the center of these changes.

TOMORROW'S GLOBAL EXECUTIVE AS A GLOBAL MOTIVATOR

An Inventory of Skills and Attitudes

- Skill to involve managers and employees in global plans and operations.
- Skill to involve managers and employees in offshore projects and enthusiasms, whatever their preconceived notions.
- Intuitive sense of other people's loyalties and priorities when they are different.
- Sense of humor under adverse conditions—and an ability to keep laughing through extended perils.
- Perception of human differences that will require special engineering, production, process, marketing, or managerial changes to make them work.
- Skill to identify, involve, and reward employees with the most creative potential, make them into global managers, too.
- Skill to perceive ways to break the traditional pattern of employee and management advancement without upsetting important elements of corporate culture.
- An unusual ability to identify, train, and promote persons with nontraditional talents, whose contribution to the company will help it to become global.
- Skill and sensitivity in selection of offshore partners, distributors, managers, or employees.
- A sense of loyalty that is different from the domestic American corporate loyalty.
- Enthusiasm for the corporate mission.
- Ambition for one's own self within the corporation.

The Global Motivator

The global executive knows that the second step along the Eightfold Path proceeds from the first, global strategy. If management does not make both domestic and foreign employees realize that it is deadly serious about the global strategy, the plan will not be taken seriously. These employees must be motivated not just to serve the company, but to be loyal to the company's global mission.

We now know that you cannot motivate someone else, but you can create the conditions under which a person becomes motivated. This chapter is about creating those conditions so that other executives, managers, employees, and offshore associates become personally and professionally involved in the company and its mission.

Recent books affirm that corporate culture can be changed. The fundamental values of any culture, including the corporate culture, are very difficult to change except over a long period of time or through cataclysmic revolution. It is easier to tinker with the everyday procedures and common attitudes. But corporate change *can* be directed. We take issue with the notion (as in Davis, 1985) that companies should not mess around with the basics. A new global corporate mission is essential and that means shifting both basics and the daily routines.

Corporate culture is different from other human cultures. Corporate culture is truncated, for it doesn't apply to the broader social functions. It does not relate to marriage and family rearing and to the general rules of a person's behavior. It is not a comprehensive culture affecting all aspects of the lives of its members. It does seriously overlap and influence home life. Workplace problems can intrude into the harmony of domestic life, and domestic tensions can lap over to influence work effectiveness. Corporate culture exists in a separate compartment for both the employee and the corporate manager. It is apart from, yet still a part of, routine family life, entertainment, and most important social events. American corporate culture has not intruded into the employee's life to the extent the corporation has in contemporary Japan. Corporate culture may be more deliberately changed, adapted, and manipulated by those who control it than is possible in a natural, community culture. The people who can influence, direct, and change corporate culture are not necessarily restricted to the level of the CEO and the Board of Directors. Line executives have a role to play.

The global plan represents a deliberate attempt to reconstruct the corporate culture, weaning it from the larger culture wherein it was founded and within which it prospered, making it ready to export to other cultural contexts around the world.

A key step in deliberately altering a corporate culture—and the one step that is absolutely indispensable to successful change—is to involve employees. The employees must be drawn into a commitment to the new culture to integrate them into its new processes and to indoctrinate them with the new values and attitudes that the global culture represents.

For any deliberate change to be brought about in corporate culture, such as globalization, *the entire workforce* has to become involved. This is what is meant by linking the corporate culture and strategy. While nothing much will happen to change corporate culture unless the CEO becomes involved and supports the effort, likewise nothing much will happen unless the change is deliberately introduced through involvement of managerial, support, and production staff. They must be motivated to want to achieve the goals of the global strategy. Executive acceptance of culture change is indispensable, but it is more critical to prevent the change being given only lip service by managers and employees *at all levels*.

Going global means involving and motivating every single employee from the mailroom up to the penthouse suite and back down to the factory floor. The global executive relishes this aspect of the challenge of global management, involves all employees, and uses some special people-management keys to bring the global plan into employee behaviors that affect operations.The global plan in operation just won't work unless everyone who works for the company has become personally and professionally committed to globalizing the mission.

> One manufacturer's marketing vice president couldn't figure out why repeat export sales were so insignificant. He had a good product and was doing a bang-up job of overseas selling. Then he discovered that small postal shipments for foreign destinations were being put aside because it took longer and caused more trouble to figure the postage and fill out customs forms. Large crates, too, sat out of sight because the clerk found the commercial invoices for customs purposes too difficult to fill out. They sat because the shipping clerk hadn't learned that exports were a high management priority.

The global executive revels in the global mission and daily demonstrates it to everyone in the company, embracing anyone who will help make the mission a success. This commitment shows in a reward system that is designed to highlight and promote the global strategy. It is apart, separate, and distinct from the established corporate reward system.

PERCEPTIONS AND MISCONCEPTIONS

Management does not have total control over how employees perceive the corporation, but management can influence those perceptions. One of the purposes of motivation programs is to change the employee's perception of both self and company. Motivation doesn't work very well if there is no commitment or only tenuous loyalty to the firm. Here the global executive has to face an even more challenging problem, not only to change the perception of employees to corporation, but also to change their perceptions of people who are not like them—specifically, the non-Americans the company will have as customers, distributors, managers, and offshore employees.

The average American regards the rest of the world as different, both different-queer and different-funny. In general, our regard for non-Americans places them in an inferior position to us. This is true of almost all societies in the world, but our geographic distance from truly different cultures (with the exception of Mexico) has made it possible for us to enjoy the luxury of this set of attitudes, unchallenged by having to deal daily with the objects of our contempt. Going global almost inevitably means closer interaction between American employees (especially managers) and non-Americans, either at home, abroad, or both. And, going global means placing offshore markets on a par with, and sometimes superior to, domestic markets.

The trick is to overwhelm the old perspectives of domestic markets coming first and of foreigners being a class beneath us.

> John sells anything and everything to the Arab part of West Asia. Through a network established over many years, he has placed friends and cousins in positions to send procurement orders through him for fulfillment in the United States.
>
> In 1985, he landed an order for 55 of the largest, most luxurious motor home RVs manufactured in the United States—an order worth several million dollars. The manufacturer took the order, with its delivery date of August 15 on the docks in New York. On July 27th, the manufacturer called John and said that orders from established U.S. distributors had been better than expected and he would be unable to meet the shipping deadline. He could deliver eight weeks late, would that be OK? John had to inform him that the Arab order would be cancelled if delivery was late.
>
> When asked what is the single worst failing among American exporters, John groaned that they tend to be late in delivery of overseas shipments. More ominously, he wondered if Americans don't treat foreign customers as if they were second class.

There is nothing at all wrong with favoring your established distributors, but there is something deeply wrong with casting offshore customers as second-class. American provincialism favors the American customer, not because there is anything against selling to a foreigner, but because there is a more comfortable feeling selling to a fellow American. And this attitude is more than just a distaste for the sometimes onerous paperwork that accompanies foreign shipments or the different ways in which exports are financed. It appears to be related to how Americans perceive non-Americans.

It's an attitude that *must* be changed, a perspective that must be altered, if American business is to succeed in a global marketplace.

Travel agents, obviously, deal with travel around the world. But American travel agents do not mix with the international members of the principal trade association when they gather for conventions. There are few relationships, formal or informal, between U.S. agents and their peers in Europe or Asia—even though collaboration would make the pie bigger for both sides. The American Society of Travel Agents has been struggling imaginatively to break down these restraints toward international cooperation.

In tracking down the reasons for this phenomenon, experts can only identify these: (1) travel agencies are mom-and-pop enterprises with little managerial depth, (2) the lack of depth is matched only by a lack of entrepreneurial imagination in marketing, and (3) vast numbers of them are located in small towns and cities across the heartland of America, and travel that takes place to exotic locales seems only half-real to them.

At heart, this is a matter of perception, a matter of attitude toward the rest of the world. Sometimes it leads to almost scandalous conduct of marketing policies overseas, as in unloading unsold American consumer goods on the developing countries at fat prices. (We often recall the warehouse in Bombay filled with softcore U.S. paperbacks, sold to the U.S. remainder merchant by the publishers by the pound to be retailed to Indian consumers at a day's pay each. We have been told that this practice in the Caribbean is even more abusive, for glamorous U.S. goods drive out necessities for a population that cannot distinguish between them.) Most of the time, offhand American attitudes toward foreigners keep us from seeing and capitalizing on market opportunities.

The global executive has a real challenge in changing employees' perspectives of America in the whole world and of foreigners as customers and as colleagues. The new attitude, while no less patriotically American, must recognize that offshore opportunities are just as rich as domestic opportunities and that the competition for them is just as intense, perhaps even more intense than at home. Success in the global marketplace will go to those who are least restrained by a nostalgic hankering for the local markets of the good old days.

A particularly troubling advertisement appeared in business publications in July of 1986. The copy is unexceptionable, arguing that it is wise to have an international insurance company write policies that have international applicability. But the headline and the 13 × 14-inch photo of a Thai insurance policy gives the impression that there can be problems buying insurance policies from foreign companies.

The reader will immediately infer that foreign insurance policies are suspect, perhaps inferior to American policies. That inference would emerge from the American preconception that things American are better. The puzzle remains whether the ad agency deliberately pandered to American preconceptions of the rest of the world or that this was an inadvertent expression of old-fashioned American ethnocentrism. The next ad in the series, appearing in September 1986 followed a similar, almost anti-foreign theme, providing some answer to the puzzle. It's particularly sad, for the company was at one time my employer, and I was among its admiring shareholders.

RECKONING WITH AMERICAN ATTITUDES

There are a good many excellent programs in predeparture orientation for executives embarking for ventures abroad, and there are some good training programs for personnel in dealing with cultural minorities in the workplace. Some references are given in the Reference Section to sources of information and programs for these culture-management purposes.

Our focus, however, is on the whole company in which our manager works and on how the global executive can help that whole company capitalize on and compete in a globalized market. To change the corporate culture means to change people's attitudes both toward the company itself and toward the company in its environment here and elsewhere. As the environments change with globalization, the culture of the company must change as it adapts to its new contexts.

For years, we have said that training people toward cultural sensitivity is little different from good education anywhere. The problem lies in the two chief obstacles to the subject matter. We have called these the Ho-Hum Syndrome and the Yuk Syndrome (Ferguson, 1987). Getting people to realize that they are victims of these diseases is the principal challenge. Once they recognize that they have been infected, they are trainable.

The Ho-Hum Syndrome is apathy. Most Americans simply do not *care* about persons in other parts of the world. The closest they come to meeting them is on the six o'clock news when the terrifying, the bizarre, and the bloody is apt to color our view of others. Not meeting many foreigners, except those who have chosen to immigrate into the United States, Americans have little care for them and less skill in communicating with them. Schoolchildren see four-color pictures of the exotic or the militant foreigners in their textbooks, but there is little reality to those images except to form hostile attitudes—or to turn the pages with bored indifference. In fact, most Americans cannot easily project themselves into the contexts in which other peoples live in order to understand them. Understanding beyond a few historical and cultural facts has not been demanded by our schools or colleges. Sensitivity toward them as people living in hope and fear is almost totally absent. American employers have a spotty record of coping with cultural sensitivities at the workplace—even where ethnic mixtures have come close to being explosive. The global executive aims higher than that, and thus may find it tougher to pull off.

After making American employees less apathetic, the next challenge is to make them less hostile toward foreigners. This, curiously, is somewhat easier than piquing their interest, but only if the interest has already been stirred. The Yuk Syndrome is hostility toward people who are not like us (or fawning over people we would like to be like—usually blonde, blue-eyed northern Europeans). Yuk is born of an ethnocentric vision of the world. In China, it spawned 5,000 years of vision that China was the center of the earth—*Xhongguo* (Middle Kingdom). In Italy, it branded foreigners as barbarians—those with red beards. Yuk in America is most commonly associated with unfamiliar, odd-tasting food or strange mannerisms, but it subtly extends to the people themselves. Yuk is hostility or distaste for what is strange and for the stranger in our midst.

The challenge once again, is to project ourselves into another's place in order to see reality from his or her perspective. It is easier to deal with people who are not like yourself if you are able to see the world through their eyes. This process should start with the global executive, who will see that other employees adopt the same kind of empathy for people who are different.

Employees who must deal with non-Americans *must* be trained to handle their interaction. Repeat: *must* be trained. It simply will not do to treat those foreign associates or customers as if they were Americans—not if you want to execute a global strategy. Sure, you can make headway with them and things *may* work out for the best. But the global executive does not take chances that Joe or Jenny will be able to pull it off without a clash of cultures marring the deal. The global executive is personally sensitive to cultural differences and will be certain that key employees on the interface are appropriately trained.

Training for interface employees ideally should be of an experiential nature. That is, trainees are given training in real or simulated cultural situations that are different from those in their own culture.

> The sweeper had finished sweeping and swabbing my office floor in New Delhi, but it was still filthy. In my best Hindi, I sarcastically ordered him to clean it until it was so clean he could eat off of it. How could he recognize the meaning of my order? He had never eaten a meal except on the floor, dirty or clean.

This is a silly incident, but it illustrates the dangers of imposing your own values on others. Analyzing critical incidents like this, especially those from the employees' own experience, makes for excellent training. By facing critical situations in which they must learn what values and standards the other people have, the trainees learn at least one basic skill that the global executive must have: judge the other person's behavior or decision by his or her society—that is what governs that behavior. Context is important in engaging in international activities. It does not mean that the other person is "right," just different. The challenge for the manager is to understand where that person is coming from before reacting to the personal behavior or to the business decision.

We would emphasize that the little things in dealing with strangers (see Copeland and Griggs, 1985) are indeed important when the manager is abroad. If you are a man, don't get into an elevator in Arabia that is already occupied by a woman. Don't eat with your left hand in most of Asia. Don't touch a Hindu woman with your hands. Don't intrude yourself on the British sharing the train compartment with you. These little things are important, but they can overwhelm the executive with worry and bothersome details.

The key ingredient to cultural training for management is much more basic and is essential to master even before going abroad. In any situation, whether personal or managerial, wait before you respond. Wait until your own perception of the person's action can be measured, not against your values, but against his or hers.

If you are an American managing in a far-off country, you are bound to get hung up between corporate policies from home and behavioral realities where you are working.

> After we had returned home, two senior managers in our Delhi office arranged for their apartment rents to be picked up by the budget. This is a very common practice and an expected management perquisite in India. What a holy row that prompted! U.S. practice is not to pay for personal living quarters except possibly for the CEO. The two managers were accused by the home office of milking the golden American cow, and they were hurt that their motives had been suspected.

The change in corporate culture must become manifest in incidents such as this. The executive has to find a middle way between one set of expectations and the other. Standards for judging a person's behavior are sometimes like American standards, but often they are wildly dissimilar. It is through too-quick reactiveness without enough sensitivity that Americans tend to get into trouble abroad or with foreign associates at home. One important illustration in particular might help understand the crucial importance of this from a management point of view.

> The trial in India of the Union Carbide cases has not told us all. There is ample evidence, however, that one of the fundamental problems was that the Bhopal plant was built to American management expectations. Certain behavior was expected of the managers, supervisors, and employees who ran it.
>
> Irrespective of how the disaster occurred, one of the most revealing disclosures in the press was that the on-duty supervisor was informed of the leak during his tea break, while he was sitting in comradely conversation with his friends. He responded that he would look into it after he finished his break, a perfectly reasonable expectation *in India* where a very high value is placed upon human intercourse and much less is placed on the workings of machinery.
>
> In a nation with little concept of preventive maintenance, a plant should be designed for the local expectations, not for the expectations of Purdue- or MIT-trained engineering designers in the United States.
>
> In our view, the Bhopal disaster represents a classic case of cultural misapprehensions in the design and management of the plant. Many American critics of the Bhopal management have cited lack of training as one of the underlying causes for the leak getting out of hand. We believe that an original, culture-specific design of the plant

would have been a more effective safety measure than any training of employees. The practices of 5,000 years of history cannot be changed by rolling out a fresh blueprint and a management manual to go with it. Whatever the decisions of the courts on culpability, we are certain that the original design was mismatched to the cultural expectations of both Indian managers and their employees.

Ignorance of local customs may have doomed more American offshore projects than just the one at Bhopal, but political incompetence has doomed many others. In spite of the most massive barrage of daily news offered in the world, news that is virtually free of controls, Americans manage to perpetuate a troublesome ignorance of the rest of the world. Almost any visitor to the United States from abroad is as well informed about American politics as Americans are. How many of us are prepared to discuss the politics of Argentina or of Bangladesh or even of the United Kingdom?

Training for all staff who will be personally interacting with non-Americans should include two elements of political preparation. First, the staffer should be briefed on the politics of the country to which he or she will be assigned or with whose nationals he or she will be working. Basic governmental structure, names of key leaders and parties, and the principal issues of the day are important for executives, managers, and other interface staffers to know.

Second, training should be provided in what those people think of the United States, both as a society and as a political power.

I was in the United Kingdom when Britain, France, and Israel invaded Egypt in 1956. Incredulous that such an outdated imperial policy could have been adopted, I pestered my British friends with provocative questions. Their response was to explain the countries' action without including their own political views of it. I first began to learn how to handle cross-national political tensions on a personal level.

The Bay of Pigs taught me an important lesson: irrespective of how I felt about the policies that led to that disaster, as an American I had to represent those policies to my Indian hosts. I learned to suppress my political opposition and to interpret the events judiciously for those who were curious. I have since returned to the United Kingdom following our involvement in the Viet Nam war, and while our government was funding and training Contras in Nicaragua. Each of these was difficult to handle under provocative, somewhat unfriendly questioning.

From these events, I also learned a lesson that everyone should learn: be ready for the obvious hostile questions, but be ready for the second and third questions, too, for the people who are interested *will* ask you and they tend to be very well informed about the United States.

ATTITUDES TOWARD THE GLOBAL MISSION

Training for the interface managers and employees is only a small part of the challenge of attitudes. Our concern, in the global corporation, is that the global strategy gets implemented. Nothing can doom it more quickly but silently than the apathy of management, support, and production staff toward the new global mission. The Ho-Hum attitude toward a global mission will sweep it under the carpet in no time. The Yuk attitude toward foreign customers and colleagues will doom the global strategy.

Beyond those who must deal personally and professionally with non-Americans, the entire workforce should become committed to the global mission. Managers' and employees' attitudes toward this mission must turn positive, and their activities and behavior become constructive. Training for these goals may be less intimate psychologically than the cross-cultural training recommended for those on the actual cultural interface, yet it must be a combination of training that attacks prevailing attitudes towards foreigners and at the same time builds enthusiasm and commitment to the global mission of the company.

Thus the global executive establishes a number of different schemes to develop involvement in the global mission by all employees. Like most good management techniques, the schemes should mix both obvious measures to attract attention to the global mission with more subtle ones. Though there may be general schemes outlined in the cross-cultural training manuals, much must be unique to the company. In our experience, there is no better way to inaugurate strategic planning than to draw all participants into brainstorming its implementation. If one of the implementation steps to the global plan is to draw employees into personal and professional involvement with the new corporate mission, then having them participate in designing an employee-involvement program makes a grand opening to the process. Some trigger-ideas for employee involvement appear in Figure 4–1.

FIGURE 4-1 _____
Trigger Ideas for Employee Involvement
_____

Brainstorming

Without criticism of any idea, draw employees into offering all their ideas for involving other employees in the global mission.

Committees

Committees tend to be ineffective in getting things done, but they are excellent for drawing out ideas. Form small groups, quality circles, small committees for eliciting ideas for involving employees.

Language Study

Offer instruction in the languages of all those countries in which you operate—at the plant and office. Have instruction on company time. If not possible, pay tuition for *any* employee to study the target languages at a local college or community college.

Vacation Package Tours

Offer cut-rate vacation package tours to all employees, only to the countries in which you are going to do business.

Incentive Tours

Offer incentive tours for performance related to the global strategy for any level of employee. Make certain that *all* tours go overseas and to the countries where you do business. (A good idea to involve your U.S. distributors.)

Contests

Try supplementing incentive awards with contests that don't relate to jobs. Make the awards as attractive as Bingo.

Visitors

Use foreign students from your target countries as interns during the college semester. Make certain that all visiting firemen and women from your target countries do more than just walk through the plant: have them eat a brown bag lunch (or better) with clerical, support, and production employees, getting to know each other as individuals.

Flags

Arrayed behind and beneath the U.S. flag, fly the flags of all countries where you do business—daily.

Entertainment

When supplemental entertainment is provided, fill it in with music, dance, and films from your target countries.

RECRUITMENT OF AMERICAN MANAGERS

The global executive must be concerned about the quality of managers he or she recruits to the company. This book might provide a profile of the executive or manager candidate to be sought, either at an entry level or from among established managers. The global mission will depend on committed and talented managers. So far, American companies do not seem to be seeking the candidate that is needed.

A study published in 1985 by the Institute of International Education reinforced earlier studies (Hayden, 1979; Hayden, 1980) about recruitment for international business. Boiled down to barest essentials, the truth is that American corporations tend not to regard undergraduate or even graduate international studies or second language capacity as important skills (a point we will treat later in Chapter Seven). A limited number of companies, and only for specifically international positions, will put some emphasis on prior overseas experience.

> We called one major pharmaceutical manufacturer that had global operations and asked the personnel director what qualifications he was looking for in new managerial talent. He replied: "Aw, we just hire army brats!" Actually, he was pretty wise, but it was quite clear that he didn't have the slightest idea what peculiar talents the army brats brought him that were valuable. Others have found that their ability to move comfortably in alien surroundings made them more effective offshore managers.

The undergraduate junior year abroad in some cases was taken as a serious achievement, but not in any guaranteed sense. In sum, American employers hire for international work according to the same standards they use for domestic management positions: skill and knowledge in finance, sales, or technology. Few look for a personality that will offer an intuited understanding of the corporate culture. We don't think American management recruitment is very foresighted.

Corporate America at any level—whether the company is now engaged in exports or imports—should be seeking to recruit the global executive now. Those who are already trained and mentally prepared to be global executives should be committing their talents to making global strategies work in companies that have made a serious commitment to going global.

The very special problems faced by the woman manager should be noted here, but because those problems relate to the management of non-American employees and the offshore operation, we have reserved them for treatment in Chapter Five.

We have made a point that the global executive, whether new recruit, in-service executive, or manager, must be able to walk the Eightfold Path of planning, involving, operating, timing, communicating, researching, networking, and negotiating. To this list might be added other personal and professional qualities.

The global executive must show an unwillingness to make snap judgments about other persons, coupled with a capacity to judge them in their cultural context. To this basic quality we would add natural intuition, used without apology but with judgment. Within the corporation, he or she should show a sensitivity toward the company's product without being sucked into unproductive management processes. An antenna should always be deployed to capture subtle signals radiating from offshore markets or from the host country. He or she should have an artist's ability to negotiate successfully with foreigners. Ultimately there is little more important than a willingness to undertake risks on behalf of both self and corporation, and in these days the risks may be of life and limb as well as of professional reputation or company career. The global executive in today's global corporation should display these attributes and should seek to recruit others that display them.

RECRUITING NON-AMERICAN PARTNERS, ASSOCIATES, AND EMPLOYEES

So far in this chapter we have dwelt on the American executive and American employees' attitudes toward both the global mission and dealing with people who are not like us. "But what about *them*?" can justifiably be asked. We, too, have felt upset at being treated beneath our dignity. We can empathize with President Nixon when Mrs. Gandhi appeared to lecture him on values, for to American eyes Indians can seem awfully arrogant. The attitudes, skills, and experiences of non-American employees can also make or break the global mission.

The most important challenge to global business expansion is recruitment. Recruitment includes identifying the right joint venture partner, regional distributor, and foreign investor, as well as ancillary personnel, interpreters, negotiators, and direct employees. We will discuss managing non-Americans in the next chapter. We will highlight one fundamental problem here—how to test "loyalty." We don't mean loyalty in the sense of patriotism or nationalism, but loyalty in the sense of how well that person will understand, empathize with, and relate to the company and its global mission. There are some important questions to ask before entering business arrangements with a person who was not the product of American culture—including employing that person.

For example, earlier we discussed the American employee's attitude toward other nations and cultures, remarking that the U.S. employee should know how to field troublesome questions about U.S. policies without being defensive. The foreigner's attitude toward the United States can be just as important. In this case, the executive should pepper the questions with some provocative ones, to test whether the person is able to respond without becoming defensive. While dedication and loyalty to the motherland may be desirable, the inability to put it into both the global context and the corporation's historical U.S. orientation may cause difficulties later.

The person engaged as a distributor or hired as an offshore manager should have had previous experience outside the home country. For U.S. companies at least some experience should have been in the United States. If this person has had no personal or professional experience outside the native land, take another look. First-hand experience offshore for foreign partners, distributors, or managers may be just as critical to your success as the same kind of experience for American managers. It doesn't help very much to move a native of Germany with five years' experience working for you in Nairobi to Peoria unless you are sure the person understands the differences between Germany, Kenya, and the United States. First-hand U.S. experience for non-Americans helps remove some of those attitudes that we take for arrogance and which make it so hard for us to manage relations with foreign associates or employees.

Is this a person with a closed mind? Is the person so immersed in the way things are done and always have been done in his or her own country that there is resistance to a new corporate culture (for even adapted to local environments, let's face it, the corporate culture will *always* reflect its origins). Ask yourself if this is a

FIGURE 4–2 _____

How Do We Test Loyalty? (offshore employees, distributors, partners, negotiators)

_____

Whom do we hire when we take that plunge overseas? Here are eight measures to take of your prospects before you engage:

1. How does he or she view the United States?

   If the person is unable to respond to provocative questions about his or her own nation without becoming defensive, don't go any further. Dedication and loyalty to the motherland is to be desired, but not the inability to put it in perspective with the company's historical U.S. orientation.

2. Has he or she had previous foreign, offshore experience?

   If this person has not had a personal or professional experience outside the native land, take another look: first hand experience may be critical to your success.

3. Does he or she demonstrate clear mental flexibility?

   Are this person's ideas open to change? Does he or she wait to listen to other's ideas before responding, and in responding does he or she show understanding of what the other person has said and why? If not, look elsewhere.

4. Can he or she change behavior in different environments?

   Is this person's behavior open to change? Can he or she respond to different signals and change behavior? Anyone without this flexibility goes on the waiting list.

5. Has the person had first-hand business experience in United States?

   Better get someone who's had personal experience here. You wouldn't want to move a person who'd spent five years in Nairobi to New York, unless you were sure he or she understood the differences between them.

6. Does the person display international savvy in general?

   Does the person show that he or she has learned how to assess the local ground rules before acting in *any* country? This is the sign of the real professional: someone who knows how to learn from experience in another country—*fast*.

7. Can he or she recognize when behavior is influenced by cultural expectations, as in negotiating situations?

   Does the person really demonstrate a general awareness and understanding of the patterns of cultural differences in human behavior? "All people are the same"? Don't touch!

8. Does he or she show sensitivity to relations between individuals?

   How does he or she respond to verbal and nonverbal signals from someone different from themselves? If he or she doesn't hold back and wait to find out what the other person is really intending, then leave 'em Stateside.

person who waits to listen to another's ideas before responding. When responding, does the person show an understanding of what the other person has said? Is there an ability to see their perspective?

For the non-American (and the American), the ability to change behavior in different environments is essential. Being able to detect signals from the host culture must be paired with an ability to change behavior and respond positively to those signals. This is a higher order of cross-cultural skill, but one that is in critically short supply in international business. Some U.S. executives, for example, have complained that Europeans tend to look down on America. If you hear such complaints among your employees it is a symptom of something wrong and it shows that they may not have what the global corporation needs. If you are convinced that the European treats the United States with condescension, you should get along without him or her. You can get along very well without this kind of sterile stereotyping.

In general, the non-American should have international savvy. The person should show that he or she has learned the local ground rules before reacting to someone else, irrespective of country—the sign of the really professional global executive. The speed at which this person picks up the local ground rules is also a clear sign of professionalism.

This implies that the person has already learned that behaviors are influenced by cultural expectations and that American expectations are going to dominate, irrespective of how global the corporate culture is intended to become. All people are not the same, but must be treated differently, including Americans.

Finally, the foreign associate should show sensitivity to relations between individuals. For those from more traditional societies, the group assumes more importance than we tend to give it in America. Their unconscious pattern is to think in group rather than in individual terms. Even if the company is a raving success at converting its corporate culture into something global, it is unlikely that the fundamental individualism of its American roots will wither. The foreign associate or employee must be able to deal with what seems like a lack of discipline and decorum among individual Americans.

There were two of us American nationals in the office in New Delhi, and there were many times when we were befuddled by the Indian response to our behavior. My colleague, always the philosopher, concluded that our Indian employees did not take us seriously because we engaged in a great deal of backslapping and bantering. We seemed to make a joke out of our work, therefore, they concluded, we ourselves didn't take it seriously.

Once we had established the truth of his perception, we took steps to demonstrate to our staff that, no matter how much fun we seemed to be having, we took our tasks, our goals, and our deadlines with grim earnestness.The message got across—and we continued to have fun.

The one attitude that simply cannot be tolerated is a fundamental political and social antipathy toward the company's home country and its culture. For the American corporation, this means the United States and its culture. No matter how hard you try and how successful the American executive may be, the company will still be at root an American growth. A prospective partner or employee who cannot live comfortably with the company's origins ought to work with a company from another country or find other employment. Enough instances will emerge in managing the offshore operation that will evoke accusations of "imperialism" without recruiting trouble.

REDUNDANCY

Embarking on a global plan does involve a number of new operations. Exports, for example, involve a great deal more documentation than domestic shipments, and financing packages are almost always different with new customers. Imports from offshore sources likewise require more paperwork and pierside inspections. To these burdens are added the cultural and communications obstacles that we have discussed.

Finding employees for these jobs is much like any other recruitment or personnel assignment task, but there are two exceptions.

First, any employee—management or support staff—who will have to interact in person, by telephone, or by correspondence with persons offshore should undergo the special training advocated earlier. Their attitudes toward non-Americans must be positive (not fawning, but positive), and they must be able to communicate. (We will see later on in Chapter Seven how important communications are, both verbal and non-verbal.) These interface persons bear a specially heavy responsibility for the success of any global plan: with a rotten egg here, even the most carefully-conceived plan can smell bad.

Second, there should be carefully-planned redundancy among the managers and staff assigned to functions that are newly established as a result of the global plan. There is a history in American business of entering global markets in a fit of absence of mind—treating exports and imports as add-ons to the basic business. The inevitable consequence is that personnel assignments are made in a haphazard fashion, often leaving the company exposed at critical times. The most obvious example is the documentation clerk, usually a person meticulous with detail who latches onto the complexities of export and import documents with relish. That clerk's enthusiasm relieves the manager of a deep worry that he or she will have to handle documentation alone or constantly spoon-feed the document clerk, but it also frequently leads to overdependence on that increasingly specialized employee. When he or she goes on vacation just when a major shipment is about to arrive at the shipping juncture, the shipment waits and the company misses its shipment date—the next order may never come.

Similarly, the Japanese language-proficient reception clerk at the downtown hotel should not be alone in that skill, especially when Japanese guests arrive during different shifts. If it is important to have the Japanese-speaking clerk in the first place, it is important to cover that need at all times.

These comments simply reinforce what we said in the last chapter: going global cannot be inadvertent or haphazard if it is going to work for the corporation. It must be carefully planned and conscientiously executed. For conscientious execution, personnel redundancy is essential so that the new positions and functions created are never left vacant or unattended.

We argue strongly for redundancy for a cultural function as well. Having duplication of trained employees for tasks related to the offshore operations commits more individuals personally and it changes more individuals' perspectives. So, the global executive sees redundancy as a tool for change, as well as insurance against being caught short-handed in an essential task.

Therefore, redundancy is to be viewed not only as a way of covering especially critical tasks, but as a means of drawing the staff into full membership in the new culture and sharing the new outlook that will guide the corporation through coming decades.

DRAWING IN MANAGERS

Another management policy that is crucial for a successful global plan is for the very best of the company's existing managers to be drawn directly into supervising its offshore operations. Global operations should not be reserved for self-styled internationalists. The global executive is not a specialist, but a person who believes the company must go global, and that what's global must come into the company's operations. Global operations should become an expected assignment of every single management employee until the company is fully staffed with people who bear the honor of being global executives.

There are a number of case histories of companies, including some of the most successful multinationals, in which the executive who succeeded offshore or who managed offshore operations from headquarters came to be regarded as a specialist. Nothing can be more insidiously counterproductive than allowing accumulated, rich, international experience to remain isolated from the corporate main stream. In part, this is because international operations of established multinational and global corporations tend to be organized into a separate division and, in the large ones, into regional divisions or sections. Once assigned to the International Division or to one of the Regional Sections, a manager often finds it impossible to break out of the mold and to move into the line functions from which promotions to the executive offices most frequently come.

> Our friend, Al, was a manager for a multinational in Karachi, Brussels, Beirut, and Tananarive. In each, he experienced great managerial success before being brought back to corporate headquarters. Al, by any reasonable standards, was a successful corporate executive, and should have been on the up-escalator on the promotion route to the penthouse suite. To outside observers he was clearly CEO material.
>
> After three years at headquarters, however, he recognized that he could not break the company's perception of him as a specialist. Al, to the brass, was the offshore executive exceptionally skilled at his job. The idea that the offshore executive brought the richest of experience and talents to the executive offices never seemed to cross the right minds.
>
> Al, discouraged, applied for and was given presidency of the Middle East subsidiary. His health broken, he died in Beirut from shattered expectations, not from its civil war.

Or take another case, the young branch manager for a big American bank in Bombay. He loved Bombay, loved working in India, loved the luxurious, laid-back life style of the foreign bank manager in a developing country. But he also knew that he would never progress into mainline banking operations in New York unless he got a transfer out of the international department. The last we heard of him, he was an account officer in the corporate business division, living in a one-bedroom apartment in Queens and detesting New York—but he had mounted the up-escalator to the penthouse suite.

Going global means integrating international operations into the strategic plan of the corporation and recasting all plans in terms of global operations. Irrespective of whether offshore operations are separately departmentalized, the global plan demands clear-headed, far-sighted, immensely talented managers. The clear implication of a global plan for management is a fluid and effortless transfer of managers between domestic and offshore operations. Senior management must recognize that the next generation of managers must be drawn from those who have become global executives. The alternative of leaving the global mission to those who like that sort of thing, but passing all of the management rewards to those who keep their careers focused on domestic matters, dooms the company to languish in that limited domestic market where the hounds of foreign competition are bound to break in and nip away at it. Restructuring, in our view, is far less important than a policy that rotates the best executives and up-and-coming managers into both global and domestic operations.

Lesson One, therefore, is to demonstrate that global experience or offshore experience is not a factor limiting upward movement of a person. The executive who has had offshore experience or who has managed exports, offshore production or procurement, or imports should be a *favored* candidate for promotion over the manager whose entire experience has been domestic. Especially dangerous in our increasingly interdependent world is favoring financial experts for highest offices. Not only does this demonstrate that the company is domestically focused, but that short-term results are favored over long-term development (We will return to this topic in Chapter Six). David Halberstam's *The Reckoning* (1986) makes this point convincingly with respect to the Ford Motor Company.

Anything management does sends messages. Messages are received by employees, including aspiring executives, in ways that may not have been intended by senior management. Thus the global executive must be certain that advancements and honors awarded are given to those who have been most involved in global operations and have contributed the most to the success of the global plan. No event is quite so compelling as the fact of promotion: management must be certain that the right message is read from that event, not the wrong one. Promote the person with global success, then make every announcement convey the message that it was *global* success that contributed to that person's advancement. Only in this way may the most talented of young managers be drawn into global operations.

Dangers of Offshore Employee Specialization

There's another danger in considering international management as a specialty. The company for which our friend, Al, worked was as much a loser as was Al himself. Look for a moment at the global strategy emerging from the process we discussed in Chapter Three. A global plan requires that international activity be an *integral* part of the corporation's mission and therefore of its operations. The point was made that treating exports or offshore operations as an add-on on top of the domestic business of the company was not a sufficiently comprehensive view of competing in the globalized marketplace. This view almost inevitably leads to decisions in which the offshore operation would come in second-best to the onshore. In short, the global plan must be comprehensive, not only in terms of its goals and objectives, but in terms of company operations and firing-line decision making.

The traditional practice of regarding executives who succeed in offshore operations as offshore specialists, then, is dysfunctional in the global corporation. It must become established policy that all upwardly-bound managers are given assignments that involve the global operation, so that they bring to the higher offices to which they are eventually promoted a more comprehensive, global view. At the same time, to respond to an employee's successful offshore management by identifying him or her as a specialist too valuable to bring back to headquarters or to reassign to a line function elsewhere cuts off an enriching process for the executive office.

People who have succeeded offshore have faced the ordinary executive responsibilities successfully, under conditions that frequently have involved great personal stress and the management of complex social and economic circumstances often packed with explosive political potential.

> I was, by any account, a low-level manager for a gigantic institution, but my position as manager of an office in New Delhi gave me experience I probably could not have gained in the United States. In many other countries, the American manager can move in circles closed to him or her at home. In three years, I had personal meetings with two successive Presidents of India and was able to speak with the Prime Minister at a morning audience. When I went to a party, I was apt to find myself rubbing elbows with Supreme Court justices and Members of Parliament. The biggest industrialists of India would see me at my request. Because of these connections, I was able to withstand a nationwide clamor for throwing out the rascally Americans that followed the 1967 CIA scandal (over CIA penetration of a number of world organizations). Two other, nonofficial American offices were ordered closed by the government of India, but not ours.
>
> When I finally took a management position in the home office, the experience I had acquired in merely keeping my operation alive in India was refocused on changing policy in the United States. Without my experience, I believe I can safely say that the home office would not have changed the way it has.

The executive who has succeeded and survived offshore should carry into higher office the highest managerial qualifications—just from surviving and prospering through such political and social challenges.

Which executive do you want running the company, one who has been able to juggle the complex political, economic, financial, cultural, and managerial responsibilities of an offshore position or someone who has succeeded mainly in the internal warfare of the corporate headquarters? For all the skills that the latter may bring to executive responsibility, the most prominent skills tend to be short-term and *ad hoc*, while the executive who has succeeded in Karachi or Jakarta or Amsterdam has a broader view of the company and has achieved a much broader managerial experience.

Studies show that American business has not yet broken from its time-honored way of recognizing merit—or presumption of merit. Presumed merit applies to those activities and managerial successes that are judged against an out-of-date frame of reference.

They are judged against Theory X management, not Theory Y. They are judged against what the Old Boys did in the 1920s, and they are as outdated as white flannels and black wool blazers at the yacht club regatta. They are judged against mostly domestic achievement when the marketplace has already turned global.

What the global executive needs (and will introduce if it does not already exist) is a promotion and reward scheme that is related to the global strategy. That means: (1) recruitment will focus on knowledge, skills, and personality that are likely to succeed either offshore or when dealing domestically with offshore problems and people; (2) periodic—but not too rapid—rotation of all management employees through assignments that are global in nature; and (3) a reward scheme that singles out those who have helped the global plan for special recognition that outshines almost any other award given by the company.

SUMMARY

The global plan requires managers to manage and staff to operate. Both managers and staff should be committed to the global plan and equipped with knowledge, skills, and attitudes to make it work. Recruitment should bring in managers with the appropriate background, and by appropriate we mean serious study of the world outside America, first-hand experience overseas, and second-language skills. Training for all employees is in order to redirect attitudes to be more positively responsive toward the rest of the world and to the strangeness of new customers, new associates, new managers, and new investors who come in from abroad. Training for the executives, managers, and staff who will be dealing with non-Americans should take on a broader dimension. Not only attitudinal exercises, but training programs that focus on the cultural differences and the ambiguities and paradoxes that abound in unfamiliar cultures should be required. Redundancy should be planned and carefully executed to cover all eventualities. Finally, an incentive and reward system should be devised for every level of employee, but especially for those who otherwise might be left in specialized positions within international business compartments. The next generation of CEOs should be drawn from among those with the broadest global experience and the greatest successes at the complex management tasks demanded in international business.

THE GLOBAL EXECUTIVE AS GLOBAL OPERATOR

An Inventory of Skills and Attitudes

- Skill to make a global strategy operational.
- The courage to break traditional patterns of corporate culture.
- An appropriate and intuitive sense of the corporate culture and an ability to manipulate it toward globalization.
- Freedom from the management cliches and shibboleths of American business.
- An entrepreneurial ability to take risks, even as an employed executive.
- Capacity to keep to objectives in spite of surprises.
- A keen sense of the similarities and differences between domestic and foreign operations.
- Ability to manage successfully in regions where the spoken word carries more importance than the written word.
- Skill to fit other people's loyalties into a context where they will not be judged by alien values, but contribute constructively to the corporate goals.
- Skill to manage people who aren't like us.
- Capacity to recognize universal rewards and know when to use them and when to use rewards of more local value.
- Firm sense of product and the overriding importance of product quality.
- Ability to manage skillfully, but without being obsessed with, the process of management.
- Sensitivity to the speed, frequency, and quality of communication with offshore customers, managers, associates.
- Ability to manage complex international transactions without being overwhelmed by the details.
- Perception of factors other than price that can be used to make an offshore sale and the ability to use them in successful transactions.

The Global Operator

Going global causes the most obvious strains in the operations area. Adjusting the home company's methods and attitudes to the environment in which it operates abroad becomes priority number one. Companies report that the most important lesson learned from international operations starts with the simple and obvious matter of managing and owning at a distance. The company must also learn to adjust to the host culture; to respect the quality of the foreign subsidiary, in spite of its differences; to put strict financial controls in place and to maintain strong technical control; to plan in more detail than anticipated; and to be able to communicate adequately (Newbould, 1978).

In spite of the unique quality of many corporate operations, there are some valid generalizations about the global company and the role of the global executive in its operations.

Once again, offshore operations have some distinctly different characteristics that make it dangerous for executives to assume that, except for export-import paperwork, business is business the world around. Business is judged according to different standards when it crosses national borders. Management faces challenges of a different sort and a different calibre when the executive is of one nationality, and the employee of another. In some world areas, businesspeople generally are looked down on, yet in many world areas American executives' heads spin because of the high level of society in which they can move.

Again permit me to draw from my Indian experience. There, *babuji* is a term meaning "revered uncle" but in practice it is used perjoratively to deride the Indian businessman. But as a Westerner I was able to move at a very high level anywhere I went in India. It could be leftover deference to the British, but I think it reflects an Indian admiration for Western achievements. In any event, the wise American executive uses it—without abusing his welcome.

Marketing also must be reshaped for offshore success. Japanese consumers, for example, have been carefully studied to ascertain their responsiveness to American imports. Not surprisingly, they display the same kind of consumer judgments that Americans had toward Japanese toys and trinkets before World War II. American goods are suspected to be of inferior quality, comes the report, a shock to our national pride. We have long thought of our goods as the most technologically superior and of highest production-line quality. Despite evidence that American quality has slipped over the past decade or two, the significant point is that the Japanese consumer administers a different standard of product judgment than the American.

Likewise, American jeans are the rage in India, a land that produces much of the world's denim. The quality standard applied has little to do with the textiles, for some of the material in U.S. jeans is made in India. The standard is that American products are desirable just because they are American.

In an era of increasingly fierce global competition, how American companies handle judgments about their products or services, how they manage the delivery and distribution of those goods and services, and how they manage relationships with their non-American distributors, partners, managers, and employees become matters of crucial importance. These soon become operational matters.

American executives simply cannot continue to assume that American tastes and judgments of quality, price, and service are going to prevail in other parts of the world. Nor can American executives presume that American management operates according to some magical, universal principles. Office procedures designed for Americans fail even with the British who superficially seem so much like us. Plants designed for American operation may lead to catastrophic failure in a culture where preventive maintenance is not commonly practiced. *Both marketing and management must change as they go overseas.*

At this point, the adaptation and manipulation of the corporate culture is the most critical—and it is here that most American companies muff it. In this chapter, we will examine some of the operating keys to global success, and the first is the manipulation of the corporate culture.

ADAPTING THE CORPORATE CULTURE

Involvement of personnel at all levels was highlighted in the last chapter as one element critical to global success. In this chapter we focus on the spirit of the company that must leap from its origin in American culture to become a lively force in cultures in which it is a stranger.

A corporation is a child of its culture. Management is affected by cultural values and attitudes, just as our own self-vision is affected by our culture. Marketing is also affected by its culture. Take the issue of employee motivation: motivation depends on the freedoms and constraints of the society in which the person has been reared. If the society is a traditional society, like many of those in Asia or Africa, a person's future is pretty well determined by birth and location of birth. The individual's role is ascribed to him or her by the society. Although the revolution of rising expectations has made some citizens of those lands try to throw off their ascribed roles and statuses, the vast bulk of the population will accept what fate has given to each individual. Thus, the individual's attitudes toward his or her role and status are affected by the expectations of that society toward the individual person and the role and status ascribed to him or her. To "manage" a person from such a society becomes an essay in determining how the society circumscribed that person's life and expectations, then managing within those limits. Management fails when it gives an individual work incentives and rewards that are based on premises brought in from a different society. Premises of American culture that each person is freely able to achieve his or her own highest potential do not operate in traditional cultures.

> An enormously successful Venezuelan was told that he had been "promoted" to the U.S. headquarters as vice president with a very handsome increase in salary. The company was shocked when he politely turned down the advancement, saying only that his first duty was to his family, and that the family belonged in Venezuela, not in the United States. What to one seemed an advancement to the other undermined what he held most dear.

What went awry? The corporate culture expected to reward this individual with advancement and increments in pay. He had been a loyal and productive employee. The gulf between the corporate culture (that expected a positive response to rewards for his own achievements) and his own native culture (that put family, friends, and familiar locale above power and salary) sent this plan askid.

The corporate culture must be understood first. A thoroughly absorbed comprehension is needed, not just awareness that the culture exists. Then the corporate culture has to be deliberately and conscientiously adapted to fit the circumstances in which it will operate outside the United States (if that is where the corporation had its origins).

When I arrived in New Delhi to manage the Center, it had been in operation just one year. The founder, who had managed it during its first year, was a man of many outstanding qualities, much admired among his colleagues. But he laid the foundation for most of my management troubles.

Using good American business practice, he had recognized that circumstances could change and that operations could be retrenched or the Center close without much warning. In every employee's letter of appointment he included a clause that carefully stated that employment could be terminated at any time without cause. He assumed when writing these letters that the employee would recognize that his or her job would last only as long as U.S. government grants kept coming.

It was my bad luck that the federal funds began to dry up almost as soon as I arrived. With little regard for budgetary constraints, my predecessor had already hired 32 officers, clerks, messengers, and night watchmen. I now had money for only 12 to 15 employees. That meant I had to lay off employees to make the budget balance. This is not an uncommon American business practice. It is not without its thorns, of course, but layoffs are familiar to any American executive and are always in the backs of employees' minds.

You wouldn't believe the hullabaloo when I told the employees of the layoff! Delegations from those employees that were kept on urged me to change my mind. Those laid off protested bitterly. As a new executive, I had some trouble wrestling with my own emotions on this one.

American workers would have spoken to the reporters outside the gates, filed grievances with the union, and tried to reverse the decision, too. The Indian employees went further, totally discounting the warnings in my predecessor's letters of appointment and assuming that their employment (like any employment in India) was to last for life. Several of them went to a communist member of Parliament. They did not just protest being laid off—they told the M.P. that I was a spy! I was a spy because I typed some of my own letters (letters home, actually)—and I rode my bicycle to deliver these letters to the U.S. Embassy. (Actually, I was riding off to a nearby ruin where a lovely park made it possible to read my papers without telephone interruptions.) I learned about their reports when I picked up a morning paper and found myself a lead article: "Notorious U.S. Spy in Defense Colony."

My predecessor had wisely employed the daughter of the civil servant in charge of law and order in India, the Home Secretary. Knowing that the attack on me was really a veiled attack on him and his boss, the Home Minister, India's second most powerful person, the government of India discounted the story. But to find myself labeled "a notorious espionage agent" came as a considerable surprise to me, for I featured myself as a pretty ordinary manager. Because I had played my political relations properly, this blew over very quickly, but the lesson should have been my predecessor's: do not hire Indian employees unless you intend to keep them for their working lives or unless you have carefully provided in advance a soft landing for them in another position of equal worth.

Fifteen years later, when I really had to close down the whole operation, we took greatest care to make certain that each and every employee had another job before we shut the doors. Layoffs are not expected in India.

In this incident, no one was at fault. It was a case of cultural expectations going awry. The administrative culture from which we had come expected that we could lay off employees as economic circumstances provided. The culture into which we had imported our own management culture did not expect layoffs under any circumstances, even if they had been anticipated in advance.

First, we failed to recognize the cultural expectations of our own management system. We acted on the presumption that the management of people is the management of people the world around. Principles that American management had never asked us to argue or justify, such as the necessity for individual self-help and individual ambition or motivation, were suddenly without any foundation. The locals didn't understand them.

Much of the glue that holds the corporate culture together in the United States is provided by U.S. culture, not by the corporation's culture. American corporate culture is the product of historical forces in Western Europe over the last few hundred years. This is especially true in Britain and Germany since the beginning of the Industrial Revolution, much modified and polished by U.S. manufacturing management. The corporate culture has unconsciously adopted or subsumed the reality of this American and Western cultural or historical glue. We expect the fabric to stay glued when we go abroad, and we are surprised, angry, and disappointed when it doesn't seem to work out that way. It is essential for the company to understand its own corporate culture within the context of American culture before any attempt is made to export it, either through export marketing or offshore management.

Second, in the illustration earlier, we failed to adapt, modify, or manipulate our management culture to fit the expectations of the people with whom we were to work. There is no more certain prescription for trouble than to expect your existing corporate culture to nestle sweetly and nicely into a foreign context. Know your corporate culture and the culture in which it was bred first, then be willing and able to adapt it in order to export it into a context which is unfamiliar.

The first and most important assignment is to understand the adaptations required for managing persons who are not themselves products of the American way of life.

MANAGING NON-AMERICAN EMPLOYEES

A recent letter to the editor in *Business Week* made the point that many products, business systems, and procedures could easily cross national borders, but those aspects of business that are people-centered do not travel as well (Sept. 15, 1986). The people side of marketing or managing continues to perplex U.S. businesses. Managing managers and other employees who are not Americans has been a monumental problem for most American managers of international companies. The dos and don'ts would fill many volumes, for the details vary perplexingly from country to country, even from city to city. There are certain precepts that will help tomorrow's global executive handle the surprises that come from managing people who are different. (Three of the better analyses are Harris, 1979; McCall, 1984; and Berenbeim, 1982.)

Edwards (1978) tells the story of the American tin mining company in Bolivia that had to compete with a French firm for a limited supply of local labor. The American company did what it would have done in the United States to attract labor: it built a movie theatre, supplied modern housing, and substantially raised accepted wage standards. There were few takers. Meanwhile the French company (with its minimal housing, long cafeteria lines, and low pay) continued to attract the workers.

The American management expected the Bolivian Indians to work regular eight-hour days for a weekly wage. They docked pay when the Indians were absent. The French, however, adapted to local customs, and expected the work would get done if the workers were paid by the hour, and no questions were asked if time was taken off for handling village concerns or celebrating a fiesta.

Look at the chart that follows. We have set it up to pose some of the most extreme opposites tomorrow's global executive can encounter. In the left-hand column are components of American business management, in the right column are some extreme, polar

U.S. Management Tasks	*Some Contrary Positions*
The executive takes charge of planning the corporation's future.	In a traditional culture, the only plan is God's Will, Allah's Will, Fate.
The executive is an organizer of other people's work.	Society is already organized, your corporate bureaucracy is just another onerous burden.
The executive recruits those who are most suited to the tasks to be done.	Take only relatives, friends.
The executive selects employees for advancement.	Promotion is based on age, sex, family.
The executive rewards employees in order to get more productivity.	Rewards are for seniority, or for status independent of the company.
The executive is a leader of employees.	You tell *our* leader, he will tell us what to do.
The executive is communicator.	Speak *our* language.
The executive helps people develop better interpersonal relationships.	Relations are fixed in stone.

U.S. Management Tasks	*Some Contrary Positions*
The executive solves problems by knowing why things went wrong, having others fix it.	Don't bother us with why, *you* solve it.
The executive makes decisions based on empirical evidence and clear, logical reasoning.	There is no difference between one course or another, Inshallah: God decides.
The executive works out ways for conflicts to be resolved.	*Our* elders solve conflicts.
The executive is negotiator of legally-binding contracts.	A whole new world where a handshake is worth a corporate lawyer's estate.
The executive controls processes in which people work.	Processes are fixed in tradition and custom; people are not free to control.
The executive is trainer.	You tell our elder, then he will tell us how to do it.
The executive uses numbers to compare and evaluate.	Numbers don't count, only God and people count.
The executive is innovator, always seeking a new and better way to do it.	Newness is the greatest danger to our community.

opposites taken from around the world to illustrate our point.

Put it another way. If management consists of moving from being a doer to being a person who gets things done—a common American description of management—then how do you face getting things done when the employee speaks another language and has no inherent drive to achieve, or where achievers are sat on by their peers and elders, have no technical skills, place family relationships ahead of job loyalty, plan to work for you for life and mean it when they say "Inshallah"—Be it God's Will?

The management challenge is colossal.

Authority. First, people in different cultures respect authority or power in different ways because power is defined in different ways. Expectations of the exercise of power are therefore going to vary considerably between regions of the world.

American authority is, generally speaking, located much closer to the individual employee than is common in most other cultures. While an individual foreman may be a tinpot dictator, American management generally tends to delegate authority to a much lower level than is common in Europe and Asia. This seems true even in a company with a rigid hierarchy and strict rules for performance. Bureaucrats in the United States routinely make decisions reserved for senior officers in other countries.

Expression of power by American executives is displayed in a wide range of managerial styles, but generally with a familiarity and collegiality—even in the Theory X corporation—than is found elsewhere. First names abound even in hidebound, hierarchical, and bureaucratic concerns. For these reasons, non-Americans are often confused, taking first-name use as an indication that power is shared with them. Similarly, American workers and middle managers like to back-talk their immediate supervisors, and American supervisors are experts in using back-talk as a means of relieving pressure in the workplace. That does not mean that in any sense they have yielded their power, a not illogical but still erroneous conclusion reached by many foreign observers.

A person's place in the accepted hierarchy of power has a profound effect on motivation. Everything learned about employee motivation (not just the myths, but the accepted realities of U.S. society) goes topsy turvy when the employee expects no advancement or never to be singled out or have control over his or her own destiny. Power is something that someone else always exercises.

The global executive has to study power and power-distance both in his or her own corporate culture and within the national culture of the employee to be able to understand it and manipulate it for the company's advantage.

Change and Innovation. Second, change has been at the heart of the American success story, not *tradition*. A nation of refugees and immigrants, we came to this continent seeking change and, once we had found change, we have revered it in the concept of progress. Change has come naturally to Americans, in spite of recent signs that we are not all that comfortable with the rapidity of change in the late 20th century.

For most other peoples, however, change represents uncertainty, and uncertainty represents danger. Most other cultures feel threatened not thrilled by the challenge of uncertainty. Our advocacy of technological development, improvements in management processes, and alterations in structure dumbfound many of our friends overseas. Thus when we come plunging into a new country, either as a marketing organization or as a production organization, we stir up gigantic waves that then hinder our ability to accomplish productive work. Coping with our apparently diffuse power structure is already a serious obstacle to performance among non-American employees, and we *add* a rambunctious addiction to change.

Managing overseas requires a great deal more subtlety in advocating and advancing change than in the United States.

> In the late 1960s, Exxon's Indian subsidiary decided to move headquarters from the stormy labor environment of Calcutta to the more serene city of Madras. All white *dhoti* (white collar) employees were offered moving allowances, company housing in Madras, and an extra stipend if they agreed to move.
>
> Virtually none of the employees, who were Bengalis, agreed to move. The change represented a fundamental threat to their order of life and to their family unity. In spite of the grim prospect of joblessness in a nation with virtually no unemployment compensation, they chose to lose their jobs rather than to change.

The presumption that employment is for life is a common reflection of the general antipathy toward change and innovation outside the United States and a few other Western countries. Security, both individual and social, has a higher value than the risk of change. Innovation, in these areas, is not an inspiration but a threat. In many other countries employees expect to spend their lives in one job, so they are not easily dislodged once appointed.

> Our son-in-law, Tony, returned to Athens to visit the travel agency where he had worked eight years ago. He reports that not a single employee other than himself had left in the intervening years, a fact that startled him because the turnover in the United States is so high and he trains new travel agents by the dozens.
>
> "My God! You're all still here!" he exclaimed. "Of course," came the answer, "Where else is there to go?"

Individualism. Third, individualism is subsumed as a given in American society and thus in American corporate life. We believe, in spite of evidence to the contrary, that role and status are achieved by individual self-help. These perceptions may be wrong in the face of reality, but we believe them and our belief makes them work as operating norms in corporate society. Certainly within certain bounds, Americans are able to advance or decline according to their own talents and efforts. Our promotional and reward systems have been established to reward individual self-help. We honor the innovative geniuses of the "skunk works" and have made them totems of excellence in contemporary America.

Watch out, then, when managing in other cultures where the individual who steps out of line to seek advancement is brought back into line by his or her own group.

When I applied for my driver's license in Hyderabad, here's how the application began:

> Name _____
> s/o _____
> Street _____
> etc.

Name and street were easy, it was the s/o that I couldn't fathom. I asked about it and was told that it meant "son of." So I declared: "Then I'll have to leave that blank, because my father is dead." The officer quickly urged, "Oh, no, Sahib, if you don't put in your father's name, how will we know who you are?"

My identity was created not by my hard-earned Harvard Ph.D., my professorship at a university, or any other accomplishments. I was who I was because of my birth—I was my father's son. All they needed to know was his name and village to know who I was. Surnames, in fact, are very recent in India.

Expectation that employees, including managers, will strive for rewards and promotions must be tempered by the practices of the host culture. Watch out for restrictions placed on individual employees by their own peer group that may not work to the company's advantage. This makes motivation and incentive schemes pretty dicey when applied to non-U.S. employees. Experimentation and a willingness to yield to local customs until alternatives can be found are indispensable when trying to manage non-Americans.

Supervision, too, creates vectors we wouldn't expect at home. Who the supervisor is may be more important than the supervisory skill the supervisor possesses. If a supervisor is really screwing up, the best American practice is to remove that supervisor (in spite of the thousands of alternatives that managers persist in trying). In another land, it simply may not be possible to remove that disastrous supervisor without losing the entire workforce. Innovative ways of inspiring effective supervision in different parts of the world are among the most creative talents in the armory of the global executive.

Do we have specific solutions to problems of motivating or supervising employees? Yes, but they are so culture-specific that they do not belong in a general book on global management. Try to build a collection of books on the culture where you will be managing as the foundation for dealing with these problems, and before departure or before starting your assignment consult an area specialist with first-hand experience in the region.

Sex. Fourth, remember the place of men and women. Few Americans fully recognize the enormous strides we have taken recently toward the radical transformation of women's roles in our society. We don't realize this until we go abroad and see how few, even among the industrialized countries, have gone so far.

The grim fact of life around the world is that women do not play the same roles in management or in corporate life generally as they do in the United States. Women executives in different parts of the world are often relatives of the controlling family. Women workers are restricted to lower, menial tasks. Even the secretaries in many countries are predominately male.

> *Business Week* recently profiled a successful Japanese bond salesperson. She is remarkable, not at all like the ubiquitous young office females, always giggling and handling routine office jobs for the men, including serving their tea. She is unlike these office women because she opted to stay beyond her mid-20s, the age when most *garu* leave. Pronounce *garu* "girl," the English word with all of its old-fashioned American office expectations prior to Women's Lib. While the thrust of the *BW* article is that things are changing in Japan, it concludes that their expectations must still be very modest.

Perceptions and expectations relative to sex roles are close to the heart of any culture. While Hindu society may be patriarchal, patrilineal, patronymic, patrilocal, and paternalistic, the key decisions—on marriage in particular—are made by women. Yet those women do not assume the mantle of family authority, no matter how well they wield their power. Likewise, in Kpelle society of West Africa, the selection of seed is made entirely by women, who thus control the survival of the society from starvation. Again, the women are self-effacing and do not strut their authority.

In business overseas it is generally true that very few women have risen to positions of authority comparable to what has happened recently in America. Business worldwide is still male-dominated for better or for worse, and our own American attitudes toward that fact are not going to change it.

For the American woman executive, this poses serious obstacles. It often means finding a male to use for representing one's professional views, particularly in negotiations where women are generally excluded, and especially if orders must be given to a male. Giving orders to senior males is even more problematical. To perform such tasks overseas demands extraordinary maturity and self-assurance on the part of the American woman. She must also muster her defenses against having a male intermediary be taken as the final authority by foreign associates or negotiators or having the subordinate male think he can defy orders. It may mean taking quietly a lot of male denigration, but at the same time working solidly, and courageously to demonstrate that women are capable of all that men are and that the women's movement in the United States carries important messages for other cultures.

All the problems are not for the woman executive, for in some countries it will be very difficult indeed for the American male to give direct orders to female workers. The intermediary is usually easy to identify, but handling one's objectives by indirection becomes a relatively highly-developed art form among American males whose operations employ large numbers of women.

The American woman executive's dilemma here is the best illustration of our argument that you have to know your corporate and parent cultures first, and then manipulate them to fit the local context—*without abandoning values that are vital.* Reflect on our earlier advice that the executive should wait to find out what influences the foreigner's behavior or decision making before reacting or deciding. Place a woman executive in a position of authority overseas with full knowledge on the part of both the company and the woman herself that the appointment is in part a message to the other country and reflects something very important about the company's own culture.

Thus the denigration of women in other parts of the world does not mean that tomorrow's global executives cannot be women. It does prescribe different approaches to the exercise of normal managerial authority in many offshore situations. It also makes it very difficult indeed to promote a local woman to a managerial post in a country where most women simply do not work as managers. We would not hesitate to assign a woman executive to a post in any part of the world, but we would be certain that she understood the constraints on her freedom of action exercised by the host culture. We would also understand that the company is going to be taking a risk, may have to face some additional problems with offshore employees and others, and yet is transmitting an important message related to the company's mission. Under any circumstances, the authority given to women should be the same as if a man were in the position. Predeparture training of women executives would have to include special techniques in getting things done overseas without actually seeming to get them done, for getting things done is what is expected of males there, not females.

> I appointed an Indian woman to manage some of our training programs in India. Some years later it became clear that to keep in the Indian government's good graces we had to have an Indian executive rather than an American and we appointed her to serve as the local director. The second in command failed to recognize her authority—he was a male and senior to her in age. Because she had had American education and training, she related well to the Americans who were in and out, and because her father had been the head of India's civil service, she was well connected in government. Once we tamed her subordinate, our little office ran pretty well.
>
> But then she was appointed to head a quasi-official binational agency, with full support from the American Board members. The three or four department managers over whom she was placed—all Indian males—tried persistently to undermine her authority. Only by playing her trump cards (which were American) did she manage to relieve their pressure on her and survive.
>
> The curious twist to this story is that the first-ever director of that same agency had been an American woman. Strong-willed and with vast experience in India, she had run a very tight ship and had always had the respect of the department heads, although she did use her fiscal officer to serve as her buffer on some occasions. But she was an outsider, an American, and so was exempt from the Indian expectation that no woman should hold an executive position.

Company support, as well as a well-developed sense of self-worth, are devices to help the offshore woman manager ride out the storms of unexpected and unwanted sexual advances, unconscious social slights, and frequent displays of lack of trust. (Copeland and Griggs, 1985, 219–24)

The Word. American managers have been reared in a society that revolves around the written word. Many people in the world are not as thoroughly tied up with the written word. We get our information from books and other written authorities, or from persons that we rely on to have acquired their knowledge from books, from wire-service teletypes, or from the written notes of first-hand reporters. We seek information from libraries and databases, both of which are written.

Moreover, in our present litigious society, we have learned not to trust the spoken word. "Get it in writing" is almost an Eleventh Commandment.

This is not true in much of the rest of the world where faith is placed in whom you are dealing with and how and is replaced by the Arab's handshake, the Japanese' expectations of an ongoing personal relationship, or the Latin embrace. Written instructions don't carry the weight of spoken, but then the spoken instructions don't carry much weight unless the line of authority has been clearly established.

Form. Form, in many parts of the world, from England to Japan to China, may be much more important than substance. We will return to this with respect to negotiation where form and substance most frequently collide for the American executive. In managing people in the office or on the shop floor, you may have to pay more attention to the formalities of communication and interpersonal behavior than to the substance. If the American executive can begin to put substance and content after the formalities, he or she will find overseas managing a whole lot more relaxing.

Language. We will devote a whole chapter to managing communications.

Time. We feel that time sense is so important that we will devote a chapter to it, as well.

Fate. Different views of divine or supernatural forces prevail in different areas of the world. Outside of Europe, look for much more reliance on Divine Will in decision making and in views of the future. Inshallah is the Arab expression given when one hopes the results are going to be favorable, but deferring to Allah's judgment. Americans have moved so far beyond taking God into account in their business lives and in their business decision making that they find it hard to deal with first-hand. It may sometimes be necessary to act as if God had decided already to back a management decision for it to work.

Authority and power, change and innovation, individualism, sex, written versus spoken word, language, time, and fate are absolutely fundamental constructs in our world of business management. There are a number of others with which the reader might want to become acquainted in the literature of cross-cultural management (especially the Harris and Moran books). Our mission is to make the global executive aware that these conflicts exist and that he or she must be prepared to meet them and manage in spite of them.

Operating Keys to Export Marketing Success

1. Reliable product quality.
2. Dependability of service, especially of technical consultation and spare parts.
3. Prompt replies to overseas inquiries and questions, preferably by telex— many foreigners don't place as much faith in the spoken word, especially over the telephone.
4. Clear, but flexible, pricing policies within a long-term goal, making sure that the difference between domestic price and offshore price is readily understandable and not capricious.
5. Dependability of delivery—the most common American export fault is late delivery or uncertain delivery.
6. Provide up-to-the-minute information to the export staff: they may not be close to home, but they are just as important as the sales staff in domestic regions.
7. Maintain open communications with offshore distributors or partners: treat them as you want to be treated.
8. Keep overseas marketing people motivated. They may respond to different motivations, but that is no reason to neglect the need to keep them going.
9. Pay close attention to credit terms: maintain a fair trade-off between the safest and the most attractive.
10. Provide good management of details: documentation, cargo, insurance, letters of credit.

When you go outside the United States, you may feel as though you have walked through the looking glass. In large measure, that is why global management is so very much fun. Now, let's turn to some specific operating challenges, with special reference to the challenges of exporting from the United States.

PRODUCT QUALITY

Product quality is a major global operations challenge.

When competing in global markets against Japanese manufacturers whose record for quality control has set new records in the world of manufacturing, product quality assumes a new importance. Unfortunately, the recent skid in American product quality has become a serious handicap to the U.S. global marketer. Quality is not an absolute, but is largely determined by reference to values and attitudes of the culture, some of which are close to global norms, but many of which are idiosyncratic to the culture doing the judging.

Theodore Levitt (1986) has argued that global standardization has led to growing world competition based on efficiency of production, distribution, marketing, and management. This, he claims, tends to make price the dominant feature of marketing. As every competitor takes a fix on price, the pressure is then on the company to assure that high quality or reliability is inherent in the product at that price.

Reliability of quality is the number one operating challenge to the global executive. In an age where U.S. manufacturing is being weaned from Theory X management, and workers in the production line are both assuming and being assigned more responsibility for creative solutions to fabrication problems and for quality control, we must recognize that the challenge is not so much productivity improvement (whatever that means) as it is enhancement of the reliability of product quality. It is quality that will sell in a world market dominated by price considerations.

Look no further than the Japanese automobile import success in the United States to confirm this. While the Japanese auto companies did deliver an economical model suited to American tastes, the trigger factor in their marketing success was an incredible record of product reliability.

As America moves more and more into a service economy, and, therefore, as exports of tradeable services assume a larger role in the American share of global trade, quality control becomes much more difficult to monitor and manage. Compared to discovering that a mistake has been made in assembly of a machine, discovering the mistake made by an insurance underwriter, travel agent, meeting planner, or banker is infinitely more difficult. Because such mistakes only come to surface much later than the transaction, they have more devastating effect than a defect in a machine which is usually covered by warranty. Thus there is a major managerial challenge in the service sector to highlight to employees the importance of initial quality control and to establish monitoring facilities to maintain it.

The global executive puts reliable product or service quality at the very top of the list of operating priorities. The global executive must recognize that "quality" is not an absolute, but a dangerously slippery variable that may easily elude definition when moving from one market to another.

DEPENDABILITY OF SERVICE

Second on the list of operating priorities is dependability of service. Distance, of course, makes service so very much harder to deliver and to monitor for quality, but global competition puts a premium on satisfactory service.

> We own a European car that has needed very few repairs. Thank God, for if we had had to order more than the few spare parts actually needed over the last eight years, both we and the car would have been broke most of the time. Spare parts have to be ordered from New Jersey. They are never in stock, few service persons know how to use them to repair the car, and the cost of parts is out of sight.

Extend our problems with the car to a European's or Latin American's problem with some other kind of product, say, a complex, one-of-a-kind machine tool. If technical consultation were not available after the sale and installation, and if spare parts were to be ordered fabricated specially, it is easy to see that the offshore buyer would be product-resistant.

I have been working with a company recently that makes a product used in the manufacture of other products for industry and consumers. To apply the product to the finished goods requires special machinery. My client does not make the application machinery himself. This company works through an export management company, so it has had no formal offshore representation on the post-sale side of a transaction, leaving customers at the mercy of the technical staffs supplied by the manufacturer of the machinery that applies the product or the export management company that handles his exports. When a problem of application arises, the customer has no recourse but to telephone or telex my client in America for advice. And the president of the company wonders why he doesn't sell more abroad?

Dependable service and readily available spare parts are part of the equation we discussed in Chapter Two. It is very difficult for a U.S. manufacturer to provide these if export operations are through domestic or indirect sales. The preferred arrangement is for an offshore distributor to provide these services and parts. That means bringing in the distributor's technical staff for training here or establishing a training program overseas until all pertinent staff are able to deliver technical advice and service. It also means finding a reliable but still cost-effective way to stock spare parts in far distant parts of the world. In this particular art, no company has succeeded like Caterpillar, and the fabled Rolls Royce. Both assure purchasers that their equipment will be down for no more than 24 hours. If spare parts are not available in that area of the world, they will be airfreighted at once.

Note that in these cases, Caterpillar and Rolls are able to export their own corporate culture around the world and elicit a positive cultural response: the customer wants service as well as quality and is happy to have the manufacturer deliver it in his own country and on terms that please him.

More imaginative shipping procedures for spare parts and the availability of small package air shipment to almost any airport in the world has made it easier to guarantee a supply of spares. The old wisdom is appropriate here: it is not the first sale you are after, but the second and third. A satisfied customer overseas will be money in the bank in a few years. A customer sitting waiting for a part with equipment and workers idle is not so likely to be a repeat customer.

DEPENDABILITY OF DELIVERY

Recall my friend, John, and his discomfort at the failure of the RV manufacturer to deliver on time 50 motor homes for the Arabs. John complains, as a freelance export agent for a variety of products, that the single most troubling failure of American firms is late delivery. Next is its cousin, uncertain delivery. Among Arabs, at least, delayed delivery amounts to no delivery.

How do American companies seem to get away with late delivery to their U.S. customers? Is there something of a cultural expectation here that is different between us and Arabia? (I wonder how an Arab would have tolerated the four-month wait I just endured for repair of my chain saw. Luckily there are few trees in Saudi Arabia!)

There will never be a world without production delays. The gremlins will find a way to foul up even the most skillful production plan. Yet there are companies that have mastered on-time delivery, and the list is growing rapidly as American firms move more boldly toward just-in-time (JIT) inventory control. JIT is made possible in American industry not just by the application of Japanese techniques. In fact, JIT in Japan depends on Japanese social affinities between suppliers and fabricators that are almost totally foreign to U.S. culture and are not easily found in U.S. business culture. JIT does work in American culture, not because we have the manufacturer-supplier social bond but because we have been able to adapt computers to help coordinate manufacture, including inventory control. A real challenge to American ingenuity might be to apply JIT to export operations.

As American companies move more stridently into global markets, they will be required to sharpen up their on-time capabilities. Once again, we refer back to the importance of establishing offshore connections with distributors, in joint ventures, or through subsidiary operations that will make it possible to assure delivery on a much more reliable basis than we Americans have been famed for. A skilled export shipping staff (with appropriate training and redundancy) working with a reliable foreign freight forwarder (or if you are going the other way, a skilled import shipping staff and reliable customs house broker) will be a precious asset in managing on-time delivery. A lot of Americans complain about the shipping companies and airlines, but their complaints would be better directed at their own understanding of how these transportation companies work and at managing the interface with them in a more effective and efficient manner.

We can make few more useful recommendations to the global executive than to get into the hands of an experienced foreign freight forwarder (outbound) and customs house broker (inbound)—often the same company but different personnel. Not only will these people help with paperwork (see later in this chapter), but they are able to calculate the safest, most economic, and most timely ways to ship goods.

With respect to the service sector, the same caveats apply, but in this case the dependable delivery should be of commitments, paperwork, contracts, and dates of service activation. Maybe it belongs in another category, but we heard this story a few days ago:

> This story may be hypothetical, but if it is, it is probably so close to a true story as to be wholly believable. A hotel general manager determined his marketing priorities for the next fiscal year. A forward-looking professional, he decided that the sales and marketing department should shoot for a target of 6 percent of the hotel's volume to be from international visitors. His sales and marketing people went right to work and were overjoyed to land a tour group for a certain date with an important client, the Japan Travel Bureau.
>
> But the general manager's budget also required 50 percent of volume to be corporate business. When one of the *Fortune* 500 suddenly decided to hold a meeting at the same time the Japanese tourists were to be there, he told the sales staff to try to postpone the JTB group, or, failing that, to cancel. They had to cancel.
>
> This hotel is no longer able to do business with the Japan Travel Bureau.

PROMPT REPLIES TO OVERSEAS INQUIRIES

> I was appalled to find that my secretary—the best secretary in the world—was saving up letters in foreign languages until she had enough to make it worth her while running down translators for them. A backlog of six week's worth of letters was in her Action Box. Although at that time I was not in the export or import businesses, it was still profoundly embarrassing to me.

Earlier, when I was in the publishing business and helping some of my overseas associates to solicit book orders from the United States, I discovered that some school districts had standing office orders that no airmail postage was authorized, effectively ruling out delivering book orders to Japan or India before the order expired.

While these may be extreme cases, we have found enough evidence to suggest that American executives ought to be more concerned not only with the quality of communications (see Chapter Seven), but with the timeliness of communications. A support staff member does not have the same sense of urgency as either the salesperson or the manager, and the support person is, for a variety of social, cultural, and educational reasons, more likely to regard foreigners as less important than Americans. A simple bottleneck like this on a clerk's desk may do more damage than an inaccurate political risk assessment in building global business, yet it is within the manager's capacity to resolve it.

First, inquiries and questions from overseas should be answered the day they are received, common sense in any market-sensitive operation. If we Americans are to take pride in our sense of time, then this is the place to begin. Show that our culture and your corporate culture values time very highly, not as a way of imposing speed on others, but as a demonstration of your interest in having the business. Reply *probably* should be by telex in the first instance—at the very least, an acknowledgement of the inquiry should be sent by telex.

Second, reply should be on paper, first by telex and with a confirmation by airmail. Americans are in the habit of conducting business over the telephone, and with a familiarity that is unexpected among other nations. It may be hard to remember that many people place little reliance on telephone communications and are offended by the "OK, Hans!" or "Attaboy, Oshiro!" familiarity, and to realize that the telephone is not an effective instrument for answering serious inquiries or crucial questions. In some parts of the world, there is greater faith placed in the word on paper than the spoken word on the telephone. Curiously, these parts of the world may also be those parts of the world that put more faith in the personal relationship than in the binding contract. But a telephone conversation is not sealed by a shaking of hands or a brotherly embrace, while a message on telex has a more substantial quality.

Airmail confirmation is essential, for sometimes telex messages go astray and sometimes, alas, they are forged. Airmail does not mean next day delivery, but often may take as long as a month to reach its destination. Alternative mailing of correspondence by "express packets" (a dodge around the federal monopoly on first class mail) may be recommended. Courier services, while very expensive, are your best guarantee that a critical document gets there: an individual carries your piece on his or her person on a scheduled airliner, walks it through customs on the other end, and the courier service delivers it to its destination.

Here the challenge is timeliness rather than cost. If you have a market-sensitive management position, you will well understand that old adage that it takes money to make money.

PRICING POLICIES

Theodore Levitt argues that price determines all in the globalized marketplace (Levitt, 1986). Whether or not Levitt's globalization of markets thesis works equally well in every part of the globe, his argument that price drives the market has to be considered carefully by the global executive, market by market.

TRADE-OFFS IN TRADE

Where it is difficult and dangerous to compromise on price:

Trade-off on terms of shipment.

Who pays land freight, ocean freight, insurance?

Trade-off on terms of payment.

Credit terms offer room for compromise.

Trade-off in barter or countertrade.

Countertrade is not unattractive, just unfamiliar. Set up with a countertrade broker and see how it can take the place of cash and facilitate compromises on price.

Trade-off on speed of delivery.

Sometimes they'll pay more if the goods come quickly.

Here, on a very practical level, however, we should be more concerned with the pricing *policy* rather than the price itself. There are three policy issues that should be considered: price changes, price flexibility, and price differentials between markets.

Price changes put off buyers. Frequent price changes confuse buyers, and offshore purchasers are going to be sensitive to frequent changes in price.

First, export prices need to be relatively stable because of the long lead time needed to book the order and have it delivered thousands of miles away. Second, perhaps unfortunately, non-Americans expect Americans to use fixed prices more consistently than might be expected of sellers from parts of the world where bargaining is a highly developed art form. Third, an old saw is important in offshore sales: "The second sale is more important than the first." Subsequent sales will determine long-term success. It is important not to convey the impression that once the foreign order is booked the supplier is going to put the squeeze on with subsequent orders. The latter practice still lingers on among some American and other industrial countries, a relic of the lost age of industrial imperialism. There are often very strong cultural and nationalistic reactions to such practices as price squeezing, dumping of unsold goods from the American domestic market on the Third World, and price gouging of other kinds. The company that has a long-range global plan will avoid taking advantage of short-term opportunities that tempt management to use such practices.

Pricing flexibility is going to become a more urgent necessity as, if, and when the market becomes even more globalized, and as you stay with fixed prices for longer periods of time. Negotiated price reductions for volume, for market-development purposes, and to meet foreign competition will be constantly on the desk of the manager of export marketing and sales, and they will always present perplexing options. In general, sticking with established prices is a better policy than being beaten down by one or another offshore customer.

This doesn't mean that there is no flexibility, but flexibility cannot come from monkeying around with price. The manager has the freedom to play with price in other customer cost factors, particularly the assumption of such expensive components in each sale as cargo insurance, freight forwarding charges, ocean or air freight, even import or export duties. In our view, pricing flexibility should be strictly limited to certain guidelines that are enforceable. Playing with delivered cost is a different matter, however, than changing price. Trade-offs on who pays for what in connection with the shipment can give the executive a margin to play with of at least 20 percent and often 30 percent of the gross delivered price to the customer. It is here that the global executive enters a world less familiar than the domestic market, but one of vital importance to success in the global market.

Price differentials between regional markets are more tricky, but are determined more by the competition than by any intrinsic factors within one or another market. Watch out for some common risks. For instance, there is a temptation to try to squeeze a little more out of the market in a developing country where your product is absolutely necessary to the government's development plans. Backfires are common in this practice, for Third World governments have been known to penalize corporations they discover are unfairly exploiting their position. To be excluded from some of those enormous markets can be a long-term disadvantage to a company with a global strategy. Be extremely cautious on this one, watching your competition carefully, but keeping an eye on non-market factors (such as political and social ones) that can hamstring your marketing efforts.

CREDIT

Like pricing, credit should be seen as a global marketing tool. And, like pricing, there are trade-offs that can be used to make your product or service more attractive. In general, international credit practices have been standardized, but the global company will also be operating within markets where credit practices are considerably different.

For example, Pakistan, a Muslim nation, has "abolished" interest which is prohibited by the Qu'ran, but a substitute is available. Credit practices in Thailand caused Ford enormous problems when they introduced some of their products there, for the customer expectations on credit could not be fulfilled by Ford which had expected more "normal," American credit practices to prevail. A general rule to follow is that cross-national transactions are governed by relatively universal credit practices, while internal transactions may be subject to traditions quite unfamiliar to American business.

International. The most attractive credit terms when crossing national boundaries are much the same as within the United States: open account, net 30 days. Because of regulations, risks, and time factors, open account is used only by those who have had extended experience with their overseas distributor or customer. We believe that open account should be the credit arrangement of preference, and that American distaste for using open account on export shipments is because of American perceptions of foreigners as somehow unworthy of their trust.

> In more than a decade of dealing with suppliers and distributors overseas, including India (which is regarded by many businesspeople as unreliable), our company dealt about 90 percent on open account and had very little real difficulty. The key to our success was a strong personal bond with our overseas colleagues.
>
> Our trust was broached in West Africa on a couple of occasions when our suppliers took our advances and used them for their own purposes. In one case, that included a three-day bender and the purchase of a new wife. But our relations with those suppliers had not been sealed into a warm, personal relationship beforehand.
>
> John, the friend mentioned a couple of times earlier, has had several requests recently for contracts from his Arab customers. Until recently, contracts were most unusual in Arab lands, but equally uncommon was dealing with someone you had never met. John has never met the Arabs who are requesting written contracts.

We believe that Americans are less trusting of non-Americans generally than is good for satisfactory business relationships. As American business goes global, it must be more willing to accept credit relationships based on mutual trust.

Letters of credit, available at any bank with an international department, like shipping terms, offer a wide scope for negotiating more or less favorable terms, and can be used as a bargaining tool. Other credit instruments, more complex than the irrevocable letter of credit also offer scope for bargaining. Because of their variety and complexities, generalizations are difficult.

Suffice it to say that international credit terms should represent a fair trade-off between what is the safest to the American exporter and what is most attractive—mainly what is the most profitable to *both* parties. Safety, like beauty, is in the eye of the beholder. Familiarity with offshore operations will change one's mind about safety as some of the unknowns disappear with experience. At some point, the desire to market successfully over a long period of years to a customer or distributor will tip the balance in favor of attractive credit terms. The global executive will seek to understand the balance between risk and attractiveness and will recognize that the balance point is constantly shifting, requiring agility on the executive's part to seek the proper balance.

Market-Specific. Copeland and Griggs (1985) maintain that credit arrangements can be difficult in some nations. Taboos of various kinds, as well as attempts to make the foreign guest comfortable, can put off discussing credit arrangements until past when they should have been considered. Remember that a new foreign arrangement is like starting business from scratch: the budding entrepreneur feels hurt if the banker denies credit or imposes limiting conditions or demands security. The same hurt can be magnified by cultural differences.

It is most comforting to nurture no firm expectations of when and how you will get your money out of a deal. While this is surely a cautious rule on which to begin operations, the veteran global executive will quickly develop a nose for credit arrangements in his or her marketplaces, and will be able eventually to find suitable arrangements. Note here the word *eventually*. While we'll discuss time later on, we should insert right here the notion that finding and using credit will not be something done in a single day or even a single visit.

Credit is also tied up with national policies on the repatriation of foreign capital and profits. These policies are particularly stringent in the Eastern Bloc and in the Third World where they were introduced to maintain local economic strength against the industrialized West and to permit local economic strength to develop. What the global executive should recognize is that these policies emphatically project the national pride and the nation's world view. To meddle with these attitudes is courting business disaster. Work with them, not against them.

Discussion of credit information is considered later under the topic of research in Chapter Eight.

IMPORTANCE OF CURRENT INFORMATION

The common practice of leaving offshore executives, partners, associates, managers, marketing personnel, distributors, and suppliers in the dark is, perhaps, understandable, but it is inexcusable. It seems that the old adage, out-of-sight, out-of-mind does indeed mean what the Japanese translation made of it: if you lose your sight, you'll go crazy!

Shortsighted though it may be, many American companies feed their overseas staff and associates information on a highly selective basis. Instructions that are directly pertinent to their responsibilities get there all right, but the offshore managers tend not to receive information as soon as it is available.

> I wasn't told of the resignation of the CEO until several months after it happened. "Oh, we thought you knew!" was the inane response I was given when I asked why they hadn't told me. The lateral movement of my boss's boss to a position outside the main line of authority obviously made a difference in how my operation would be regarded when priorities were set. But I learned of it months after the event, when I had spent days working on plans I hoped he would be able to sell to senior management at home.

Of critical importance, too, is up-to-date information that relates to the corporate culture, the company's mission, developments in product and process, and important second-level personnel changes. To expect the same kind of service or better from staff posted overseas when information crucial to their long-term success is held back is a particular failing of medium-sized companies. It may be the cost of postage, telex, or telephone that deters communicating information that everyone else in the company has, but it may be something much more basic in the corporate culture.

For whatever reason, communicating insufficient information—and particularly current, up-to-the-minute information—imposes a serious limitation on the overseas staff's effectiveness. And this criticism applies to those companies that have no overseas staff of their own but rely on local or regional distributors, and to those in joint ventures with non-American partners. How can the people over there represent the company if they are not fully apprised of what's going on at headquarters?

We'll go one step further: we believe it is important to draw overseas staff and associates into the generative process that goes before all new products, services, and processes come to the marketing stage. It isn't just informing them that's important, it's involving them, too (see Chapter Four). Just because they are not physically present should not condemn overseas staff and associates to being merely message-recipients. These people are crucial to the global marketing effort of the global corporation. Their assessment, therefore, of market, product, service, pricing, and other factors associated with product development not only should be solicited, but should be built into the creative process out of which corporate changes are made.

Because the global marketplace has been produced by ease of communications and transportation, it should be seen as extraordinarily sensitive to corporate information. Bad news travels faster around the world today than ever before. It is vital, therefore, to get any news that may adversely affect marketing and management staff overseas to them as quickly as possible. Otherwise, they may discover the news from your competitors.

OPEN COMMUNICATIONS

Related to rapidity of communication is openness of communication. While this is more pertinent to personnel and organizations that are not employed by the company, such as distributors and joint venture partners, it also applies to employed managers and other remote, offshore staff. Offshore staff seem to become second-class citizens, more remote cousins than brothers and sisters, when they go offshore. Absence, in most corporations, *doth not* make the heart grow fonder. Distance from the informal communications network makes those posted overseas feel left out, even hostile. Experienced offshore executives often make it a badge of honor that they are not caught up in the politicking and gossiping and the backbiting of the home office, but don't let that fool you: they also feel aggrieved that they are left out. The same exclusion of foreign nationals reduces their loyalty to the company and their willingness to take risks, in particular when they have to confront their own national government or fellow nationals.

It is vital for the global corporation to treat its offshore personnel, partners, and distributors as it would wish to be treated in similar circumstances. The company must transmit news (even of the washing of dirty linen) of any information that is to be shared with domestic staff and distributors. If those overseas do not learn in a timely fashion of important changes at headquarters that will affect their effectiveness in the offshore markets, they will be operating with hands tied behind their backs.

Sharing company gossip is never easy. The boss doesn't want any gossip to circulate because it undermines his or her control of the company. Yet gossip is one important way to communicate corporate culture. When gossip validates the corporate mission and supports the policies of senior management, it is a useful and even productive function of the corporate culture. Even when gossip is used for its own purposes by the executive suite, it works to grease the skids for the corporate launchings. Gossip, however, depends on personal contact or at least the capacity to use the telephone for protracted discussions. The offshore staff, American and non-American, are normally left out.

Then there is the exclusion of non-American executives, managers, employees, and associates from the informal communications network. This is a normal phenomenon in any living culture: there is information that is, by its very nature, esoteric—limited to the in-group. As non-American employees are not automatically seen as members of the in-group, they tend to be excluded from the gossip transmitted through the informal network. Sometimes this natural exclusion is tightened by cultural strains and even hostilities between nationalities within the organization.

On the other side, it is important for corporate headquarters to regard communications from *offshore* to be as vital as communications from regional sites around the United States.

I have been an offshore executive. Nothing made me madder than some of the decisions made at the home office that simply paid no attention at all to my on-the-site advice. We'd spend days or weeks preparing careful analyses and recommendations, then see a decision coming our way that showed no respect for our advice.

Frustrating, but less stinging, were decisions emerging from other agenda within the gigantic institution that was our parent, where our advice would have been of little relevance irrespective of how hard the decisions may have hit us.

The global mission of the company demands that information from abroad be received openly and given as high a priority as information on markets at home. Only if their information is accorded the same kind of respect as domestic information will offshore sources be able and willing to produce what they are expected to produce.

OVERSEAS MOTIVATION

Motivation of managerial, support, and production employees has received a great deal of attention through writings, speeches, books, and training programs in the last decade. Analysis of the "motivation" discussed suggests that the concept of motivation is about as strongly influenced by American cultural attitudes as are the concepts of management and marketing.

Not long ago we heard of a presentation by a pair of friends of ours that had been prepared for corporate seminars in the United States. The thrust of their program was that employees are motivated by a desire to "be happy." While experts in the field of business psychology will immediately indict this as overly simplistic, it is a not uncommon motivation program theme on the meeting circuit. "Happiness," however, is a term that does not easily translate into other languages and cultures.

> For example, in the 1960s, a high-powered American media team went to India to help promote family planning (population management). After much study, discussion and debate among themselves, they recommended to the Indians the slogan "A small family is a happy family," and asked that it be translated into Hindi. Nervously, the Indians laughed that it would be impossible to translate, for the only Hindi equivalent to "happy family" was "big family." The slogan, then, would have been: "A small family is a big family," which doesn't make too much sense.

Motivation is strongly influenced by cultural factors, including the corporation's own culture. How can one company turn around its productivity by worker involvement while another company still is plagued by lack of worker motivation on the production line? Motivation is a personal matter in America, something that individuals do, often in response to general stimuli, including peer pressure and power influences from management. In other cultures, motivation is not so much an individual as a group matter.

> There was a controversy going on when I visited Balama, a West African village. Problem? One farmer had planted wet rice. The rest of the society was organized around cooperative work groups that slashed and burned the tropical forest to plant upland or dry rice. Upland rice yielded very meager returns, and both the national government and international aid agencies were trying to get the farmers to move into paddyfield cultivation (wet rice) for higher yields. But

guess who was the object of ridicule? Was it the people who persisted in an inefficient cultivating pattern that resulted in marginal diets or the man who had individually broken from the time-honored pattern in order to bring in a cash crop? Obviously, it was the loner. No one actually disturbed the solitary paddyfield planter, but no one worked for him, either.

Culture influences motivation so strongly and with such variety of consequences that it would be presumptuous for us to lay out any ground rules for managing motivation in other cultures. But just because we avoid giving advice here does not mean that the subject is not important. For a global plan to work, it must rest on offshore employees, distributors, and others who are motivated to seek the company's goals *within the context of their own culture.* Because helping to generate motivation among persons who are so different from us presents a major managerial challenge, all too many companies simply put it aside.

Disregarding an overseas management problem as important as employee motivation is a very dangerous practice. It presumes that the American way of encouraging productivity is universal and will apply anywhere. This means, however, that employee behavior is generally expected to conform to Western standards. To export this baggage intact overseas is not only presumptuous but clearly impossible. The corporate culture simply must be re-tuned to the culture in which it is going to try to fit if it is outside the land of the company's birth. Employee motivation is the most clear-cut cultural challenge in the management area.

The global executive, during the offshore phase of his or her career, will make a special effort to ascertain the hierarchy of motivations that prevail among local employees. Use Maslow's model if that helps (Maslow, 1970), with physiological motivations at base, personal and psychological safety next, social security third, ego satisfaction fourth, and self-actualization at the apex. But in cultures that are no more distant from the American than the culture of the United Kingdom, the Maslow model runs into trouble, so something else must be constructed if one needs a model. The motivational diagram will be skewed in societies that ascribe role and status to the individual rather than permit an individual to strive for and achieve role and status. Where class and rigid hierarchy are easily visible, watch out for lack of enthusiasm for motivational rewards and incentives. In West African cultures generally, the cooperative work group, normally a form of extended family group, will govern an individual's motivation more than any of Maslow's steps. In rural India, carried over into much of city life, there is an intricate system of personal interdependencies that mutes the effect of both monetary and personal rewards that are aimed at the individual.

General rules are dangerous, except for the rule that should be universal: know the culture before you start to manage in it. Learn its corollaries. First, know the motivational structure of that culture before establishing goals, incentives, and rewards. Second, remember that setting new goals, incentives, and rewards to fit the motivational patterns of another culture is nothing more or less than adapting and manipulating your own corporate culture to fit the new context.

Basically, however, the global executive will know that finding a basis for motivating the offshore staff is every bit as important as motivating the domestic or headquarters staff.

GOOD MANAGEMENT OF DETAILS

Finally, success in global operations will depend on how well managed are the details of exports and imports. The paperwork of international trade has created a whole industry independent of those who manage their own. About $5 billion is spent on paperwork in the United States each year and slightly less in Europe. Worldwide, the total is perhaps $12 to $15 billion, making it a major enterprise in itself. And, like any enterprise, it ought to be managed well.

Documentation cannot be entirely delegated to foreign freight forwarders and customs house brokers, although for small- and medium-sized firms those agencies offer excellent service at a fair price. Management of documentation will depend on how well your employees have become involved and to what extent you have created redundancy to be certain the job gets done well and on time (Chapter Four). It would be wise to set up a systematic reporting system to track the flow of paperwork, however, in order to be certain that it is accomplished according to the highest standards. Remember that your customer may not come back to you if the paperwork gets bungled and causes trouble on the other end— even once.

Cargo handling, not simply its effect on the delivered cost of your items, but the thoroughness and efficiency with which it is booked, expedited, and managed, will have an effect on your repeat orders.

In our business, we discovered, for example, that the port of New York was too expensive for our small import shipments from Asia and Africa. Little tricks that labor unions, stevedoring firms, and the truckers got away with playing on the big boys in New York amounted to big bucks for us: delayed pick-up by the trucker on the dock so that extra demurrage would have to be paid, pilferage, transfer charges. Even the customs house broker's fees were heavier. So we insisted that offshore procurements be shipped to us either through the port of Boston or the port of Baltimore. It took the same length of time under ordinary conditions, and the Baltimore shipments went in bond to Boston for clearance. But it saved us money in the long run. When therefore, one of our suppliers shipped to us— against our explicit orders—through the port of New York, we were sufficiently upset to question whether we would reorder through him.

Insurance coverage, irrespective of who pays for it, ordinarily is taken out by the shipper. So the exporter has to be certain that the coverage suits the risks involved and that the carrier has a reputation for fair and speedy settlement. The settlement may not amount to many dollars, but if the offshore customer thinks the carrier is giving him a run-around in settling, the burden of that dissatisfaction will come back to haunt the shipper rather than the insurance company.

Letters of credit (and other instruments) likewise require fine attention to detail. Banks in the United States have not been famous for the high salaries they pay their clerical employees, so no one should be surprised by some slip-ups in complex international transactions.

I had a call from the international division of the regional bank we dealt with about a letter of credit we had applied for. "Mr. Ferguson, you've asked for the shipment to come in through the port of Boston, is that right?" "Yes," I replied. "But, Mr. Ferguson," asked the puzzled voice, "is Boston a *port*?"

On another occasion, we applied at the local branch of the same bank for a bank draft in dollars to be cabled to India. After 10 minutes leafing through a big reference book, the assistant vice president looked up in desperation and asked: "Mr. Ferguson, India *is* in Europe, isn't it?"

After these incidents, we spent a great deal more time looking over how we had filled in the blanks on the letter of credit application—and at how the bank had translated them into the terms of the letter itself.

On letters of credit coming the other way, there are management details that ought to be followed to assure that what is specified in the document is what was agreed on in advance. Banks in certain countries have been known to play games with both their local customers and the importers of their nation's goods. The eagle eyes of staff have to be focused on the documents to spot the pitfalls, and the manager has to erect safeguards to be certain that those eyes are keen.

Recently, we worked with a trade association whose members had been having trouble with Korean import agents for their commodity. The American exporters complained that the Koreans were violating the terms of their letters of credit. When we investigated, it turned out that the Korean importers were indeed using the standard terms of the letter of credit against the American suppliers, but were using the terms to their own advantage. The Koreans complained of short-weighting and of substandard materials, claiming the shipments were not what had been ordered in the letters of credit. Of course, bankers are not there to open crates or containers—they only attest that the documents are in order. The Americans, furious, were casting nasty imprecations at the Koreans, and the situation was deteriorating. Each needed the other, but each felt used and abused. There was no violation except to the spirit of the documents.

While this was not so much a matter of management of export details as it was a matter for negotiation between the American exporters and Korean importers, it does suggest that the global executive be aware of the dangers in misinterpreting international documents and establish office procedures for spotting irregularities at an early stage.

SUMMARY

Whether the executive is in a service business with tradeable service exports or in manufacturing, there are some basic operating keys to global success. The first and most persistently troublesome problem is understanding how cultural expectation of executives, managers, employees, distributors, and customers change from one region of the world to another. The second perplexing problem is to adapt the company's own corporate culture to fit into sometimes paradoxical situations abroad. Knowledge of the company's history and culture must therefore be matched by knowledge of the history and culture of the environment into which the company's operations are to be exported. Reliable product quality, dependability of service, and on-time delivery come first.

There are certain key operating procedures that must be carried out effectively. While each of these may be stated independently of the cultural contexts in which business is to be conducted, each is influenced by the particular context of each transaction. The executive who forgets that may only be limiting the growth potential of the global business, but will often find much worse difficulties emerging from failure to understand operating procedure within operating context.

Clear, but flexible pricing policies, current product or service information, open communications with all of those offshore, whether employees or associates, and motivation of offshore personnel are equally a concern for the service and the manufacturing industry. A fair trade-off in credit terms between what is safest and what is most attractive should be sought. And, last but not least, good management of details of international transactions will keep details from assuming a larger-than-life importance in global transactions.

THE GLOBAL EXECUTIVE AS MASTER OF GLOBAL TIME

An Inventory of Skills and Attitudes

- Sensitivity to differences in views of time and its movement among different cultures.
- Ability to set one's own schedule to different perceptions of time.
- Ability to set one's corporate schedule to different realities of time.
- Skill to negotiate patience within the financial community to which the corporation is oriented.
- Skill to negotiate and enforce executive rewards on a long-term rather than a short-term basis, while preserving their incentive character.
- Skill in moving within the financial marketplace for long-term results.
- Skill in using time as a managerial tool.
- Ability to take risks in scheduling all aspects of management.

The Global Timer

The Dance of Life is the title of Edward T. Hall's latest major work on human culture. While all of Hall's brilliant books should be on the global executive's reading list *(The Silent Language, The Hidden Dimension, Beyond Culture)*, this one is about *time*, that most elusive of all abstractions but the most real and ever-present challenge to the American executive. Hall debunks some common concepts of time—that it is a constant and that it is singular. He takes clear aim at our Western notion that time is linear, a single entity running in a straight line from past to future.

In another book entitled *Ceremonial Time: Fifteen Thousand Years on One Square Mile* (Mitchell, 1984), the author muses about time, the eternal mystery, and finds satisfaction in a concept of ceremonial time he has borrowed from some American Indians. In 1987, *Discover* magazine ran a feature article on the mysteries of time. Mitchell, Hall, and the scientists in *Discover* all question our Western, and specifically American, concept of time; Mitchell in a philosophical vein, and Hall in a comprehensive study that compares how time is perceived and used in many different cultures. Our purpose, to equip the global executive with the skills and attitudes needed to compete in the globalized marketplace, is to point out how time must be controlled quite differently—and much more imaginatively—when one goes offshore with business.

In Mexico, *mañana* does mean "tomorrow," but only in the dictionary. In conversation, it only means "soon." When I called this to the attention of an audience recently, a participant said that a Mexican had asked his Arab friend if the Arabic language had the concept of *mañana*. "Of course, came the reply, *bukara*, but it doesn't have the same sense of urgency!"

In Hindi and Urdu languages, *kal* means not only tomorrow, it also means *yesterday*. Trying to set a timetable with such a cultural mindset suggests that patience must come before dates and deadlines.

Copeland and Griggs tell the story of an American oil executive told by a Chinese official that China would one day be the leading nation of the world. The American asked when that would be. The answer was in several hundred years (Copeland, 1985, 10).

Americans watched the evening news for 444 days after the Iranians took hostages, waiting for the news that they had been released. Most Americans were not aware that the captors had been holding a grudge since the seventh century when Ali, son-in-law of the Prophet, had been murdered. If they had anything more than desire to wipe out the infidel, it was patience, monumental patience.

These examples from several languages and cultures may give a hint of the challenges faced by the global executive, whether managing at an overseas installation or from the home office. Irrespective of where one is posted, the management of people and processes will be strongly influenced by both American and foreign concepts and uses of time.

Americans are driven by time. The whole key to the lately fashionable "management by objectives" was to tie specific "timelines" (as well as budget allocations) to objectives and strategies. Note the coined word, *timeline*, which amply confirms Hall's point that Western peoples think of time in linear fashion. Our linear concept of time was shocked a couple of years ago when a British physicist suggested that it had been an accident at the origin of the universe, the "Big Bang," that time had gone the way it had and not the other way. Think about that in your spare time!

The global executive will have to be a new kind of global timer to be able to maintain a sense of purpose and direction in parts of the world where time ticks to a different beat. The first obstacle is internal: can you, the American executive, shed your presuppositions about time in order to get your work done effectively in settings where the *feeling* for time is substantially different? Can you exercise the appropriate managerial response to how your offshore employees and associates treat deadlines and timelines? If you are posted overseas for either a short or long time, can you establish a schedule for yourself, professionally and even personally, that adapts to the time-base of the local culture and keeps schedules set by the home office? If you are managing offshore operations from the home office, can you apply the requisite amount of corporate patience to allow projects to develop at a different pace overseas?

Many Americans posted to foreign bases become intensely frustrated by time, yet few of them ever blame the conflict of time-concepts for their frustration. Even fewer of their office-bound bosses in the United States understand that time itself may be uncontrollable.

> Jim, our frustrated manager in India, was stymied because "things don't get done here." What he really was saying was that Indian decision making did not move at the same pace that he was used to—or that his superiors were pressing on him from the United States. His first challenge, which I believe he bobbled, was to make peace within himself over the pace of life and business in South Asia. Jim continued to pursue the same hours he had followed at home. He complained about how his Indian staff wandered in late and spread out to catch a snooze on the bare floor for an hour or so after lunch. Curiously, he also complained about the fact that the office was open from 9 to 1 on Saturday, which he regarded as some God-given day for golf.
>
> I will concede that time frustrated me on my first visit to South Asia. But I also recognize that, when I returned to the Northeastern part of the United States in the first brisk days of autumn, I was equally frustrated by the speed with which my fellow Americans walked, talked, and conducted their affairs. By the end of the first month back home, I was again moving at the same pace as I had before I had gone abroad, and I was surprised to find myself getting to appointments and dinner dates at the hour scheduled.

Each of the world's locations has at least a slightly different pace. So the first task for the offshore manager is to identify what is that pace and make the personal adjustments that will be necessary in his or her own life. The parallel task for the executive at home is to understand that this change of pace must be accepted for the offshore manager to become effective.

The second challenge won't be as hard if the global executive has faced and conquered the first one. This challenge is to set one's *corporate* schedule to different realities of time. If you've passed the first test, this one will be easier to handle, for at least you will have understood that time is a different commodity where you are working. Again, although the culture is far from typical of what business executives will meet in Europe or Japan, we use our own experience in India to illustrate.

> History—which after all is time past—moves downward in India. The Golden Age is not just a nostalgic hankering for a bygone era, it is real in the sense that it is a guiding ideal of Indian life. It is represented in the principal festival, Dusshera, when Hindus celebrate the victory of Rama (representing Good) over Ravanna (representing Evil). Today is not in the Golden Age, but is in Kala Yuga, the Era of Darkness, the last phase of history before total destruction overtakes the Universe.
>
> In contrast, Americans have been raised for at least a hundred or more years with the notion that history is the story of *progress* from the cave to "higher" life. Though our faith in progress seems to be wavering at the moment, it forms our attitude toward time as history and makes a strong impact on our decision making.

How do your reach decisions in a society that is dominated by the notion that anything we do is bound to be less satisfactory than what was done earlier? How do you explain to your superiors or board at home that it will take more time?

GETTING THINGS DONE

> Three successful U.S. exporters reported to our breakfast meeting on the reasons for their success. One of them said that there were three keys: "patience, ability to relate personally to the foreign distributor, and understanding their way of life." The second also said that there were three keys: "Patience, patience, and patience." The third said, "Yes!"

Patience is certainly a quality we neglect in preparing Americans for management positions. We budget our time as we budget our money; we spend time and waste it. Patience is not our long suit, but it must become a stronger suit if we are to win in offshore management.

Understanding *their* time concept comes first. Then comes understanding the actual rhythm of life. Start with the day itself. Prepare a little exercise for yourself, even if you are only on a short visit to an offshore city. This exercise is to recast the common clock-bound questions about life into society-linked questions. Here are a few examples to start with:

Clock-bound Thinking	Culture-linked Thinking
What time do they get up?	What triggers their awakening?
What time do they arrive at the office?	Is there any generalization about when business starts?
How long is lunch break?	Is there siesta?
What time do they quit?	What signals the day's end?

The key is to adjust your wristwatch-thinking to a clockless world. Even if they do use watches and clocks, such an exercise helps reprogram your own day.

> The Methodist minister stood on the Chief's porch where I had been drinking palm wine with the elders of an African village. "Now we will have our service," he said.
> "What time is church?" I asked, the innocent American.
> "How can I know, you're the only person in the village with a watch," the minister replied. "We gather when everyone is in from the fields."

When you've adjusted to thinking of life-rhythms without a clock, then probe some other areas. For instance, find out the expectations for appointments, both business dates and entertainment dates. Avoid embarrassment and frustration by knowing what *they* expect you to do.

Once you have their day down to a watch-free rhythm, turn to the weekly cycle and see if you can find any patterns in it that are distinctive. Then turn to the cycle of feast days and national holidays. In America, are any decisions made between the 23rd of December and January 2? We shut down almost completely during that 10-day period, but only Christmas Day and New Year's Day are actual holidays.

The same is true elsewhere in the world. Know it in advance, before you find yourself in China during Spring Festival, or in Pakistan, Egypt, or Indonesia during Ramadan, France during August, or Sweden on a summer Friday. Advance knowledge avoids frustration. It also can work to your advantage to know that certain cultures practice the repayment of debts on a certain day—usually the day before the first day of the new year. While it is impolitic to push too hard, such pauses in the annual cycle can be used to your advantage in completing transactions, repaying debts, and negotiating.

Our American attitude toward decision making is related to time. We link the two. For success overseas, try to break that link. Reformulate your approach to decision making so that you and all of your employees at home or abroad can be happy with this definition: *A decision is made when all the factors, of which time may or may not be one, have been taken into consideration.* Time should not be the major consideration for the American manager of offshore operations, for it often is not an important consideration for non-American associates or employees. If time is a consideration to them, then recognize that the consideration may relate to some event in the family of the decision maker (a name-day, or a death-day, or an auspicious day in the personal calendar), or it may relate to some traditional regard for particularly auspicious hours. Take another personal example from India:

> It was a Sunday afternoon when I took my daughter to a renowned South Indian flute player to engage him for lessons. We arrived a little after the time we had set because we had lost our way. Try as I might to talk about music and about Jeannie and about music lessons, Mr. Srinivasan would always direct the conversation aside. But he did keep looking at the large, imported watch on his wrist.
>
> Finally at six o'clock, he smiled and started talking about music. He volunteered that he had steered the conversation away from the expected topic because the period between 4:30 and 6:00 on a Sunday is exceedingly inauspicious for beginning a new endeavor. He must have been right, for she became a star performer.

Deadline-setting, therefore, becomes a much more hazardous part of the manager's occupation in many parts of the world. For the most part, it is better to tailor expectations of decisions made and projects executed according to markers on the chart of the local rhythm rather than to set specific dates, established arbitrarily according to the corporate rhythm at home. Achievement will be much more up to expectations if agreement on the time-frame is reached in advance with some sort of mutual understanding if not consent.

Getting things accomplished in another part of the world, however, is more than managing time. Just as important are some constraints on time that don't relate to how time is regarded. Many perfectly ordinary business tasks have been so streamlined in

American business that when the executive goes into another country he or she stumbles over the time it takes to get things done. Research is a part of the executive's work expectations, whether related to marketing or production. Research forms an entirely separate chapter later on, where we will point out some obstacles to anticipate. But here the point to be made is that fundamental and basic research takes much longer to accomplish outside the United States.

Take such basic research as running down credit information. It is not only the fact that the U.S. executive is unfamiliar with information sources and has to identify them first. It is that we have massaged the delivery of information to impressive rapidity. In the United States, we call D & B or another credit agency and have a report in our hands overnight or electronically. In most countries outside North America, running down credit information can be a major consumer of time. Checking references on a potential distributor is not something done on a three-day visit. A check of competitors should be on the agenda, as well as bank checks—in person, not by letter or phone—on the reliability of the distributor, and spot-checks with customers, satisfied and not satisfied. The ready reference resources are absent, and a lot has to be done on foot with corresponding consumption of managerial time.

Many American businesspersons believe they can do these tasks in less than a week, or, more often, in 48 to 72 hours. In almost every country outside of Western Europe, it is a much longer proposition.

We heard Victor Kiam interviewed on National Public Radio after his—eventually—successful effort to gain distribution for Remington razors in Japan. He had thought it would be quick: he went to his bank contact, asked for references in major department stores, then went off to try to sell them. One big department store's buyer was more than polite, but gave no decision, nor could he be prompted into a decision on subsequent days.

No sale. Nice words, pleasant company, but no sale.

Kiam had operated on the presupposition that his Japanese bank contact was the same kind of official, performing the same sort of services as in the United States, including introductions to such people as department store buyers. Kiam eventually learned that this conception was utterly false. He learned at last that it was essential that he meet not just with his company's account officer in the bank, but with the Managing Director, the CEO, himself. When Kiam met with this august elder, the Managing Director picked up the phone and called his old friend, the Managing Director of the department store, who set up an appointment for the American entrepreneur. When he kept the appointment, he found himself with the same person who had resisted his sales pitch earlier. But this time, the buyer was ready to buy.

Elapsed time? About three times what he had budgeted for.

Experienced international executives who have come to know their world area well will work out schedules for accomplishing certain tasks. Then they will put in a fudge factor such as doubling the time allotted the task for Southern Europe or tripling it for Asia, Africa, or Latin America. Research, negotiation, and bargaining for a deal all take much, much more time even after you are familiar with the turf—and that takes the most time of all.

The global executive who visits or works abroad has to budget time to learn the lay of the land thoroughly, then allot more time than is customary at home to arrange credit, conduct simple research, and conclude negotiations. Meanwhile, he or she has to be certain that the CEO isn't wondering what edge of the world the executive has dropped off. The global executive or CEO at home has to see the other side of this coin and hold the patience required for the job to be done.

CORPORATE PATIENCE

Time in the American corporation is governed by both the American culture around it and the corporate culture within.

> I worked in government for awhile, personally frustrated at the pressure, pressure, pressure to respond to memoranda from higher up and from legislators within 24 or 48 hours, but at the same time taking six years to get my own project approved and funded at the highest levels. It reminded me of my Navy days when the order of the day was to hurry up and wait. It also frustrated me because the very setting of automatic deadlines (set and enforced, alas, by secretaries and executive assistants) tended to confuse senior managers between what was urgent and what was important.

In our catalog of devils plaguing American business, one of the most irksome is this tendency to confuse what is urgent with what is important. The word *urgency* derives from *to urge*: to press on, to hasten. It has within its meaning a sense of time, especially of short-deadline time. *Importance*, on the other hand, springs from the verb *to import*, to bring in. In a business sense, it means to bring up and become weighty. Importance, therefore, is a matter of substance, not time. To confuse the two often means to fly off solving transient issues when the key decisions are left unresolved.

> The young English official was required to pay courtesy calls on the governor and chief justice when reporting for duty. His wife was required to accompany him for each visit, and it was expected that each visit be no less than 15 minutes in length. The visit with the governor, an English gentleman, was easy, and the couple tarried beyond the 15 minutes in comfortable, expatriate ease.
>
> But the chief justice was the first Indian chief justice, and he had not moved into the cantonment area. The way to his house was crowded and dirty. The road narrowed so they had to walk the last furlong or two on foot. The judge's home was a small bungalow with a tiny compound out front marked only by a stone bench across its end. They were not invited inside.
>
> As they sat on the stone bench waiting for the judge, the young bride expressed her horror of the city and the house. Looking at her watch, she extracted her husband's promise to rise, take their leave, and flee back to the cantonment at the instant 15 minutes had been reached. Her urge to run mounted when the chief justice emerged, for he seemed to her obscene in his *lungi* (wrapped skirt), bare chest, sacred thread, and *tilak* (red marks of the worshipper) on his brow.
>
> The eminent jurist did not invite them into his house, but sat with them on the stone bench. They began to converse.
>
> Forty-five minutes later, the lady noted the time, but showed no inclination to flee.

What had happened here? What happened was that importance outweighed urgency. What was important was human discourse, the sharing of the wealth of experience, the judge's hospitable welcoming foreigners to his land and to his home. Time ceased to be urgent. Social intercourse became important.

Our American tendency to confuse urgency with importance was aggravated by the pressures of war in the 1940s when urgency and importance became closer to being the same. But it has been aggravated in the last 30 years by a number of factors.

First, our accounting procedures have become much more standardized, and generally accepted procedures have assumed a force of such strength that few honest executives will challenge them. CPAs want to prepare their reports in a *timely* fashion—

audits for the shareholders, board, and management; tax returns for federal and state authorities.

Second, our financial markets have come to depend much more heavily on quarterly and annual reports on which investment decisions are made.

Third, our private sector has become immensely more dependent on government decisions, especially funding decisions which are made on an annual basis.

Fourth, and less obviously important, employment decisions tend to be made in an annual rhythm tied to children's school years, vacations, and the general summer slowdown, making renewal more obvious by the appearance after Labor Day of new faces at both the entry and advanced levels.

Our markets open and close at the same time, and although it is now possible to buy and sell securities 24 hours a day through offshore markets, few take advantage of the facility. Our offices open and close at the same time, with quite different expectations of promptness on the part of management and staff: management can be expected to drift in a little late—or be there at dawn—but is also expected to stay until the work is done even if into the night or on weekends; staff can be expected to come promptly and leave promptly. There is a circadian rhythm to U.S. office and shop life that is blurred only on the edges. And this rhythm is reinforced by the time tyranny of our radio and television systems. Bryant Gumble and David Hartman will chop off an interview with one of the world's most important and powerful persons because of the tyranny of the stopwatch and the necessity to go on to the next message from the sponsors.

Short-term thinking runs head-on into the long time spans necessary to get things really cooking offshore, whether a marketing plan or a manufacturing scheme. Short-term thinking springs from some of these facts of American business life. Several are worth exploring, for they are especially important to the global executive when he or she occupies a senior executive position while trying to implement a global strategy.

THE GOVERNMENT CYCLE

The American government cycle impels U.S. business toward short-term thinking. American government is less volatile than many other governments in the free world, but it is tied much more firmly to time than any other. Our elective cycle is rigid and unbreakable, rendering many governments ineffective as the last date at which they will be in office approaches. There is no pressure for effectiveness on a lame duck administration at any level, for the constituency is looking toward the next government for results.

Yet the cycle of government has had a profound effect on American decision making, especially since the war years. The heavy reliance of much American industry on contracts from the Pentagon and on other government contracts, federal, state, and local, makes business keenly aware of the funding cycle. That cycle operates on an annual basis, year after year. While our rule of thumb in government was that it took three years to get any new program through the legislative process, once authorization is given, the focus is on the annual funding cycle. Annual, rarely any longer than that.

"Long-term" thinking with respect to government then becomes "next session," which is next year, or "next administration," which constitutionally cannot be more than four years away. With the single most important national document being the *annual* federal budget, we lack substantial incentive to look further into the future. All advocates of some kind of national or industrial planning have been greeted with adamant, if understandable, resistance. While five-year plans have received a bad name from the Eastern Bloc, and while they have rarely achieved their goals in the developing world, they do have a significant influence that might well be helpful in the United States: they force thinking out of short-term molds into at least a regular five-year cycle. That kind of discipline is lacking as long as both the government of the country and its industry work according to the annual cycle. We believe that the global executive will begin to disassociate his or her business rhythm from the annual federal cycle and make some longer-term plans and commitments.

THE FINANCIAL CYCLE

Even more compelling than the annual, biennial, and quadrennial cycles of U.S. government are the pressures of the financial marketplace. If betrothal to the government cycle is an annoying vexation, marriage to the short-term prospects of the financial markets seems close to becoming an intractable problem.

Executives clearly must be responsible to shareholders' interests. That is basically what they are hired and paid to do. They, too, are major shareholders and are immediately responsible to a board of directors consisting of shareholder representatives. There is no way to dodge this responsibility.

Nevertheless, in our view, American business has become too bound up with the vagaries of the financial marketplace and the needs and desires of major investment portfolio managers. The reason is simple: investment managers, especially those who are retained by enormous pension funds and mutual investment trusts, are given goals of improving the value as well as the income of their investments. Because modern technology makes it possible to monitor investments by computer, to trade shares, bonds, or foreign currencies day and night, and to go in and out of investments with the greatest of ease, there are premiums placed on the day-by-day increment in value of the portfolio and its income potential.

Ellsworth (1985) reported that the Fidelity Magellan Fund, one of the best performers among growth mutual funds, had a portfolio turnover of 338 percent in 1979. More recent figures suggest 1986 to be the year in which, for the first time, New York Stock Exchange turnover of total shares was more than 50 percent, meaning that investors were, as a whole, tied to particular investments for less than six months.

Investing for improved value day-by-day or month-by-month may make good sense for portfolio management, but it puts a higher value on short-term gains than on long-term investment. Worse, it puts real pressure on the CEO to achieve short-term results. The exigencies of the marketplace flow over into management of American business, turning executive attention increasingly toward the short term rather than the long.

This trend has had a devastating effect on American competitiveness, one ailment the global executive has to seek to relieve, then to cure. Ellsworth, comparing the effects of the short-term focus of our investment world with the comfortable long-term competitive postures of the Germans and Japanese, says that the American concentration on the welfare of stockholders is quite different from both the Germans and the Japanese. They are more concerned with returns, steady employment, and global competitiveness.

Ellsworth's thesis is that Japanese and German corporations are much more heavily leveraged with debt, relieving them of day-to-day responsiveness to market fortunes of their shares. While this does put them at the mercy of their lenders, both German and

Japanese banks tend to be cozy with their corporate borrowers, their officers serve on boards of directors, and they are generally willing to ride out short cycles in favor of long-term growth. There is, specifically, no legal obstacle to close, even immediate relationships between corporate borrowers and their bankers, as there is in the United States.

This is an important competitive advantage to German and Japanese firms, for they may focus on longer-term decisions rather than on the immediate. There is evidence that the wave of mergers and acquisitions, which has sucked up much of the cash left available for investment after the U.S. deficit has already drained the pool, is in large measure a response to the generally short-term thinking that afflicts our financial markets.

What does the global executive do about short-term pressures from Wall Street? A series of imaginative steps might be recommended. The imagination and the steps must come from global executives, but the series notion must be there from the start. Following a program similar to that recommended in drawing managers and employees into the global strategy, the global executive conceives a long-term, step-by-step program that emphasizes and reemphasizes for shareholders and portfolio managers alike the long-range nature of the global plan and its payoff potential.

The global corporation in our terms must be committed to long-term growth. It must be willing and able to risk a series of successive quarters where offshore investment is dragging down the bottom line. It must have the self-assurance to stick with its commitment even when it results in "weakness" in the short term. This means that the company and its executives must be unrelentingly up-beat and positive about the long-range prospects. The first step is to illustrate with facts and figures that the long-range prospects of the global strategy are to be demonstrably better than if the company stayed domestic. Soft figures may have to be used, but the commitment to the long haul must be hard.

Clearly, a solidly-constructed global strategy backed by an implementation schedule is a first defense. This might become the centerpiece for presentations to securities analysts and portfolio managers by the CEO of a company going global. A clear forecast of how offshore operations are going to contribute to increased profitability, which after all is the principal reason to go global in the first place, should be designed to take off some of the heat. But it will not take all of the heat. Wall Street memories are very short.

Global executives, it seems to us, ought to be organizing their own network to put pressure on the financial world where it counts. For example, CEOs of corporations, executives who recognize that they *must* be applying better long-term thinking, might collaboratively organize to put their own investments into highly visible long-term funds. A mutual fund that emphasizes global accomplishment over many years could at least gain some public relations exposure for this point of view, especially if the names associated with its organization belonged to corporations making global commitments. This alone won't take off the pressure, but it is offered as an illustration of the aggressive posture we believe that executives should be taking against short-term, domestic thinking in the financial marketplace.

Bring in significant portfolio managers, then draw them into the process of global planning (which of course should involve the board as well as management). Force them into a personal and professional commitment to *your* global plan and to your long-term objectives as a way of easing some of the short-term pressure on the company for always wanting quarterly earnings growth.

It is clear by now, we hope, that export growth and growth of a presence in global markets is going to be the result of a long and arduous process, immune to quick fixes. Organizing within the company, and with other companies committed to long-term global growth to counter American short-term decision making, is among the more challenging tasks of today's CEO. It is a challenge, too, for the global executive to be certain that the commitment sticks.

EXECUTIVE INCENTIVES

We discussed rewards and incentives in the last chapter. We did not discuss the special rewards to the persons at the top who can be promoted no higher and for whom increments in annual salary are dysfunctional. We did not discuss stock options, stock bonuses, and other incentives to performance that are tied to the value of the company's shares.

The senior executive who looks more to the end-of-year stock reward than to cash salary inevitably becomes caught up in the short-term thinking of the portfolio manager. He or she becomes more concerned to see that each quarter—in some cases, each month—shows an increment in earnings of the company. This distracts vision from the long term, and is certain to hurt the development of global markets where profits take so long to be realized.

The global corporation should include as part of its global planning process a way of attacking the issue of executive incentives. There are ways that a company could institute an incentive system based on 3-, 5-, or even 10-year growth patterns. While the CEO may be long retired by the time the rewards come, those rewards should outdo the annual incentives by some quantum leap.

For example, if a stock option is offered for meeting annual earnings performance targets at, say, a 20 percent discount from market, how about raising the discount for performance 3 or 5 or 10 years out? *Give* it to them without charge if the long-term target is met, for by that time the pie will have become larger, the wealth of the corporation enhanced, and all of the shareholders will benefit.

Imagination is called for here, imagination that has been in short supply in recent years.

SUMMARY

Outside the United States, it takes longer to get things done and time stretches out in unexpected ways. The global executive who is operating offshore has to adjust personally and professionally to differences in time concept and to realistic expectations of getting things done. The global executive who is managing offshore operations from the home base has to balance time as a factor in decision making with the realities his or her offshore executives, managers, or associates are facing. He or she also must create a kind of corporate patience which is rare in the United States, but which must be found if the company is to compete against Japanese companies that are, with government help, planning 30 years out into the future. Short-term constraints must be removed if the company is to compete with foreign corporations that are not so immediately responsible or responsive to the stock market.

The global executive therefore must not only be a resilient personality when operating abroad, but a person with immense imaginative and creative capacity when operating in the United States to be able to counter short-term thinking with long-term. The way to do it is to assure higher profits from global activities and long-run commitments around the world.

THE GLOBAL EXECUTIVE AS GLOBAL COMMUNICATOR

An Inventory of Skills and Attitudes

- Recognition that business *is* communication.
- Awareness that communication is not automatic, but deserves hard work and constant attention.
- Willingness to undertake new communicative techniques, including mastery of new languages.
- Ability to use more than one language with enough proficiency to conduct professional business.
- Ability to communicate to other executives, managers and staff, irrespective of their mother tongues.
- Sensitivity to nonverbal signals.
- Awareness that the language of business is the customer's language—whatever that may be.
- Enthusiasm for using languages of other nations, especially of customers.
- Skill to handle all of the social preliminaries to negotiations in a language other than own.
- Ability to identify, train, and motivate interpreters and translators for the good of the corporation.
- Intuition to separate the cultural particulars from the universals.
- Skill to use cultural particulars to one's own managerial ends.

The Global Communicator

Business is a series of transactions. A transaction is an act of communication. Business is a series of communications. Business management *is* communication that gets services performed or products manufactured, distributed, marketed, and sold, and it is the communication that draws profit out of the transaction to be used to increase the shareholders' wealth and for other purposes. Business, seen as communication, is a lot easier to export than if business is seen in its normal everyday, tangible meaning because it predisposes the executive to prepare for adaptation in new environments. This perspective makes it easier to understand the dimensions of the management challenge we have been discussing, the challenge to adapt, modify, and manipulate the corporate culture as it changes among the cultural settings in which it operates.

Language makes culture possible. Language lies at the very heart of culture, as its first and most obvious artifact. Language therefore includes not only the names of things and of people and describes their movements in space and time, but language makes possible the abstractions that govern people's behavior and their beliefs, values, and attitudes. It is those abstractions—like friendship, loyalty, trust, permanence, and quality—that make business possible within any culture. To go global means to be able to find common understanding of what those abstractions mean in other languages and other cultures. Once the meanings are comprehended, then corporate operations have to be fine-tuned so as to be able to operate according to the new values those abstractions represent. This is the toughest part of the Theory Q challenge: to export the corporate culture in such a way that it slides smoothly into a cultural context that holds different values and sees the world in fundamentally different ways.

The way executives use language acts as either the grease that slides this adaptation into place or the grit that keeps it from fitting. The global executive is, if anything at all, a global communicator, using spoken language, written language, and nonverbal communications to the advantage of his or her business.

THE UNIVERSAL LANGUAGE OF BUSINESS

The global executive shakes his head in disbelief when hearing again that most pervasive, U.S.-based myth: "English is the universal language of business." It's a myth that continues to blind American businesspersons to the realities of business and bedevil their chances of success. It is baldly false. Leonard A. Lauder, President of Estee Lauder, Inc., who masterminded a major gift to the University of Pennsylvania's Wharton School for the Joseph H. Lauder Institute of Management and International Studies, raised the question (*The New York Times,* October 7, 1985) of how can Americans sell to people unless we can talk to them—product demand notwithstanding. Our lack of communication ability could be seen as both arrogant and self-weakening.

The language of business is *your customer's language*, whatever it is.

English has, of course, grown rapidly as a medium of communication, paralleling the U.S. rise to world economic dominance. It is a useful language because it is alive and changing all the time, making it possible to fit new perspectives, rapid global changes, and advances in technology into understandable communication. Because of its wide use in business and government, many nations of the world require their students to study English. Some even require that students meet minimum proficiency standards, as in the Soviet Union, Germany, and Japan. But that very quality, the quality that makes English so adaptable also makes it possible for many kinds of English to exist side-by-side, some of which are only barely intelligible to each other.

A Japanese "fluent" in English may not necessarily be able to communicate in English when visiting the United States or with U.S. visitors to Japan. Like this author, who can listen to his son-in-law's French-speaking parents and understand almost everything they say, he cannot effectively communicate back in the same language. An Australian, Indian, or Pakistani, born to English as a mother tongue, may not be intelligible in Brooklyn or Atlanta. Translation is needed, especially translation of key attitudes and values that do not translate as easily as the words that represent them.

> I like to tell the story of Ron, my neighbor in Connecticut, who returned from his business trip to Japan where he tried to introduce new production procedures in the Japanese affiliate. I asked him, "How was the trip?"
>
> "I played some great golf," he replied.
>
> "Was it a business success?" I asked.
>
> "Well, you know it's funny, Henry, but for two weeks, they 'yessed' me to death, but when I got back to the home office, nothing seemed to have changed in the Japanese operation."
>
> "Do you know Japanese?" I asked.
>
> "I didn't have to. They all spoke perfect English."
>
> "But do you know 'Japanese English'?" I persisted.
>
> "What do you mean?" he responded, puzzled.
>
> "Did you know that the Japanese—in any language—cannot say 'No,' especially to a distinguished visitor?" I queried him. "Did they say they would study it?"
>
> "Oh, yeah, they said that a lot!"
>
> "If they said they'd study it, Ron, they meant 'No!' "

The executive who presumes that English words mean the same thing to English-speakers from different nations is in for a rude shock before very long.

> Even English speaking countries don't speak American. One American banker was asked to be after-dinner speaker in Australia. He blundered in the first sentence, when he said he was "full." When he heard the nervous laughter, he changed that to say he was "stuffed." In Australia, "full" means "drunk" and "stuffed" means being on the receiving end, so to speak, of sexual intercourse. (Ricks, 1983, 57)

English is not spreading and flourishing as many Americans like to believe. In a recent survey we conducted, one upper-level manager stated: "Why should we teach American kids other languages, when all the rest of the world is going to be using English?" Such a statement reflects not only ignorance but arrogance of the kind that feeds anti-Americanism. In fact, there is evidence that resurgent nationalism in many parts of the world is making

English *less* acceptable as a medium of serious communication rather than more. Many of those areas are markets not seriously tapped by American business.

Yes, English *is* taught around most of the world, but that should not mislead the American executive into believing that people prefer to use it over their own language. Don't we prefer to use our own language in business? Why not expect others to feel the same way? We expect non-Americans even to speak English with us when we are guests in their countries. Speaking only English can be taken as imperialistic and arrogant. Yes, communication continues to be a question for American executives outside the United States.

Someone mentioned to us that, because of tax laws and threat of terrorism, the number of Americans working overseas had shrunk dramatically, so there was no need for this language capacity. Our reply was that there still exists an interface between the American executive and the non-American, though it has moved to the United States. Wherever that interface exists, communication problems will emerge. Naturally, on our own home turf we would prefer to speak English, but we must keep thinking about the sale. The sale is the thing, irrespective of what language it takes to bring it off and on whose turf the bargaining goes on.

LEARNING THE CUSTOMER'S LANGUAGE

The answer: American global executives are simply going to have to learn to use more than English. It should become a high career goal for anyone at or near the entry level. Take Kathy, a hypothetical but representative young American businesswoman. She was a college major in business, but she took a minor in Spanish, a communicative skill she reinforced through a junior year in Spain and two years working for a development agency in Latin America. She came into business with first-hand overseas experience, experience living *and communicating* in another culture and language. A recent study (Kobrin, 1984) showed that multinational recruiters looked first and foremost for college graduates with courses in economics, finance, and accounting. At the same time, they valued credentials like Kathy's above those candidates who had been either business majors without foreign language training or foreign language majors without business courses. Candidates with overseas experience as well as business courses and formal language preparation came in ahead of those who had overseas experience without the business courses. So far, in contrast with the multinationals, employers from medium-sized and smaller companies have generally failed to recognize the importance of the language training and overseas experiences as significantly powerful additional skills among those management employees whom they recruit. This, clearly, is a reflection of the domestic focus of most American business.

It may also reflect a traditional American allergy to second language study. And who can blame them when the language teachers and professors in U.S. schools and colleges have concentrated on drilling them in the past pluperfect subjunctive and not on establishing communicative proficiency? We applaud the recent movement in the language profession toward much more useful goals of communication rather than reading literature and honing skills in literary criticism and historical analysis. For many years, U.S. language teaching has been misdirected to literary objectives, and U.S. attitudes toward language learning have reflected this reality. Americans tend to be convinced that learning another language is inherently difficult. If so, how is it that so many Europeans, Soviets, Asians, and Africans can flip from one language to another without batting an eye or slipping a syllable? Are those people smarter than we are?

Those American beliefs that "languages are hard to learn" and that a person "doesn't have an ear for languages" are also dangerous myths in global business development. Both are poppycock, springing from a century of abysmally bad American language teaching. That is changing rapidly right now, and plenty of enjoyable, exciting language learning opportunities are around.

> When I went into the business of importing Indian books, I had the advantage of already knowing Hindi reasonably well. Thus, if my Indian suppliers didn't know this, I had a tremendous advantage, for I could understand what they said to each other privately in Hindi thinking I couldn't understand. If they did know I spoke Hindi, they would avoid those private asides, considerably limiting their freedom to talk behind my back, so to speak.

There is clear evidence that a person who has mastered a second language (without being born to a bilingual situation) has mastered something more than a capacity to use it for communicating. The act of learning the second language has been, in fact, the act of learning how to learn another—any other—language, for it has been undertaken as a conscious, intellectual exercise. Thus the third language comes much faster than the second, and the psychological hangup most Americans suffer when they lurch into another language begins to ease and they don't feel so self-conscious or fear criticism of errors in grammar, pronunciation, or timing.

The global executive tries to get to a level of minimal communicative proficiency in at least one other language before launching overseas ventures simply because it is good mental preparation. He or she is also receptive to the challenge of learning others. The proficiency level aimed at can be defined as the capacity to carry out *routine* business tasks in a language other than the mother tongue. It does *not* mean being able to conduct delicate negotiations or discuss highly technical or abstruse matters with fluency. It does imply knowing most of the nonverbal clues that go along with the second language in routine business situations.

NONVERBAL COMMUNICATION

Spoken language is only part of the human communication system. Signs and signals without words are sometimes every bit as important as verbal language. Take the brake lights on your car, or the unspoken nod of assent from your boss, or the look of your lover's eyes as powerful signals that are said without words.

Each set of nonverbal signals, however, is as close and particular to a culture as its spoken or written language. Body language, including how close you stand to the person you are speaking with and the movements of your body, arms, fingers, head, and other body parts, can transmit signals that can be misinterpreted with dire consequences. There are many hand signals in the United States, perfectly nice in polite company, that become grossly offensive elsewhere.

The global executive does not presume to learn all the signals any more than he or she presumes to learn all of the world's thousands of languages. But he or she will learn to watch how signals are transmitted nonverbally when visiting or living in another country. Judgment on the meaning of the signals will be reserved until he or she has examined the context, or perhaps talked about the signal with a friendly member of the other culture. Likewise, the global executive will hold back from using casual American signals just as he or she would refrain from deliberately throwing American slang into a business conversation with strangers.

Nonverbal communication is vitally important, and the global executive learns how to read it and use it to business advantage, wherever in the world business demands, even at the home office.

LANGUAGE AND CULTURE

We started this chapter with some comments about how language and culture are closely related social phenomena. They both perpetuate a culture and make it possible for people to live together in a society. The values, beliefs, and attitudes of a culture are carried from person to person through language—spoken and unspoken.

Decisions of any kind, personal, professional, political, or business, are always affected by the values of the culture in which they take place, and by the values of the different cultures represented, if the decision is a cross-cultural one. Behavior coming out of a decision is judged by other people according to the norms of behavior they have been led to expect by their upbringing and education. Behavior is different and the norms are different when cultural lines are crossed, although there is some fundamental overlap between all humans. Murder, rape, and arson, for example, are universally condemned.

Yet the major portion of the arena in which we behave does not overlap with other cultures because the norms, the social values, and perspectives do not overlap. We show this in the first diagram in Figure 7–1. Note the shaded overlap in both diagram 7–a and 7–b. This is the area in which persons of different cultures have mutual understanding. This is where one of them will give the appropriate attribution to why the other behaves the way he or she does. The unshaded area is where people run into trouble in communication and tend to misjudge each other, because the values by which each judges the other are different and unknown to the other. Note that there will *always* be an area of uncertainty, even between two persons of the same culture and even the same family, but the ideal in any society is to enlarge the shaded area, where people can interact without misunderstanding or conflict.

The challenge for the global executive is to expand the shaded

FIGURE 7–1 _____
Enlarging Mutual Understanding
_____

(a) This is the way we are when we meet:

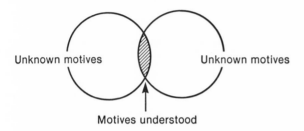

There is a very small area inside of which we accurately attribute motives to the other person's behavior.

(b) This is the mission: to enlarge the area within which we understand what prompts the other person to act or make decisions in a certain way.

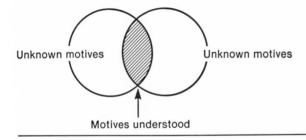

area as widely as possible—and as fast as possible (diagram 7–b). This means that the global executive doesn't just fly in on the Redeye Express and bound right straight into business transactions with the "natives," even if they are English-speaking and seem so much like us. Instead, he or she arrives several days or several weeks before serious business action is expected, using the extra time to push back the unshaded portion, to learn more about what has been in the shadows. The executive should become at least partially acculturated (as well as acclimatized if going from a temperate zone into the tropics—a little feature many executives discount as unimportant, much to their later dismay).

Acculturation means specifically to restrict the area of difference and magnify the area of identity of understanding and of interests. This does not require anyone to throw off all the signs of American identity and go native, a mistake of another kind, but it does mean to empathize very actively. Empathy, remember, means to crawl into another person's place, into their personality and into their culture, in order to be able to see the situation (including your presence) from their point of view. Empathy and acculturation does *not* mean to become more like them or to agree with them, only to understand why they are acting and making decisions the way they are.

Understanding the roots of any behavior that directly affects negotiations and decision making is the most critical element of acculturation for an executive. But it is wise to keep a notebook or diary in which a checklist may be compiled, allotting one column for the cultural particulars of this country and one column to universals. This can be done also by writing little biographical sketches of the people you talk to, including the bellhop, the waiter, the taxi driver, and others. The purpose is to build up your own ability to distinguish what is peculiar or particular to this society and what seems to be more universal to human society as a whole. This sensitivity becomes especially important when you are into your negotiations, and you need to know what influences are going to affect the decisions of your opponents.

On the next page, there is a checklist (Figure 7–2) of things to do when you arrive in another country to do business. It is shorthand, so there's a lot left out, but it may suggest some things you'd like to do. Modify it to suit your personality, profession, and mission. We do not believe that there is any substantial difference between the requirements for communication and cultural understanding between the long-term offshore employee and the executive who flies in and out on the corporate jet. Both have an obligation to their global mission to get their act in proper order before serious business is transacted.

WHAT TO LEARN AND HOW TO APPLY IT

Language, nonverbal communications, and culture form a learning agenda for the global executive that may faze someone who is already in service as an executive. But if there is not the time or the resources for a serious learning program are missing, there are some minimums that ought to be sought.

We have been asked at seminars and speeches what part of the

FIGURE 7–2 _____
How to Get in Step Quickly without Wasting Time (a checklist of things to do on arrival)
_____

- Walk around, just like at home.
- Get to know the neighborhood.
- Learn how to get around on public transportation: taxis, buses, subways, trains, motorscooters, rickshaws.
- Do some shopping—even if you don't buy anything: salespeople are often extremely well informed, especially about the marketplace.
- Learn how to bargain if you're in a bazaar economy.
- Stop converting local currency into dollars, learning local values.
- Do the museums, especially the historical and cultural.
- Talk with everyone who will give you an ear, but especially with host country nationals.
- Sightseeing is good, guides rarely have reliable data.
- Talk to people standing in queues.
- Go to the university and talk with faculty and students.
- Accept as many social invitations as you can.
- Follow up on all contacts from home, even if they are from people you don't really care about back there, for every one counts. Do the social contacts first, then the business when you're a better-informed guest.
- Read the local papers if in a language you understand, picking up on the issues of the day: informing yourself on the latest scandals shows you care about what's going on, but avoid talking about the political scandals.
- Establish your bank account.
- Locate the post office.
- Eat out at restaurants, outside the hotel, and learn to read the menus, learn the meaning of various dishes.
- Read signs on the street, above shops, on houses.
- Look for signs of national identity in symbols, signs, flags, etc.; learn political party signs.
- Listen to the radio in your spare time; watch television.
- Go to the movies, but avoid American flicks.
- Go to the theatre, listen to the living local language.
- Attend musical and dance performances, concentrating on the indigenous music and dance.
- Identify the most popular sports and attend games.
- Go to religious services, even if it is not your faith.
- Keep a notebook or diary, and write in it biographical sketches of people you have talked with. Write down questions you think of afterwards that you want to ask someone else.
- Write letters home and ask them to ask you questions. Be sure they save your letters.
- Write down _only_ positive statements or neutrals. Avoid negatives in anything written.
- Never talk negatively even when alone with your spouse.
_____

language is most important for the manager to learn. Our answer has been: the parts dealing with *preliminaries* to negotiation. Without pushing material on offshore negotiations from Chapter Ten up here, we should at least make two points: don't try to negotiate in another language unless you are the equal in fluency to a native-speaker of that language who is a college graduate—a level you are not likely to reach without many years of offshore living; but learn to engage personally as far as possible in the exchanges that go on *before* you actually negotiate with your offshore associates.

In the United States, negotiation preliminaries are brief and relatively perfunctory: arrive at 10:00, introductions and coffee, two hours of solid bargaining around the conference table, adjourn for two martinis and lunch at the Athletic Club, wind up the deal by 2:30. In most other countries, there is a great deal more up-front-getting-to-know-each-other activity. Entertainment, especially dinner in the evening, is a normal preliminary outside the United States.

Knowing what to do and what to say in these getting-acquainted parties is the most important single learning you can master. For this reason, we have put together a list of matters for which you might well prepare in the language of your hosts: start out with learning simple, declarative sentences about yourself in that language, how you describe yourself, where and how you live, what you like to do, and something about the weather and life in your home town. From this simple start, go on toward matters that are apt to arise in conversation with educated, important people. A good target to shoot at is to be able to talk about yourself or a third person with respect to: age, nationality, address and phone number, family members, occupation, place and date of birth, height, weight, complexion, facial features, body shape, and color of hair and eyes.

If you can master those, then go on to psychological characteristics and more particular elements of personal appearance: your character, personality, likes and dislikes, tastes and interests. business clothes that Americans wear, their casual clothes, cosmetics and perfumes (useful when shopping), special devices such as glasses or hearing aids (for emergencies). Related matters are climate and topography of the area you are visiting as well as those of your home for comparative purposes. Words and phrases related to the weather are particularly useful in so-called temperate climates.

Conversations often revolve around physical locations, such as home, apartment, hotel room, office, factory, room sizes and functions, furnishings, layout, and equipment. These matters become important if you have a role in setting up the room for either negotiations or entertainment.

Before negotiations in most countries, there is entertainment. During negotiations, it is common for the visitors to entertain the other team. Thus language about meal taking and entertaining assumes a critical importance in pre-negotiation posturing and positioning, and intra-negotiation repositioning. Learn something about the types of food and drink and when certain dishes and drinks are served. Know the taboos on alcohol and tobacco, pork or beef. Learn the formalities of mealtime interaction, including the niceties of handling your food, for in some countries you eat with your fingers in good company, in some with chopsticks. (We had to eat a pork chop with chopsticks last night!)

It is not necessary to go into business vocabulary except to describe your office building or factory, its location, and some elements about it that are at the chitchat level. As we will point out later, it is generally not a good idea to launch into a business discussion during the pre-negotiation preliminaries. Their purpose is quite clear: both parties are getting to know each other as persons and as professionals, with the company and the business put carefully aside until a personal bond of some kind is struck up.

We have checked out these recommendations with language professionals who are leaders in language proficiency standards in this nation. They have told us that what is on this list can be learned rapidly and that there are some fun learning programs around that allow you to accomplish this goal pleasantly.

A couple of words of advice from a professional student of language who has no language teaching credentials: concentrate on the verbs first, but don't become obsessed with tenses. Tense doesn't much matter unless you are catching a train or plane, and speakers of the other language will understand why you are speaking only in the present tense or simple past. Second, concentrate on "honorifics." Learn the terms of address which are going to please your foreign associates and that are appropriate from a person of your age, rank, status, and sex. With the special exception of Chinese, there is no language as uninflected as English—that is, we have the fewest terms in our language that signify honor and respect to elders, to superiors, to males, to females. If you want a warm welcome during those negotiation preliminaries, be sure you use honorifics, but be certain that you use them accurately.

INTERPRETERS AND TRANSLATORS

There are times when even the most proficient speaker of another language cannot speak the language or cannot interpret accurately the nonverbal signals of the nation where negotiations are being conducted or where business has been opened. And even proficient speakers of other languages have learned that it is a powerful help to negotiations to have an interpreter present, for it allows time for thought and reconsideration of issues while the interpretation is begin made. Gromyko, that most dour Soviet statesman, speaks and understands English with near-perfect proficiency, but he never used his own English in diplomatic contacts with the Americans. The third party is a very useful presence, too, for misunderstandings that might have explosive consequences can be muted by a simple explanation later: "The translation was not accurate." Interpreters are useful because, if they are native speakers of the other language or have had long experience in its culture, they can "read" the nonverbal signals.

The global executive learns the advantages and limitations of professional language assistance. He or she also routinely pays for the interpreter to spend some time at the home office learning the basics of the industry and specifics of the corporation before a major round of negotiations. And then he or she tries always to use the same persons, rather than rely on new ones each time out in Korea, Germany, or Thailand. While superiors may grouse about the expense at first, the bottom line results of bringing first-class language skills into negotiations can be demonstrated without much difficulty. Not to train interpreters in advance is shortsighted and essentially taking yourself into negotiations with a blindfold on.

> Our daughter was hired by a manufacturer to help with interpretation during a visit by some Chinese. Had she been more familiar with the company and its executives, she might have been able to translate the chairman's jokes into Chinese—or, better, would have been able to

warn him not to try to tell jokes at the formal banquet. She and the Chinese' own interpreter shook their heads and shrugged their shoulders at the impossible task, much to the embarrassment of the chairman.

The importance of trustworthiness among interpreters and translators has been underrated by American firms, which tend to pick up interpreters hastily and only when they need them. Think about the confidentiality of company bargaining positions or of its technology. If you were an interpreter being paid less than $10 an hour and the other side was a company run by fellow nationals of your country who were willing to pay for a little inside information, the temptation would be very strong indeed. We believe that hiring interpreters and translators long in advance to train them in the company's business makes good sense because it gives the interpreter an opportunity to develop a loyalty toward the company and it gives the executive time to test the interpreter's loyalty and trustworthiness.

To assure loyalty, preparedness, and continuity, interpreters should be retained in advance, paid more than the going rate for piece work of this kind, and perhaps given an annual minimum retainer against which the first actual hours may be charged. Costly? Yes, but it is an insurance policy against even greater losses.

Some companies have native speakers of other languages on staff in managerial or technical positions already. It is easy to use such people because they are obliged to obey orders.

One of America's industrial giants has had a run of bad luck in its China trade. One reason may be that its permanent staff in Beijing includes only one Chinese-speaking professional. Negotiating teams from many different departments coming to China would ask for the services of an engineer in Massachusetts who happened to be a native of China, but not a native speaker of Kuo-yu, the language of North China. Even though he brought amusement to some of the North Chinese by his southernisms, he was a good sport and had the capacity to translate difficult technical terms that were essential to the missions. But after spending three or four weeks out of every month on the plane to or from China or actually in China unable to do the technical work that he enjoyed, he took early retirement, leaving the giant dependent on outside interpreters—or, worse, interpreters provided by the Chinese government who would work for their own employer, the Chinese government.

Besides, there are all the embarrassments possible. More big business blunders relate to language than to any other area of international business. Ricks' chapter on language blunders is the biggest in the book (Ricks, 1983).

Trusting just any old interpreter has given us some good stories.

Otis Elevator exhibiting in Moscow had its "completion equipment" translated into Russian as "equipment for orgasm." (Ricks, 75)

Many years ago, Parker Pen promoted a truly reliable fountain pen that could be carried without leaking and creating embarrassing ink stains. The advertisement worked wonderfully and everyone knew it in the United States, so it was shortened, simply saying that Parker Pens prevented embarrassment. But when the condensed version was translated into Portuguese (by a Portuguese, not a Brazilian), it said "Parker Pens prevent embarrassment." Alas, in slang Brazilian Portuguese, "embarrassment" means an unwanted pregnancy, one out of wedlock. (Adapted from Ricks, 80)

And General Motors, the champion marketer of the world: translated "Body by Fisher" into Flemish as "Corpse by Fisher," (Ricks, 83) and found that, while *Nova* written as one word is understood to mean "new" in Latin America, Puerto Ricans were joking about it as "*no va*"—two words meaning "doesn't go." It was renamed the Caribe. (Ricks, 38–39)

LANGUAGE TRAINING AT THE PLANT OR OFFICE

If American business is to become competitive again in global markets, it is going to have to be able to communicate. Global executives will have to know language and culture. Corporations should start now with formalized language training for the inservice and entry-level managers.

The obvious reason, of course, is that the company will eventually need executives and managers who are able to use other languages in order to get the company's business done. And that is a valid reason to invest (not spend) the money to provide training.

There's another reason that harks back to Chapter Four. By offering language training opportunities, the company is sending a very powerful message that it is serious when it says it has a global plan. Few messages are as effective in changing a corporate culture as putting money where the mouth is. You can say you're going global, but it takes a long time for that to happen and for the results to show up at headquarters or on the production line. But if every employee of the company is offered the opportunity to learn another language, or brush up on one studied in school or college, the message is unmistakable. If there are already course offerings, then make the language offering have some special quality that makes it more attractive than the rest.

In-house study is the best way to involve the most employees because they don't have to make any special effort to get to classes. If that is not possible, then try offering free tuition to classes that are designed for "communicative language proficiency" at a local college. Or give free tuition and expenses to weekend or vacation "total immersion" programs such as those offered at Mohonk Manor House by the State University of New York at New Paltz or the Monterey Institute for International Studies. To acquire a language then becomes a matter of pleasant reward, not bitter pill.

Finally, be certain that the instruction is aimed at communicative proficiency. Check the syllabus with the American Council of Foreign Language Teachers (Hastings-on-Hudson, New York 10706) or the Council on Applied Linguistics (35th St., NW, Washington, DC 20007). Check quality by whatever means are available to be certain that what you have bought is light and lively and living, not read-and-repeat drill. It is an investment in involvement and motivation, while at the same time accomplishing an important training task for executives, managers, and staff.

SUMMARY

Learn to love language and love to use it. Learn that language is the doorway to culture and that culture will determine the success or failure of decisions you make in another part of the globe—or for that matter right at home if negotiations take place here. Take language seriously, especially when dealing with customers: use theirs, not yours.

Explore the host culture of the nation where you are going to be doing business before you start to do business. Just as most businesspersons explore a new city on foot when they arrive, explore the culture "on foot" for at least several days before engaging in any business. And try to broaden the area of agreement in decision-making and behavior between you and your international associates.

Translators and interpreters should be recruited in advance, paid well, and their loyalty purchased. Treat them as valued allies and colleagues, not as necessary nuisances.

Introduce a broad program of language training in the company to reinforce the global plan and its meaning, and to give your employees and your company a leg up in the global competition.

THE GLOBAL EXECUTIVE AS GLOBAL RESEARCHER

An Inventory of Skills and Attitudes

- Intuitive sense of business potential in another nation or culture.
- Skill to identify and use global sources of information without being distracted by U.S. perceptions, values, or attitudes.
- Ability to assess offshore prospects from standardized resources within the United States.
- Skill to use oral information resources and informal networks in place of written resources and formalized information networks.
- Ability to separate unjustified expectations in another country from actual market or sourcing potential.
- Ability to assess market and source research in various countries in the light of global objectives.
- Skill to identify information resources in a country where databases of all kinds are different or undeveloped.
- Skill to relate familiar databases to actual information resources in another country without permitting scientific method to overrule fact.
- Ability to personally conduct or manage research in an unfamiliar business context.
- Skill to detect subtle warnings and fresh opportunities from other world areas and from general economic, social, and political trends.
- Keen sense of what is politically and socially possible in an unfamiliar context.

The Global Researcher

Few marketing efforts have ever succeeded without significant input from the target market itself. Few production plans work unless the manufacturer knows the geographic features of the plant location, including labor, natural resources, transportation, taxes, and many other key facts. These matters are so important for decision making that market research and plant- and office-location research have become developed as highly technical sciences in the United States.

There are several fundamental problems facing the global executive, especially in the crucial sector of market research, but that also limit sourcing, production, and technological research.

First, there is no organization or association that effectively encourages international market research. Thus, what standardization exists tends to be narrowly built on presuppositions emerging from Western experience, often quite inappropriate and off-target in non-Western areas.

Second, the complexity of transnational market research has discouraged some very talented people from entering the field. Market research performed by Americans is actively discouraged in some developing countries. Where it is not discouraged, market research becomes daunting for the American-trained practitioner. Greener pastures attract most U.S. market research specialists.

Third, the lag of market research behind marketing need has led to a "What the heck" response from both the executive who needs the research and the market researcher. (This may lead to "winging" it. For an amusing but insightful perspective, see van Mesdag, 1987.)

Fourth—and this applies to market, technological, and plant location research—there is the unavoidable fact of management's location here in North America. The domestic executive is *here* and can supervise the research through speedy mail and direct-dial telephone from headquarters or by hopping on a plane and visiting the key site then jetting home again immediately. For the global executive the challenge is much more substantial simply because of distance and time.

Finally, there are cultural problems. A number of business failures have resulted from inadequate on-site research before an overseas commitment was made, or from research that was adequate by commonly accepted U.S. standards but that didn't fit the non-U.S. environment. Further, American business has been lamentably slow in identifying key advances in technology or production techniques fashioned overseas. Our failure to stay up on technology has been largely because our vision is local and is focused inward on American technology, American manufacturing techniques, and American service inventions. Here again, we are the victims of our preconception that foreigners are not as "advanced" as we are. Then, too, our language translation capacities are limited, leaving many crucial, published articles and monographs on new processes untranslated from their original languages, especially Japanese, but also Russian.

This chapter and the next one, The Global Networker, concentrate on the problems of information generation, retrieval, and evaluation as foundations for business decision making in a globalized marketplace. This chapter concentrates on the impersonal aspects, the next on the personal aspects of information seeking.

There are several basic business research problems. First, we Americans have been trained throughout our years in school and college to rely on the written word and on the printed wisdom of certified experts of various kinds, communicated through rather formal networks. Second, outside of northern Europe and Japan there is neither the love affair with scientific data we Americans favor nor the basic demographic information that makes it reliable. Third, there are both structural and cultural obstacles to research in each country of the world (Kaynak, 1982).

LIMITS TO WRITTEN INFORMATION

The problem is tough to solve. Virtually any American executive is the product of the American schooling system, and most of them are going to be graduates of American universities. Our entire structure of learning is based on the written word and on the spoken word of a recognized authority, namely the teacher, the professor, the preacher from the pulpit, the president, or the authoritative anchor who reads the teleprompter on the six o'clock news. We have been taught that when we need information, we go to the library, take down a book and look up what we need. We are taught not only to go to the library, but to do a database search on a computer. It is still the written word that we are after for authority, for fact, for hard foundation to our research.

Because the greatest potential over the long haul will lie in the developing areas of the world, in Asia, Africa, and Latin America, it is important to note the importance of unwritten information sources. American executives, taught to rely on the written word, are uncomfortable when they have to operate research projects in countries where the most reliable information is conveyed by word of mouth. This phenomenon is surely a product of a non-literate tradition in some countries, but even India, where the business class has been literate for at least a century, clings very hard to the value of the spoken word, and the written word is often used in business communications to leave open options one wouldn't think should be left open. So the global executive has to expect to rely on the spoken word and will have to rely on how the offshore staff interprets and puts onto paper that spoken word.

The most challenging aspect of locating and accessing oral information is to identify the most reliable source, namely a person. This topic will be attacked in the next chapter, but the singular talent necessary to deal in nonwritten communication of information should be high on the priority list for anyone who wants to run a corporation as the global executive.

ACCESS TO INFORMATION

Go outside the United States and try to run down the same kind of information we get from books and computers, and you may have the feeling that you've walked back into the Dark Ages. The American passion for information of all kinds has generated a remarkable data-delivery system that we take for granted, walking into our publicly-supported libraries, calling up advanced databases and accessing shared information, and using mammoth reference volumes prepared for sale by commercial publishers.

In many other lands, the information seeker is left in the dark, with only limited access to data sources. Scholars love and admire the major reference libraries abroad. Those reference libraries are not as user-friendly as Americans expect them to be from their own experience using university and reference libraries at home. Catalogs are often out-of-date and use reference systems we find difficult to grasp. Sometimes they have large gaps, and reference assistants seem relatively casual about them. Newspaper archives are not as accessible as at home.

Custodians of records and archives in many other countries are not oriented to serve the outside user. Access to offshore computer databases is much more limited because the databases are more proprietary than are some of the major research databases in the United States. The general market for information is so underdeveloped in many parts of the world that commercial publication of directories and other reference works would be unprofitable. Finally, particularly in the developing countries and the Eastern Bloc, governments regard information as a precious national resource and will share it with foreigners only under severely restrictive conditions. In short, our very access to information resources is limited and, even when gained, the resources do not readily yield the kind of information we sought. And, when we find it, it is apt to be in a language we can't read!

Much of the basic printed information on which we in the United States rely so heavily—such as information provided in yellow pages, city directories, and corporate reference volumes— is available only in the developed nations of Europe. It is not remarkable that one of the first frustrations of the American executive posted overseas is the lack of telephone yellow pages, or, where they do exist, their inadequacy. What is more surprising is how angry they get at this lack. Other directories, like *Moody's*, *Standard & Poor's*, and *Who's Who* have few parallels when you move out of the developed nations. There are some excellent, but limited, international parallels to these resources that are available in the United States mentioned later in this chapter under "Before You Leave Home."

Although it may seem tangential, the dearth of foreign technical information in the United States may become a serious barrier to the success of the global executive. Much high technology research is being conducted in Japan, Germany, and USSR. Even a developing country like India has a large body of educated scientists and engineers who are often found on the frontiers of new knowledge. Indian technical writing is in English, but it is not available generally unless it gets picked up by a U.S. periodical. A law, passed by Congress in 1986, will provide federal funds for massive translation of Japanese technical literature, but it may be too little or too late. We urge trade associations to take on as their responsibility a systematic and continuing search of foreign periodicals and publishers' lists for the latest technological and production information disseminated abroad and, if it is not in English, translate it or at least provide abstracts for members to keep up with what's taking place outside the United States (Ferguson, 1987–2).

On locating plants overseas, research obstacles are similar to those faced by marketing managers. Because governments are generally enthusiastic about building new factories, introducing new technology, or employing more labor in their countries, site-location information is more generally available than market or technical information.

Securing information on financial resources available sometimes proves more difficult than expected. Some potential sources of funding are less than forward in trotting out details of their resources, for fear of government intrusion into their business affairs, most normally for unpaid taxes. For this and a variety of structural reasons (see later in this chapter), financial resources may ordinarily be identified and accessed through interpersonal networks rather than formal information resources. The reality of American finance is much the same, but we tend to do our initial research by looking up possible sources in the financial market's reference works.

The other really difficult area of plant location research relates to labor. Though the government may freely inform the prospective manufacturer or service industry that labor of certain training quality is available, there are sometimes constraints on sharing information about how labor is organized. Maybe unique local power systems provide labor organized around families, but the information provided by the government may make this old-fashioned system appear to be a modern labor union. Labor troubles are persistently hard to define unless one can find a noncompetitor who uses similar workers in his factories and offices and who might be willing to share insights into labor problems. Newspaper reporters are often more helpful in this respect than are the articles that appear in newspapers, for newspaper editors are frequently subjected to heavy pressure from advertisers and government to keep the news looking rosy.

Lack of available and sufficiently extensive printed information resources on markets and site location puts a premium on the overseas executive's ability to find information in the United States first. When he or she goes abroad, the premium is on being able to identify substitutes for the familiar U.S. resources.

SCIENTIFIC RESEARCH

Scientific method, so highly valued by American market researchers and those planning production facilities, is in short supply outside of Northern and Western Europe. A cynic might wonder what difference it might make, for all the attention paid to scientific market surveys by leading executives who have ordered them completed and then ignored them in decision making. Such scientific market research in the United States consists largely of telephone interview or personal interview surveys. Ninety percent of all market research expenditure falls into those two categories, according to estimates by market research experts (figure cited by Ron Brutlag in oral presentation, August 12, 1986).

What happens then when you get to a country where (1) a much smaller percentage of the consumer market has telephones, and (2) people are not as open with telephone interviewers as Americans are? What happens when you try to interview consumers in a culture where such interviews are regarded as an inexcusable intrusion into personal privacy? What happens when interviews are conducted by a person of one sex to which members of the other sex have been conditioned not to talk at all, much less reveal family confidences? What happens in a country where only the outward characteristics of a scientific survey are familiar, so imaginary statistics are inserted into the expected format and delivered as "scientific?"

Much business research outside the United States is conducted on the same scientific basis as in the United States. That means not only that its scientific basis is the same, but that its cultural basis is the same. Inevitably, that means that the fundamental assumptions of the research methods are bound up with perspectives of Western cultures and U.S. business—which may not match local reality.

There is nothing wrong with this—as long as the executive knows that culture biases the research conclusions. Any research should, therefore, be validated for its application according to the way people live, move, behave, and look at things before it is accepted as reliable. Ricks (1983) gives some wonderful examples of solid, Western scientific marketing research yielding expensive conclusions. Here are a few of his samples of the misapplication of research or the misinterpretation of research results:

A Swedish pharmaceutical firm did an elaborate market research job and discovered a large market for its product in Southeast Asia, because similar drugs were available only on the black market. It didn't find out until a large investment had been made that the corrupt government controlled the black market, making it all but impossible to do business there. (Ricks, 135)

Automobile surveys in the Netherlands suggested an appropriate spot for a fast-food emporium, according to patterns of American auto traffic. Unfortunately, the average Dutchman does not pop in the car with the kids to run out for a burger and fries. Better locations in the Low Countries are those reached by pedestrians out strolling.

A famous American fast-food chain did a standard, American-style traffic-count in Hamburg, West Germany, obviously taking account of foot as well as automobile traffic, and found the ideal place to build a hamburger restaurant—ideal by American standards. It, too, bombed. The heavy traffic discovered was not out looking for snacks, but was walking next door to the city's largest bordello. (Ricks, 4)

Kentucky Fried Chicken did the same kind of market research in Brazil that had made the company a success in the United States. Their researchers, because they were using standardized American research procedures, didn't apprise the company of a most significant fact: that a zesty, barbequed chicken, a traditional favorite of Brazilians, was sold by street vendors on virtually every corner, including the one next to the Colonel's stand. (Ricks, 128)

Finally, there's the famous story of *Reader's Digest's* market survey that "proved" that West Germans and Frenchmen ate more spaghetti than Italians. What was measured, however, was the purchase of prepackaged spaghetti. The Italians, in fact, consumed far more, as you might expect, but either bought it in bulk or made it at home. (Ricks, 137)

Marketing and management are both closely tied to the cultures of their origin. Because both emerged from American business, and we are Americans, we tend to regard them as universals. American marketers tend to believe that American marketing principles and methods, especially marketing research practices, can be applied anywhere in the world equally well as at home. These horror stories—and many more like them—demonstrate that this is not the case. Market research, sourcing research, and location research all are influenced by factors and perspectives that are local to the place where the research is being done.

Even if the researchers have been trained in reliable sampling and other research techniques, there are many nations in the world, including some in Europe, which, for a variety of historical, cultural, and national security reasons do not produce the kind of demographic data on which much market and labor pool research depends. Italy, by any standards, is an advanced, industrial nation; yet its published census information is still suspected by some market researchers of being too soft and having gaps too large to make the whole body of it as usable as it might be. India's census, one of the world's great wonders when it was inaugurated in the first decade of the 19th century, still reports information which, while interesting to governments, revenue departments, and demographers, is hardly the concrete on which one would base a marketing campaign for consumer goods. A census is government-produced data, reflecting the biases of the governments, one of which may be to limit knowledge of those particular things that most interest American managers.

Lack of up-to-date maps is a common problem. Even a country as industrialized as Taiwan does not publish a clear, usable map of its capital city, Taipei (Kaynak, 1982). While in Taiwan this may be the result of a fearful, even somewhat paranoid, national government, in other areas it may be because maps are simply a luxury that few need or can afford.

The research infrastructure is also narrow. In many nations, there are very few market researchers, for reasons we will mention shortly. Those who do exist generally do not work for business, but enjoy government or academic appointments that are generally much more secure. The academic researcher may seek information too esoteric for the use of the entrepreneur, while the government researcher is not available to business. Their research training outside the United States tends to be fearfully academic as well, limiting the usefulness of their research to the manager. Sixteen years ago in Peru, there were only four advertising and market research firms in the whole country, leading several researchers to conclude that there was no market for market research in Peru (Glade, 1970). The marketing surveys prepared by commercial research firms in many parts of the world may be expected to be designed more for the pleasure of the customer than for dedication to scientific research methods and reliability of conclusions.

What goes for scientific method may be flawed and scientific method may be misinterpreted, but there may be an even deeper flaw that the American executive will not be able to perceive.

> I have conducted field research on two different continents, Asia and Africa. I have, over the years, reached the firm conviction that the methods I was applying to my research were fundamentally flawed. The basic flaw was that my research methods were those I learned at Harvard and the London School of Economics in the 1950s. My research in India was on the values used by administrators in managing; in Africa I worked with John Gay on an interpretation of village modernization. In both instances, I found that the preconceptions I had about research itself just didn't fit the realities of life in the society studied.
>
> My research methods were themselves the products of the examination of Western societies, an academic pursuit of great interest since the early 19th century. The methods were then enhanced in value by the departmentalization of German, British, and American universities and, more recently in America, by the "publish or perish" pressure on professors, forcing them to publish more and more articles and books about narrower and narrower subjects. As a consequence, while our research methods in the social sciences have gained vastly in their value as tools for examining *Western* societies, they at the same time have become so Westernized that they largely miss the fundamental differences when applied to studying other societies.

In short, we cannot rely on "scientific methods" that matured in U.S. universities to yield reliable results when they are directed at studying non-Western societies. We cannot emphasize too strongly the dangers of this misperception, a mistake that has led to pratfalls of many distinguished American corporations. Our position is surely a minority one, for few American social scientists agree with us, but our argument that the Western social science methods themselves will distort reality when you move them from the culture of their origin to a non-Western culture under study deserves careful reflection by the global executive who has no academic turf to protect.

As a result of these limitations, many plastic-bound market and site-location surveys in southern Europe, Africa, Asia, or Latin America may not be worth the paper they're copied onto. The global executive knows what to watch out for.

But there are other, fundamental research problems.

STRUCTURAL BIASES

The researcher has to beware of structural biases, especially to market research, biases that have little to do with research itself but which emerge from social conditions. (Though academic, Kayak 1982 covers the subject in some detail, from which the executive can draw his or her own warnings about market research overseas.)

First, some governments in the developing countries discourage competition for political reasons. This means that marketing research has little reason to grow, very few researchers will be found, the data will be hard to access, and surveys will overwhelm the native population. In some countries, government approval is required before a market survey may be undertaken. Check in advance: it may take a long time to get the OK.

Second, such restrictions imposed from the top exaggerate inherent resistance to market research that comes from the small number of independent companies conducting most of a country's business. Many companies are owned by large, extended families that exercise influence if not control over even larger sectors of business. These companies have little need for advanced market research, and they tend to employ managers who have no academic training in marketing or market research. Management tends to be ingrown, with little diversity to create a sense of competitiveness. The small, closed group is favored over outsiders.

Because they constitute an elite group in their country, they have a natural desire to perpetuate the *status quo*. A foreign company coming in with a marketing research program represents change of an unpleasant sort, for it presumes that the next step will be actual marketing of products or services that may upset the applecart. Change of any sort is unwelcome in an insecure environment. With limited capital formation and fear of economic instability, business in the developing countries focuses on short-term profits from small units of production within a known market. The return on market research in relation to its cost, therefore, is always questioned. One consequence is that highly skilled market researchers go to work for government or universities, while those less skilled continue to suffer low social and business status. Marketing, of course, suffers from the general antipathy toward effective market research and the impracticability of concluding it successfully.

Third, in the developing countries, there are built-in conditions that have created a seller's market. A seller's market tends to stifle research because the demand for goods is already guaranteed by other conditions. A number of factors create this seller's market. There is frequently an increasing supply of money which, coupled with a shortage of foreign exchange, makes buyers seek rare goods. Increased demand for imports relative to exports draws the government in to restrict the supply of available goods. At the same time, increased government planning and expenditures, and a rigid, cumbersome administrative control apparatus stifle the development of more enterprise. Sellers' markets do not require active marketing: just stick it on the shelf and it will sell.

Fourth, there are structural social obstacles to objective scientific research. The basic problem is finding interviewers who are trained or experienced—or who can be expected to be unbiased. Respondents in many countries are not conditioned to respond to surveys and resent the intrusion of surveyors into their lives. Access to homes and to women may be limited, even for a native interviewer. The surveyor who is able to get the interview often finds it hard to obtain information on what the interviewee may regard as personal: personal information is not shared with strangers from outside the family. *Opinion* is totally absent in some classes of society, for their "opinions" are formed by the classes that have kept them where they are, thus biasing any measurement the researcher wishes to take. Illiteracy makes it impossible to sample a population using a written instrument, and local language peculiarities faze interviewers who use a rarified, citified form of speech.

Surveys that seek information from retailers face similar problems, for the small size and precarious financial position of retailers in many developing countries, and their survival at the mercy of large family-owned wholesale and manufacturing suppliers make them reluctant to release information on competition. And few businesses will release information on sales or profits, even if the researcher has assured them of a noncompetitive intent (such as using the same distributor).

Finally, there is a common problem outside the United States and some Northwestern European countries: the dishonesty of the researchers. An elaborate unwritten set of controls, principally sanctioned by competitiveness, operates in the West, forcing most researchers to render objective or reasonably objective reports. The absence of these controls makes it possible for a research firm to render blatantly false information, neatly wrapped in a plastic binder. The global executive quickly learns that it is safer in many parts of the world to rely on government information, for at least the biases to that information can be known.

It seems absurd under these conditions to invest money in marketing research. In turn, this means that local executives in developing nations tend to generally underestimate how much market research might help in improving the match between production and demand. They also tend to underestimate the possible contribution that research might make toward coordinating channels of distribution. Both underestimates lead them to downplay the significance of marketing itself for developing broader market shares and establishing better trade relations with the outside world.

Answers? First, the global executive does solid homework on both macro and micro levels right here in the United States. Second, the global executive gets out there and uses all the skills available to sniff out the conditions that will affect marketing, site location, or technological advances.

BEFORE YOU LEAVE HOME

The global executive knows that, although resources are improving rapidly in all parts of the world, it is wise to begin research at home where the sources are (1) reasonably comprehensive, (2) scientific, and (3) in English. Our Resources section at the end of the book lists names of some organizations that will supply information free or for a fee.

Start with the company's own library. Honor the corporate librarian—one of America's most unsung assets—with your interest and your compliments. He or she can do wonders for any research project using the miracles of on-line databases and interlibrary loan. The special librarian at the large company will know the value of the local public library, particularly in the larger cities, and will refer the executive to those resources. Executives from smaller companies should seek reference assistance from the nearest reference library, university library, or the state library. Macro information is expanding rapidly and access to it is relatively easy and not very expensive.

Specific country information is available from foreign embassies and consulates, but we would suggest starting with the United States Department of Commerce. The International Trade Administration has regional offices of its U.S. and Foreign Commercial Service whose addresses are available through your regional Commerce Department office. Overseas offices are maintained in certain major cities, as well. Because the service is specifically aimed at helping American exporters develop their exports, their advice and counsel and their references to other information sources are invaluable. Make personal friends with your area trade representative—and show your Congressman how pleased you are with the service.

There are many other sources right here in the United States. The U.S. Area Handbooks, available from the Superintendent of Documents, are a rich source of in-country information hard to get for many countries. The State Department makes available free its overseas post briefings, country reports, and policy papers with respect to specific countries, a good source to review before making either marketing or plant location decisions overseas. The United Nations supplies vast quantities of relatively reliable statistical data. The OECD (Organization for Economic Cooperation and Development) makes available very useful economic data. The World Bank and the Inter-American Bank provide useful information.

Consultants of various strengths and talents are ready to supply predeparture information. One of the richest sources is Business

International which publishes a periodical of the same name, occa-sional checklists, and other publications and provides for-fee con-sultancy services.

Then there are the risk managers. There are important uses for political risk assessments, and an executive should obtain one be-fore locating an expensive plant in another country. We do scoff a bit at the computerized risk analyses available for so much money from such distinguished former senior officers of government. The main flaw to watch out for in the computerized analysis may be that it is not sufficiently tailor-made to the specifications of the client company and the client company's industry niche. In any event, these analyses are quite superior to going out there and getting thrown in jail for insulting the local dictator or the air force corporal who will be tomorrow's *junta* leader.

Before you invest a lot of money in a political risk analysis, ask yourself whether you will really base decisions on the analysis and whether it will really help your decisions. Ask which, if any of the following categories of risk analysis is what you want or need: a quantitative, econometric analysis of the country; a quantitative, weighted checklist on the country; a structural analysis in which qualitative and quantitative ratings are applied to each factor; or a qualitative analysis reflecting mature judgments of the risks by professionals with experience in the country. The main question, though, is the first: "Am I going to pay attention to it or am I using it to cover my posterior in the event I go ahead and things turn out different from expectations?"

We have a hunch (without empirical evidence) that the political risk analysis is more effective with the larger firm. The CEO of a medium-sized or small company will lack the kind of sophistication needed to make business decisions on the basis of the risk analysis. There are already so many problems in going international, the tendency is to retreat to the old comfort of the domestic market. The computer-generated analysis sometimes makes the obstacles seem much larger than they really are. The neophyte, exposed to a printout outlining restrictions on the repatriation of capital and profits, will say to heck with it, even though most restrictions have significant loopholes that permit profits to be brought home.

Political risk analyses are weak on the kinds of information that field managers (in contrast to CEOs) need to know. They are weak on the cultural and micro-level economic factors that will be the daily challenge of the on-site offshore executive. CEOs must, by the nature of their jobs, deal with the great issues of state that will make or break the company. But, let's face it, most business will be made or broken by factors at a much more mundane level. The global executive orders political risk analyses and heeds their advice, but at the same time spends time learning political, social, and economic forces from the micro level. The micro level can only be learned on-site and from the ground up. The macro can be learned best before departing the United States.

Before turning to the specific research challenges of finding a distributor and soliciting credit information, there are a few approaches to research at home in the United States that deserve comment. Export trading companies, internal international marketing research groups, and prospecting contribute to the manager's knowledge of offshore conditions, especially for marketing.

Export trading companies (ETCs) do offer the potential for performing marketing research for their client members. If the ETC is established within a particular industry segment (in contrast to one organized by a bank or a multinational), resources may be concentrated on serious offshore research.

Larger companies may wish to organize an offshore marketing research group independent of the operating divisions and covering all global areas. This makes it possible to rationalize market data-gathering and processing by the marketing staffs of all the overseas subsidiaries and divisions. Standardization is provided by the research group. Recommendations can then be fed back to the subsidiaries from the sophisticated research group at the home office. For management, the offshore marketing research group offers a method of monitoring and controlling market research expenditures and activities of the offshore subsidiaries. More important, it dispels in the headquarters offices the creaky old notion that knowledge of domestic markets can automatically be transferred to offshore situations (Business International, 1974).

Don't leave home without having done serious homework on the macro economic level, but do as much of the micro as you can possibly do. For example, significant micro research of certain kinds is possible to perform here. There are excellent studies available for most parts of the world. Compile your own bibliography and try to become familiar with the key works on that list. Here's where the university's federally-funded National Research Center in International Studies can help, for its staff will be familiar with ephemeral or periodical literature which becomes pretty minute in its focus. Ask for a list of National Resource Centers from the Center for International Education, U.S. Department of Education, Washington, DC 20202. There are over 80 such centers, divided among a half-dozen world regional specialties.

Such simple preparation on the micro level will avoid some expensive mistakes like this one cited by Ricks (1983, 4):

> An American pineapple company saw that a pineapple processing plant could be conveniently located closer to the North American markets than its existing plants, but downstream from the plantations of Mexico so the fruit could be floated downriver. It built the cannery all right, but discovered that harvest time was also floodtime, and the river was too turbulent to float the fruit.

The checklist below will help steer the global executive's thinking toward some homework research that will pay off.

Then there is good old-fashioned prospecting, using the mail. Translate your letters into the language of your target country and send them out to a broad selection of persons and institutions that will benefit from your proposed venture. Get as many names in the greatest depth in the target organizations as you can, and, even at

---

FIGURE 8-1
Research to Do before Leaving Home (a checklist for managers planning offshore ventures)

- Make yourself known to your regional representative of the International Trade Administration, U.S. Department of Commerce, through your regional office of the DOC.
- Identify the best international banker for your proposed venture: a strong international department, a presence in those countries where you'll be doing business.
- Check in at the major U.S. university center that specializes in the part of the world where you'll be doing business.
- Order a political risk analysis (See text).
- Check the local chamber of commerce for nationals or companies from the country where you are going, meet them and see what they can do to help you.
- Use U.S. government, U.N., OECD, World Bank, and independent information on the target country.
- Use available U.S.-based credit information sources.
- Introduce yourself to the nation's Washington Embassy, regional consulate, or trade mission. Make the acquaintance of the commercial officers.

---

the risk of duplication, mail to them. If you don't get answers within a month, don't be afraid to write the same people again. And again. Persistence is much more highly regarded outside the United States. It shows your determination.

Our sincere advice is to use telex for merely making mechanical arrangements for your arrival and hotel accommodations. Telex is too impersonal for most international communications when the company's offshore enterprise is in the sowing, planting, or germination stages. Comments on the telephone have been made earlier: it is simply not an appropriate way to inaugurate business relations that you hope will prosper.

Comments on predeparture networking are reserved for the next chapter.

FINDING A DISTRIBUTOR

Research to find a distributor should start at home, but should not be completed without an on-site visit. Identifying a potential distributor requires research that overlaps with credit information research, so be certain to read the next section in conjunction with this one.

Start out with country and regional business directories of which there are several, such as *Kompass* for Europe, *Bottin International* for the world, *Nordisk Handelskalendar* for Scandinavia, and the *Japan Trade Directory* for Japan. Yellow pages *do* exist, however limited they may be. Jaeger and Waldmann publishes an *International Telex Directory* that may be useful to identify names of firms in particular locations. Company lists by country, line of business, or both may be ordered from Dun & Bradstreet, the U.S. Department of Commerce International Trade Administration, Reuben R. Donnelly, Kelly's Directory, or Johnston Publishing. Obviously, scanning the advertisements in international trade journals, especially the journals of the trade associations, is useful. (Much of this and other useful checklists may be found in *Business International*, 1985.)

Likewise, establishing your company's presence offshore by advertising in selected trade publications may attract distributors to you, rather than you having to chase them down. Trade publications and exporters' associations sometimes help their members or subscribers find foreign dealers. Trade fairs held by the U.S. Department of Commerce, your state commerce department, or your trade association can help spot potential distributors.

American firms seeking export distributors may advertise a new product or distribution requirements at very modest cost through the U.S. Department of Commerce Trade Opportunities Program (available through subscription or on-line through DIA-LOG database).

The U.S. banks are sensitive to U.S. corporate customers' referral requirements. Don't expect highly sophisticated referrals, for banks are in the banking business first, and information second. Local, foreign-owned banks may be less useful, but should be contacted as if they were major information resources—you never can tell how a bank may help you plug into the local network (and banks are better at that than they are at specific, research-targeted information).

Some of the more aggressive national airlines, air cargo companies, and foreign freight forwarders will make trade contacts for potential exporters whose business they may thereby secure. Some even publish trade leads for their customers.

Some foreign consulates are better than others in serving as brokers between manufacturers and distributors. A thorough search for offshore distribution will certainly touch base with a consulate or trade office, for networking purposes at the very least.

Chambers of commerce abroad, like their kin in the United States, vary widely in their effectiveness in information brokering. Most major cities have American chambers of commerce or binational or international chambers of commerce, but it may be necessary for you to join to use their facilities. Many of them publish annual directories of members that are available for sale, many publish newsletters in which local companies list their needs, and some publish manuals on how to do business in that country. Our information from experienced U.S. exporters is that the chambers are not as useful as one might wish.

Whatever sources to which one turns for offshore distribution information, it seems advisable to prepare a precise procedure for following up on any unsolicited or isolated inquiries or orders from abroad. An order is hard evidence that someone is interested in the product, and a follow-up by mail, telex, or phone is clearly a priority. Reputable offshore companies have good research operations and may have picked up your advertisement in U.S. or foreign publications.

Finally—and in our view at least 80 percent of the research—is the field trip. Just as Peters recommends "management by walking around" we will recommend "research by world travel." The global executive does not sit behind a desk in the home office, but creates a corporate presence even in those countries where the company does not presently market or manufacture. We agree with the advice of the old hands that a carefully conceived, meticulously planned, and unhurried trip to selected markets abroad constitutes the best long-range investment you can make. We would emphasize that haste indeed does make waste.

The personal aspects of researching offshore distributorship is covered in the next chapter.

CREDIT INFORMATION

Earlier, the critical importance of selecting the right distributor or partner was emphasized. Before dealing with an overseas distributor, entering into a joint venture, or selling goods or services directly, it is good business practice to procure reliable credit information. For the U.S. company seeking offshore distribution, it is well to undertake a thorough evaluation of the potential distributor that includes but goes beyond credit information. In the United States, we dial up credit information from the reporting companies or from banks. In many parts of the world, this process is not available, putting an additional burden on the on-site executive. Credit research becomes almost as significant as market research, and may consume what Americans regard as inordinate amounts of the executive's precious time.

Check the other suppliers—American, local, and other foreign suppliers—who have dealt with your prospective customer or distributor. Firms that are not direct competitors of yours are apt to share credit information. If you can identify the prospective distributor's or customer's bank, then get your international banker to request a credit check. Remember, though, that credit checks are often limited by restrictive government policies as well as national traditions within many countries. Be careful with credit reports sought from local banks, as well, for the company's and the banker's ties within the local network may distort the quality of the information communicated.

Some credit information is available in the United States. If it is a distributor's credit that needs checking, it may be worth the price to order a World Trade Data Report from the U.S. Department of Commerce. The reports cost $75. They are compiled by offshore U.S. commercial specialists who gather detailed information, often on a custom basis. The problem with the WTDRs is that, if the company being researched is new to the database, it may take six months or a year to get the report, although new procedures seem to be speeding up this process. The same kind of service from their own governments is available to companies domiciled in the United Kingdom, Japan, or Sweden.

The old hands at global operations also seek the WTDRs in order to protect them from U.S. Justice Department inquiries with reference to the Foreign Corrupt Practices Act. We'll talk in more detail about the Act in the final chapter, but calling up a WTDR is a way of demonstrating to the Attorney General that the company did not deliberately enter into a corrupt arrangement with the brother of the president of the other country or the queen's consort. In this respect, a WTDR is an insurance policy rather than credit information.

The Foreign Credit Interchange Bureau in New York City provides its members with low-cost credit reports on foreign companies. It also publishes bulletins on offshore credit conditions and credit practices. For companies with major needs, membership is recommended. Alternatively, try Dun & Bradstreet which does operate from offices in principal cities around the world. There are also local credit agencies in principal cities, lists of which are available through Trade Data Reports, Inc., of New York.

Finally, remember our injunctions earlier about offshore market research: much of it is based on your needs rather than on credit realities. Credit reporting agencies may want to please you as a customer for the service by feeding you good, if inaccurate, information.

ROLE OF THE ON-SITE EXECUTIVE

When I was managing a 32-employee office in India, I quickly learned that I had to reallocate my time dramatically from what I had expected. I found myself spending about one third of my time conducting what were essentially political fence-mending tasks which required that I know who was who in government as well as what were current government policies. Another portion of my time was devoted to simply learning how to get things done in that country. Neither political nosing around nor learning the nitty-gritties of how to get things done could have been accomplished as effectively without going out there.

The global executive is out there, on-site, getting as much information, formal and informal, hard and soft, as he or she possibly can. There is no substitute for this. Information gathered from host-country nationals is, of course, useful, but by itself it is not adequate. The American executive must go out and settle into the country for long enough to be able to sense what is not spoken or not written about the market or its potential as a source of goods. The checklist on the next page (Figure 8-2) gives some obvious pointers on what the on-site manager should do *before* marketing or production gets started.

Once on-site, either temporarily or for a long while, the manager has a number of immediately useful information resources. Local attorneys, either American or host nationals, are looking for international business. One of their services is information brokerage, general or specific, including introductions, representation, and compliance with local laws. Similar information is available from the banks, as noted. Public relations and advertising firms, both international and local, can be helpful in providing general and specific information, including introductions. General information, of course, comes from the public media and other formal publishing sources. American embassies over there are also at your service if you are seeking business opportunities that will help correct our trade balance. Business and professional associations make information available that is sometimes superior to that received from the chambers of commerce. Host governments, as noted, are precious sources of information, especially when they see your project as being in their own good—thus they are especially useful for plant location or the import of technology.

A local distributor or partner provides an immensely valuable information resource on the marketplace, other customers, and other potential connections for your business. A local partner can help you identify potential market researchers, perhaps through connections with the local university or business college. But remember to be open and above board with your partner in how you plan to use the information provided by him or her.

FIGURE 8–2
Things to Do *before* Operating Offshore (a checklist for the visiting or permanent offshore manager)

- Brief yourself on the national government: power, status of political parties and groups. Verify the risk analysis you have bought by doing your own.
- Put together your own briefing manual on the state of the country's economy, prepared as if for your replacement.
- Identify the major social movements that may affect your business; look for minor ones, for they may have escaped the risk analyst and they may destroy you.
- Do your own assessment of national transportation facilities by travelling extensively *before* opening for business; learn the geography.
- Estimate your company's position with the tax authorities: are there implications for your personal finances if you are to be an offshore manager?
- Get the local banks in on your intentions. Use them to find out about financing sources and limitations.
- Call at the U.S. Embassy or Consulate and introduce yourself to the chief commercial officer. Ask their advice on dealing with the national and local governments. Find out rules and regulations that affect your intended business—the ones no one would tell you before you left home.
- Join the American or international chamber of commerce.
- Learn all you can about labor: unions, nonunion groups, relation to political parties, relation to social groupings, relation to religious groupings; study any alternatives to the way others employ workers.
- Learn about labor law and employee rights and benefits.
- Identify the options for marketing, for distribution, for purchasing goods or manufacturing yourself—on-site.
- Check out secondary sources in the host country: books that never got as far as the United States.
- Identify relevant trade associations.
- Find an attorney who has had experience with U.S. business but who is well-connected yet not dependent on the political party that is in power.
- Identify an advertising, public relations, and market research agency.
- Make yourself known by news releases, even advertising.
- Explore the credit information system, if any. Learn how to get reliable credit information. Take the time to acquire credit information on distributors, partners.
- Hire an insurance agent, learning about insurance and potential liabilities.
- Accept social invitations from prospective business associates. In general, avoid accepting too many invitations from resident Americans: their information is helpful, but not as helpful as what you learn from business acquaintances locally. Begin to network.

INTUITION AS A MANAGEMENT TOOL

Intuition has a bad reputation in our rational, American business society in spite of its obvious role in the success of some of America's entrepreneurial giants. Intuition, in fact, may be that ingredient that most separates an entrepreneur from a manager.

Intuition is that immediate knowledge that seems to bound in upon consciousness without any reasoning process. It is what teacher used to frown on in arithmetic class when you *did* know the right answer but couldn't tell her how you got to it. Intuition, poorly understood in scientific circles, is apparently knowledge that the mind summons up from past experiences. As such, it should not be dismissed as bad information.

The executive of the offshore business, who has dealt with a series of crises in a series of different countries, is apt to be able to draw intuitive responses to new challenges from rich, personal experience. Some young persons who have yet to acquire that rich experience nonetheless are innately gifted with an ability to penetrate through the details of a situation to grasp the subtle but important inner meanings, an intuitive sense that grows more valuable with experience.

The global executive will be a person who has that intuitive gift and cultivates it in moving through business experiences at home and abroad. Intuition will supplement another skill, the ability to detect subtle signs emanating from other countries and cultures.

Every business, every organization, and every government emits signals of change. Lobbyists in the United States are trained to detect early warnings of governmental change, as certain managers are in corporate America. But when you transport the executive to a country where the language and culture are different, those early warning signals become harder to detect. The executive with an intuitive sense, coupled with a hounddog's nose for dim signals in government, economy, and business, will be a valued employee both overseas and in the executive suite. In a world caught up in exponential change, these skills are precious resources of immense potential value to the company.

SUMMARY

Research outside the United States is limited by written information resources, absence of sound demographic data, and lack of solid scientific research. This puts a premium on the executive as a researcher—far beyond what would be expected of the person in a parallel position in the information-rich United States.

The global executive, whether located at home or overseas, knows where to seek information and uses an intuitive skill to detect trends, opportunities, and danger signals from the host country's environment. He or she also knows how to identify decision makers and move into their network for effective management.

CHAPTER NINE

THE GLOBAL EXECUTIVE AS GLOBAL NETWORKER

An Inventory of Skills and Attitudes

- Ability to discover how decision makers are identified in another country.
- Ability to identify specific decision makers when the identifiers are known.
- Ability to identify interpersonal and interbusiness networks to which decision makers belong.
- Skill to enter another, unfamiliar network.
- Skill to merge one's own and others' networks without forcing one on the other.
- Skill to enter into personal relationships with persons unlike oneself with intention to create enduring relationships.
- Skill to use local networks for local purposes.
- Skill to use local networks for global purposes.
- Skill to use a global network for local purposes.
- Skill to use a global network for global purposes.

The Global Networker

"Who makes decisions?" "How are decisions made?" There are few more important questions an executive can ask when embarking on a new undertaking or entering a new market. In particular, identifying a decision maker as your partner, distributor, or agent becomes critical to success.

"In this country, how are decision makers identified?" is one question we don't ask here at home but that must be asked when moving offshore. Once identified, the decision makers are used to help carry out the corporate objectives, not only through their individual judgments but especially through the networks into which they are plugged. The two basic questions about decision making remain the same in global business, but other cultures do not identify the real power brokers, the real decision makers, the same way we do. Applying American standards for identifying people in other countries can be misleading, sometimes dangerous to your business. The global executive recognizes the significance of the answers to these questions. Once the decision-making process has been mastered, the global executive has effective control over the success of the offshore operation, whether it is a marketing or a production function.

In the United States, we know how to identify the decision maker. We react intuitively to a number of easily-identifiable clues—the Bigelow rug on the floor, the Man or Woman of Distinction bearing, access to the executive dining room, the hot-shot parking place, distinctive pin-stripe suit and French cuffs (male or female), and speech characteristics including accent. We also tell by how other people in the office react when he or she comes in, how they converse, and how they respond to suggestions, orders, or commands. There are clear signs that we normally (but not always) read accurately, even though we are an unusually casual, even jocular, first-name people. The following story, although perverse, does illustrate the point.

> Bernie Picotte, a big office-building developer in Albany, was visiting Hartford some years ago for a weekend convention. In a spare moment, he wandered around looking at new office construction, and he found himself at the Phoenix Mutual Life Insurance Company's unusual, ellipsoid building. He pressed the buzzer and explained to the guard who he was and asked if he could look around. The guard shrugged the question over to a man standing nearby in jeans and lumberman's shirt. "I'll take him around," said the second man. The tour, according to Bernie, was terrific, from the mechanical rooms to the board room. When the tour was over, he thanked his guide with a compliment: "You sure do know this building!" The reply was unexpected: "I should know it, I built it. I'm Chairman of the Board of Phoenix Mutual."

Sometimes our clues fool us, even at home! All the more reason to seek clues to how decision makers are identified in countries that are new to us.

Networking has become something of a buzzword in American society in the last few years. We tried without success to find out who first made "to network" a verb and applied it to contemporary American life. The noun's social meaning has for many years been conveyed in the phrase "the old boys' network." Old boys or new boys and girls, its importance cannot be gainsaid.

We either find the key decision maker and try to use his or her network to reach other important persons, or we find someone within the network who has access to the decision makers. Until we began to recognize its importance and dynamism, and we began to use networking systematically, we used the decision-maker network feature of our business world unconsciously and naturally to spread the word about our products, enhance our image, or get things done. Now, especially with respect to getting things done in Washington or in state capitals, networking has become a conscious part of every executive's daily work.

American society has made identifying the decision makers and the networks relatively easy, too, through the rapid growth of associations and societies that hold frequent meetings, conferences, and conventions. The decision makers are asked to give the principal addresses and they serve on boards of directors or as advisors. The network is formalized by the association, although networks as informal institutions remain largely independent of the association. The network uses the annual convention or trade show as its means of renewing its alliances and communication points. Networks can be identified by associations, and, conversely, associations themselves can usually be quickly identified for the importance of their members' networks. Subtle hints give us clues that are difficult to define to others. How we know that the Business Roundtable or the Trilateral Commission or the Conference Board are important is not a function of their names but of the reputation we have been able to sniff out or others have told us about.

Americans also publish directories, membership lists, and encyclopedias of decision makers, national leaders, corporate officers, and directors. We can buy a mailing list of executives of corporations beyond a certain size who live in houses in certain special suburbs where the family income is above a certain average. And these lists work, too, or they would not continue to be available and grow in precision and sophistication.

American businesspersons use their information on people most likely to be key decision makers to plug into their networks, using the telephone as well as the meeting as their instruments of choice. The telephone call to a person that we think will know an identified decision maker may not yield immediate access to the decision maker we seek. "Why don't you call A.?" But the process started by that phone call most often will lead us to someone who is even closer to the big person, and this process continues until we finally get the access we want. "Hello, Mr. Big, A. suggested that I call you. . . . "

Our business world is built around a web of elaborate information strands, interconnected and related to a number of key decision makers. With these processes—much abbreviated here—we are able to make our objectives work, and keep our companies functioning in the American market.

Now, as we go global, we have to export this aspect of American corporate culture. That means the global executive has to learn how to use the web wherever he or she is working.

In no other realm of global management are there so many

unknowables, so many mysteries, because the relationships and clues that create the web and make it usable are so different from the United States. Roy Herberger (*Dallas Morning News*, August 26, 1985) believes that overseas market research is a particularly acute problem for the small to medium-sized company. His point is that these companies do not routinely have access to data sources familiar to the multinationals. These companies not only do not know the available research resources, they do not routinely plug into the international networks. Thus the country-specific networks that they have to work with in particular countries are even more remote for them than for the industrial giants. The small operator simply does not have access to insiders in other countries.

Insiders are the keys to successful offshore business. Insiders may be important here, but at least printed sources and growing electronic databases are available. The public resources in most other countries are still limited and structural restraints can hamstring research efforts.

The network that leads to the insider and the network that leads from the insider to others critical to business success must be identified and used if the global executive is to make the most of offshore opportunities.

HOW DECISION MAKERS ARE IDENTIFIED

The major offshore challenge is to find out who makes the key decisions in another country and how those decisions are made. Without this information, even the most sophisticated global plan can go awry. In order to find the decision maker, the executive has to construct a whole new set of clues and hints that are not used in American business. A few examples illustrate the dangers of assuming that decision makers are identified the same way we Americans would identify them:

> The United States and United Nations pumped millions and millions of dollars into promoting wet rice cultivation in West Africa, sending experts from village to village to talk with the elders and the medicine men. They discovered too late that the men knew nothing at all about seed selection. My friend, John Gay, discovered that seeds and seed selection were tasks reserved exclusively for the women. No one had been sent out to talk to the women.
>
> I learned in India that virtually no decisions are made except at

the very highest level. A friend of mine, N., in the Indian Administrative Service won a Parvin Fellowship to Princeton, but clearance from the head of the civil service didn't come through. When the president of India visited the district my friend was administering at the time, he asked N. how things were going. N. mentioned the hold-up on approval for his study leave, and the president said he'd find out about it when he returned to Delhi. The president asked the prime minister for a report. The decision was then made in the Cabinet of India. This is not an exceptional case.

In Japan, corporate consensus involving senior executives and even middle managers must be achieved before a decision is announced. The notion of consensus runs through the whole corporate decision-making process. So, while the seniormost executive is crucially important in your negotiations and will attract most of the attention of his Japanese subordinates while he speaks, he alone does not make a decision and to try N.'s Indian end-run in Japan may ruin your prospects.

A major power equipment manufacturer won a contract, as I recall the story, with the Ministry of Irrigation and Power in India, to supply a gas turbine installation in Agra. A team of their expert engineers and trainers went jetting off to India, with an expensive array of equipment following by air freight. The company executive in charge was dismayed—and understandably rather furious—when he learned that the equipment had been impounded by Indian Customs at Delhi Airport for lack of an import license. But, he argued, we have a contract with the Government of India to install this equipment. No, came the reply (eventually and not in this simple form), you have a contract with the Ministry of Irrigation and Power, but the Ministry of Finance controls import licenses. Besides, the Ministry of Finance regards itself as the seniormost ministry and jealously guards its prerogatives. While all this was being sorted out and the company was birddogging its import license application through the corridors of the Ministry of Finance, its group of engineers and technicians was eating up per diems in bored idleness in the shadow of the Taj Mahal.

The common element to each of these horror stories is that the key decision makers were not the persons that the Americans had expected them to be. Therefore you must find out how the decision makers are identified before you can find those insiders who can provide the key information you need.

Whether you are planning a trip to a country overseas or are actually assigned to the site, the first and most basic challenge is to learn the identifying clues to the decision makers and their networks.

The process for identification of power brokers and decision makers is an interactive one: what you learn in the United States helps define the scope of the inquiry, what you learn on-site allows you to establish underlying principles of identification clues—both enable you to spot and then use the decision makers.

Some clues to identifying decision makers outside the United States are included in Figure 9–1. We make no claims that the questions asked are universal, but the questions may trigger some of your own thinking about how positively to identify the decision makers. It may work less well in some of the developing societies where family is more important than any other social group, and the family patriarch or matriarch is not ever visible to you. And it certainly will work less well in Japan where decision making is fundamentally decentralized in a system of consensus building. The Japanese company's management consensus is often reached with few external signs that it is happening, sort of like the Quaker's "sense of the meeting" that is reached without a formal vote. Whatever you do, whatever your assignment, follow the clues to power *systematically*.

Obviously, start with the same networks or the same kind of networks you use at home in the United States: clubs, service clubs, banks, trade associations, fellow Americans including the U.S. embassy, chambers of commerce, and the like. Remember, however, that sliding into these organizations may *seem* as easy as at home, but you are still the outsider. A Rotary, chamber of commerce, trade association, or country club may *seem* the same, but it is governed by relationships and unwritten standards that you cannot automatically know. The reasons why people belong may be substantially different from why Americans are drawn into such organizations. The acceptability of certain individuals to their peers in these organizations may rely on factors that are totally foreign to you. The geniality and generosity the members or associates will almost invariably show toward you may be simply the normal hospitality of the country, not an indication that they have accepted you personally much less embraced your professional business program.

If you are going to use these networks for corporate purposes, then be systematic about how you use them. If you join the local Rotary or country club, be certain that you get a list of members. Then mine that list as systematically as you would *The Wall Street Journal*. You are engaged in collecting names, but are not after

FIGURE 9–1
Decision-Maker's Identification Kit

Offshore decision makers are crucial to the success of a global business, but are not identified the same way they are at home. Here is a form to use when you are exploring a business opportunity abroad and have to assess whether your contact is a decision maker. Fill it out when you get back to the hotel or office, but be sure to update it and seek out feedback from old hands in the country.

How old is this person? (Is age highly honored/makes no difference?)

How is the person dressed?

What personal possessions are on him/her or in his/her room?

Describe the office setting.

What title does the person have?

How does this title compare with others you know are decision makers?

How did the person handle time: was he/she late/early?

If among a group of persons, who entered the office/room first?

What could the seating order tell you about this person's importance?

How did managers in the office relate to this person?

How did support staff relate to this person?

Did this person defer to others as decisions had to be made, reflecting a need for consensus or respect for subordinates?

What kind of car does this person use? Drive self or is driven?

(If you got to his/her home) What do the house and its furnishings tell you about this person's tastes? Do those tastes square with general tastes of the power group from what you have learned about the social structure of that society?

FIGURE 9–1 (concluded)

What engagements outside of business does this person maintain (social or political leadership)?

What kind of education did this person have, and does he/she show it?

What did you learn about this person's relatives? Are they important?

What did you learn about the spouse's connections?

What did you learn about this person's contacts with government and do they prove out from what you have learned?

What sex is this person, and how does this society usually regard persons of that sex in decision-making roles? Is this an exception?

Is there another corporation to which this firm is beholden?
A government office? A group of investors/owners? A labor union or work group? A family?

If decision making is *decentralized,* how does this person fit into the pattern by which decisions are arrived at?

Is this person's power local, regional, or wider?

specific names as first task. The first hurdle is to find out the underlying principles beneath *why the who is important.* The why comes before the who. The how are they identified comes along with the why. Ask questions.

Persistently asking questions (a key to offshore success) is not only acceptable, but expected. You are a foreigner, maybe even a dumb foreigner, and you are expected to seek information through questioning. So keep at it, especially when asking about people.

Make lists—few American businesspeople actually make lists of their contacts and what each one is worth in business terms. Try the trick of noting on the back of business cards the occasion when you met the person and what that person can possibly offer you. For the offshore operator, such lists are invaluable and should be annotated with new and deeper information as it is gathered. That information should, as far as possible, be aimed at outlining the distinguishing features of decision makers in that society. Be certain, however, that the lists include no information that you would not want someone else to see, a competitor or a government agent, for example. Any personal judgments should be as neutral as possible and as closely related to specific business concerns as you can make them. Security for this kind of information is important to preserve, but avoid using codes to hide your purpose: some countries do nasty things to people who use codes, making innocent purposes appear sinister.

Whether you are going for a short visit or are being posted to an offshore location, make it a practice to seek answers to the basic decision-making question: how are decision makers identified in this society? By using the experience and wisdom of others before you leave your office in the United States, you can have a reasonably good list of clues to identities. When you get on-site, open your eyes and ears to the more subtle clues that your informants forgot to tell you about. Your lists of apparent decision makers tell you the underlying principles of identification. After a short time, if the task is undertaken systematically and is reinforced by constant questioning of those who should have the answers, the pattern of identification is yours to use to your business advantage.

IDENTIFYING WHO: BEFORE LEAVING HOME

The place to start identifying decision makers, of course, is before you go abroad in the first place. Check your own board of directors. Network through the influentials in your own company first, then expand to companies that you know do business in the part of the world where you are going. Unless asked, few of these important people will remember to tell you about their French roommate at Harvard or their Kenyan-exchange-student-now-Minister-of-Finance. Because you are generally not going to be able to find the kind of published, in-depth lists of executives in most other nations of the world, these informal references are crucially important. Do it systematically and keep a record of names, addresses, titles, and phone numbers.

A particularly important group of persons to try to identify before leaving home are those who have been involved in overseas work, projects, living, or study in the past. Start within the company, asking if anyone at any level has had first-hand experience in the target country. In your corporation, you may have employees who were born and raised in the target country. If these employees are management or technical professionals, it is likely that they came from important sections of their society. However, no matter how inconsequential that person's company job may be, he or she may have some important clues to share with you (and you can offer ownership in the global plan by consulting him or her).

Many persons with first-hand offshore experiences are university-based, but most of them have extensive experience with government and corporate types in the target country. Seek out returned diplomats, military attachés, and even ex-missionaries, for in many parts of the world Americans of any occupation tend to move in higher social circles than they might at home. You'd be surprised the contacts many of these people have who can serve as conduits for you into contact with the real decision makers when you get out there. There are some dangers. Some Americans lived their expatriate lives in golden ghettoes, cut off from the society at large. They are reasonably easy to spot. Harder are those who had a particular axe to grind about their posting overseas, their bosses, their host-national relations, anti-Americanism, or the like. Their antagonisms may so subtly color their vision that references given by them may be less useful, perhaps even politically dangerous.

INTRODUCTIONS

Most important, however, is getting an introduction. In many parts of the world, you simply cannot telephone, telex, or write for an appointment in advance, much less walk into someone's office without a proper introduction. Even where you can, you will find the reception a great deal warmer if you arrive after an introduction has been received. If your introducer is an American at home, be sure your American contact at home has in fact already written, phoned, or telexed the fact that you are on the up-and-up, that you are coming, and that he or she expects you to receive the same treatment as would be accorded the American contact. If you cannot engineer such a formal introduction, make certain that you can use the contact's name when you generate your own introduction. Use the people you meet on arrival to seek written or phoned introductions where you do not already have them. Virtually the entire rest of the world is more formal in such matters than we are.

Respect that formality by resisting referrals without the referee giving a formal introduction.

Bankers and attorneys are the first choice for making contacts when arriving abroad.

I arranged for the correspondent bank of my American bankers to identify some potential distributors for my goods before I arrived in London. They did exactly as I had instructed, and the managing director took a half hour out of his busy schedule to brief me on them.

For years I complained that it had been a waste of my time, for the firms I was referred to were inappropriate for my product line. In retrospect, however, I realize that the fault was not the bank's, it was mine. The bank is in the banking business first. It is in the information brokering business as an adjunct to the banking business, not as its first line. It was up to me to use the contacts provided as a way of building *my own* network. Even though they were off-target as potential U.K. distributors for me, they were in the same general line of business and some hours spent with them would have helped me to identify the persons who really could have helped me.

The bank had done its job. I was too impatient, in London for too short a time, and too ignorant of the networking possibilities that might have resulted from finding alternative decision makers to make the trip worthwhile. My company was the loser.

Certain cautions should condition how you pursue contacts abroad. A relationship, once established, creates obligations as well as benefits. This is true in the United States, of course: If I ask you for a reference, I expect to be able to render a favor to you of about the same worth if and when you ask for it. In many countries, however, the relationship may require a more enduring and a deeper commitment than you might expect in the United States. Knowing how deep one has penetrated in a relationship is often very difficult to assess without help from a "native."

My wife took lessons (an American term for the study of music) from an Indian Muslim, a young man on his way to international recognition. I was included in events within his family as much as she was. But when he asked Joan to serve as hostess to the international guests at his sister's wedding (his women were all in *purdah*—behind the veil), I said that she would not be able to, for I had tickets to the Music Festival in Madras at the same time and we were planning a family trip down there. He was deeply upset.

It wasn't until five years later that a mutual friend, in Amjad's presence, explained to me that we had passed from being "friends"—

bhai-bhai means "brother-brother" but it's more a backslapping camaraderie than kinship—to being actual members of the family. As members of the family, we were *expected* to sacrifice our trip to Madras for the benefit of the sister's wedding.

We had assumed an obligation that went with the privilege of Joan's learning music from him that was far greater than we had recognized.

In some countries, also, there are persons who regard providing information about decision makers and networks as their bread and butter. Their role in the negotiation process has become quite formalized in professions. In Korea and Japan, information brokers are absolutely essential to getting the right introductions and serving as go-betweens. In Japan, it would be difficult to enter a business transaction without a *shokai-sha* or introducer and possibly a *chukai-sha* or mediator. Both are outside, third or neutral parties, thus their usefulness. But the information they provide requires appropriate recognition, perhaps compensation. While not printed in any fee schedule, the remuneration required will tend to be quite specific—something you learn from a mutual acquaintance of both you and the information broker.

In China, the interpersonal network known as *guanxi* is the route to accomplishing your mission, often through roundabout or back-door routes. But using a *guanxi* is not only a way to facilitate your process but an integral part of your business relationships and operations, an end as well as the means to it (Copeland, 1985, 176). In Latin American societies there is the *compadre* relation, and in India a lingering element of *jajmani* personal interdependencies can be used for networking if their local meanings are understood and they are not used for arrogant manipulation.

In many countries, it would be grossly improper for an American *not* to follow up on referrals given by a national of that country before departure. Any referrals by a member of the culture ought to be taken very seriously, even if they are presumably more social than business. Remember that many business and professional emigrés may be very well connected indeed.

Before leaving for my assignment in India, I was given several names by Indian friends in the United States. My wife and I had several enchanting social evenings from these referrals. One referral, to one of the most important contractors in India, proved to be little more than an informative social occasion at which we met India's greatest cricket star.

Another introduction, however, led to a number of different ramifications that were to be important to us in India. Because of who had given the reference and the location and title of the person to whom we were referred, we had absolutely no idea how important that contact might become. In this case, the person to whom we were introduced was a powerful politician (of the in-power party), an extremely well-connected businessman in our business (publishing). His wife ran a school and was a published author whose books we later distributed in the United States. As a result, I take such referrals very seriously now.

In the last chapter, we suggested using certain agencies for information useful to research. Many of them also provide introductions. To recap briefly here, the principal ones are: attorneys, bankers, embassy commercial attachés, public relations and advertising firms, chambers of commerce, and trade associations.

IDENTIFYING SPECIFIC DECISION MAKERS

When you have learned the signals by which local businesspersons and others identify the decision makers, then you have to apply that knowledge to single out the ones who are of importance to you. There are some cautions here, too. Did we follow these cautions when we first went abroad to do business? The answer is no, but having done business abroad, we now know how important they are. Our more recent offshore ventures have followed reasonably closely the following pattern of cautious inquiry.

First, ascertain how the decision-making authority has been acquired. Second, ascertain to what extent that decision-making authority is shared. Third, if decision making must be shared, find out under what particular circumstances and when it must be shared. Fourth, ascertain what informal channels—if any—are used by host-country nationals to go around this decision maker. Fifth, determine whether there are channels open to you, as a foreigner, that are distinct from locally-accepted channels and whether the local ones are open to you.

If the company is planning a long-term commitment in a particular country, checking out these implications of leadership is fundamental to success. While some executives are better at intuiting such relationships and practices than others, almost any executive had better find out the parameters of any person's decision-making authority. This is a different matter from discovering the clues to who are the decision makers, but the information gathered in that inquiry may be applied here as well.

Power is never distributed or exercised alike between two countries. This truth applies to business as much as to government. "National character" may be a figment of our imaginations, but there are identifiable national practices with respect to power and decision making. Watch out for misleading stereotypes. It may be argued that the Swedes and Australians are very much like us in some respects, and that the African and Arab executives share strong traditions of consulting with each other in making decisions, while the East Asian cultures emphasize harmony and consensus in group decision making (Copeland, 1985, 123-6). The wise executive makes his or her own judgments from experience. The successful global executive does not accept anyone else's stereotypes, maybe because one of these cultural boobytraps has already exploded on him or her. Always judge people on *their* terms, individual and group.

In otherwise unexceptionable books on doing business abroad, we often find unsettling drifts from solid, verifiable information toward apparently harmless (but useful) stereotypes. We are sure that some stereotypes have crept into this book, which only proves that stereotypes creep in unconsciously and in spite of best intentions. Stereotypes are useful social devices, but they are a social device that protects one's own group. In the interdependent world, which is the natural habitat of the global executive, stereotypes should be used with extraordinary caution. And, the reader should seriously challenge any stereotypes we are guilty of perpetuating in these pages.

Government decision makers are identified in many of the same ways as private-sector authority figures. Their titles give away their rank in the hierarchy, a rough indication of how much clout they may have—if you understand that the hierarchy may be different from its American parallels. Knowing who makes decisions in the bureaucracy or among the governmental ministers can make the key difference to your success in an overseas business venture. Government decision makers can make or break a business venture more thoroughly than almost any other single factor.

Government authorities should be built into your local network in the host country. You also have to know what may limit their power or authority. Ask (cautiously) by whom or what means have these persons been challenged or threatened in their decision-making authority, either by means of subtle influences on government, by free election, or by *coup d'état*. Knowing who will replace the government decision maker in the event of a change of government is almost as important as knowing who makes decisions now. Government influence on purely business decisions tends to be more pronounced outside the United States, so the global executive makes it a priority to ascertain the power of decision makers and the potential of their possible replacements.

Also, because authority is frequently delegated, the global executive finds out what are the traditions of delegating authority to make decisions. Knowing practices of delegation will most certainly affect your ability to know where you stand with government, with your offshore business associates, and with your counterparts in negotiations. In offshore operations, you may have to delegate authority to others in your management of the offshore operation. To impose an imported form of either delegation or decision making can be catastrophic.

> My predecessor in the office in New Delhi was wonderful in one particular respect: once he had appointed a person to a position, he left that person entirely alone to execute responsibilities without interference.
>
> Unfortunately, there is no tradition of such delegation in India. Employees expect to be told what to do and expect to be held on a very short string. A key employee in our office was utterly unable to handle the responsibility on his own. While I had evidence that he was venal shortly after I took command, it was the utter chaos that had developed in his administration that was the real problem. He had not been supervised, so, in spite of his obviously great intelligence and relevant experience, he was unable to manage his office without constant supervision. Quite simply, he had had no experience having authority delegated to him, so he misused it.

The case in point is taken from operations, but let's turn it around: If delegation is not widely practiced, as in India, doesn't that mean that the executive should seek the highest level official he or she can identify? The answer is yes. If delegation is widely practiced, then the chain of command should be followed out to see at what level one should most effectively concentrate one's attention.

Finally, find out what sort of relationship a person of your role and status would bear to the decision maker if you were a fellownational of that country. Then see if you can figure out how you, as a foreign executive, are different from a fellow national. What you want to seek is a relationship with the decision maker—whether he or she is in business, banking, or government—that will help you get your work done effectively. Involved will be a whole new set of personal commitments, many of which may be unfamiliar to you.

Often the new relationships are not as close as we would expect them to become in the United States. In Japan, for example, you should never expect to be entertained in the home of a Japanese executive, nor should you entertain the Japanese executive in your home if you live in Japan. In France or England, you should not mix people from different segments of society in an informal, party atmosphere. If they don't mix in their own lives, it is not up to you to change that. You may, of course, demonstrate American ways of doing things, but do so with extreme caution that you are not going to cause yourself more trouble than it is worth.

In short, find those subtleties that govern your own *personal* relationship with the decision maker, ascertain how your company relates to the decision maker's organization, then operate very carefully according to the rules you've discovered.

PLUGGING INTO THEIR NETWORK

The essence of breaking into *their* network is to recognize that your own network won't work. How hard that is to do is demonstrated on any business day by the numbers of American business executives eating lunch *with each other* in any of the world's capitals outside the United States or playing golf with each other. That was part of my friend Jim's problem in getting his job done in India: he networked with fellow Americans and Englishmen, and avoided building the network he needed with Indians. This isn't a feature only of India, but our examples come from where we have had the most experience.

Networking is more than a cute abstraction. By using your personal and professional networks, you are able to gain information that is not part of the public record and to communicate some of your needs to those who may be able to satisfy them. Networking is like an army in being: its very presence is a strength to the person who has built up strong connections, especially with the power structure of the country. Power and information go together and both are accessible through networking. Networking, at the same time, tends to make playing with power and information less dangerous, for the network shares some of the hazards, making a single member of the network less exposed. The keys to networks are decision makers, persons who are able to use both power and information effectively.

Once the decision maker has been identified by using the clues from their identification system for decision makers, the executive's task is to ease himself or herself into that network. Here again, unfortunately, it will be easier for *him* than for *her* in virtually every country of the world outside of the United States. Networks may rely on women to keep their unity and their communications, but entrance into the networks of business and governing politics in most of the world is very much in the hands of the men. An American woman will be at a significant disadvantage, no matter how adept she is at using the identifiers. If she is aggressive, she may well be sending the wrong signals.

Some generalized clues may be helpful. First, aggressiveness in general will not be helpful in networking. A pose of studied respect for your decision maker is much more likely to pay off. That does not mean that you cannot ask questions or express honest interest in the customs and practices of the host country. It does not mean that you should not display that you have done your homework on the country before you came out. Questions and evidence of deep interest will usually engage your contact's attention and lead to an invitation to join him for a social occasion or the meeting of a club or association. At the club or meal, watchful attention to what is happening and why it is happening and who is making it happen is much more important than representing yourself for anything other than an interested foreigner. Let your behavior mold itself to the glove of the other nation.

Second, while you must represent your company, try not to make a big thing out of your rank. Rank *is* important in most societies, but rank should be displayed with subtle, preferably muted, signals. Our experience is that we have been accorded higher rank by the fact of our being American than if we had paraded exactly how important a rank we carried. In this case, let the glove fit itself to you instead of vice versa.

Third, take people at their face value when they offer to serve as intermediaries for you. Not all may work out, but don't insult a person by failing to take him up on the offer, for there is no telling how well-connected a person may be, even someone for whom you can generate little personal respect.

Finally, follow the local rules for gift giving, entertaining, and socializing. Doing what you do at home is more often a disaster than not.

> I made a point of personally meeting with an army wife, a dozen or more years ago, who had been written up in the *Christian Science Monitor* for her efforts to better train army wives for overseas posts. She told me of the first entertaining done by a senior military couple in Indonesia in the late 1960s: a cocktail party where the wife greeted the guests in her hot pants. Indonesia is a Muslim country where alcohol is forbidden by religious law, frowned on among government officials, and where women are kept hidden from view by Believers. Nothing the American couple could have done would have offended the host nationals more thoroughly.
>
> I failed miserably to meet Japanese expectations of me as a business visitor when I did not present my Japanese associates with gifts. The head of the Japanese company, who happened to be a woman, but was the Emperor's first cousin and a cousin to the Empress as well, gave me a sterling silver *sake* cup, inscribed with my name and the date of the event, crowned by the chrysanthemum, a symbol reserved for the Imperial family. What a dope I felt! What insult I did her not to return an appropriate gift!

Suitability of gifts and of entertainment rank as the most important feature of fitting in to a new culture, being the most immediately obvious. This includes knowing how to eat, how to drink, how to toast, how to express thanks, how to exit properly. So, in before-departure preparations, learn the gift-giving and entertaining expectations of your host nationals as thoroughly as possible.

Remember, when you aren't in the United States, you will not be judged by American standards which tend to be very casual. You will be judged according to the rules of the local culture, and you cannot possibly know all the nuances and graces of their rules. Do your very best.

It is especially important to avoid casual comment about the rules and practices. Never say *anything*, says Eric Herz, head of the Institute of Electrical and Electronic Engineers, that cannot be safely overheard. Even in the privacy of your own hotel room or apartment, keep comments and criticisms of how they do business or how they behave to those that are inoffensive and that cannot be misinterpreted. You never know who is listening. Never put negative evaluations of the local situation on paper; you never know who may read it.

NODAL POINTS

Nodal points connect your networks with theirs. We believe that the global executive will use nodal points to plug into another network, but will also use those points to deliberately connect two local networks into a more global network. If the future lies in globalization, to deliberately make your networks multinational will eventually become an important component in your global success.

Start at home. Prior to departure, try to make some fresh network connections. A good source of these may be through the university. The faculty has good international connections and can refer you to colleagues who are plugged into your target country. Don't forget the alumni office at your college. College alumni, even those from abroad, have fierce loyalty to the institution that may be used to leapfrog a fellow alumnus into networks in other countries. And don't forget that many U.S. universities have been engaged in overseas programs for many years and have a band of "hidden alumni" among persons who worked with those projects. Oftentimes these are persons who have never been to America, but if they can swing it they will send their favorite child or children to the university with which they worked in their own land. This loyalty can be enormously useful.

Relatives in the United States are also an easy plug-in, but this connection is more difficult because it is difficult for you to assess to what social group they belong. If they are professional people, you may infer that they started out from the educated classes of the target country. Sometimes immigrants to the United States are connected with heady reaches of their motherland's society. If they are immigrants who have struggled for a toehold in the United States, you may find that their group were outcasts in the homeland. Thus you may find their network overseas is not suitable to your mission. The same may be true of members of your religious denomination, who may be persons from an oppressed minority that joined your group in order to gain freedom from the oppression of just those classes you may have to work with in your business. Do some careful homework on what their contacts mean in order to assess the importance of their networks to your purposes.

Persons that you meet as they come through at chamber of commerce meetings, world trade councils, world affairs councils, councils of international visitors can be of great importance later on, even if you have no plans to go to their countries right away.

> Several years ago, we were asked by our local foreign visitors center to host a visiting couple from abroad. They had not been comfortable guests to their American hosts in other cities. We had a lovely weekend at our home, for we accepted them as they were. When we later visited their country, they had laid out an elaborate, five-day, red-carpet tour of a major region, complete with banquets, performances, and meetings with key people.

Keep your doors open to professional visitors, for their doors may later be open to you.

Politicians are likely among those whom you have met when they visited the United States. With this one, be careful, for you do not understand political machinations and subtleties in their country. They may have fallen from favor since you saw them, or be under secret police observation. A visit to them may taint you in the eyes of the present government. Be very cautious in following up political connections. Bureaucratic ones are apt to be less dangerous, but then again they may be less helpful.

It should go almost without saying that you should join, then maintain your membership in any American clubs or professional or trade associations that have overseas chapters, for they do provide networking entry points.

When established in your foreign base, make it your business to become involved in community activities. Make certain that they are nonpolitical as far as possible, and that your involvement will not be regarded as one more sign of American imperialism. But highly respected community activities are a good way to prove your innocence of imperialistic interests or subversive ones.

> Fortuitously, before I left for my assignment, I agreed to do some work in India for an American voluntary association that was con-

cerned with rural development. Through that connection, I ended up working behind the scenes in the initial stages of the foundation of the Appropriate Technology Group in India. I thereby established my credentials in a network that reached into the planning commission, the universities, the research institutes, the Council for Scientific and Industrial Research. I was happy to be of service and was flattered by the compliments I received, but the importance to me was that I had both performed a useful public service and plugged into an important network.

MERGING NETWORKS INTO A GLOBAL NETWORK

It is our position that, for the long haul, your chief goal in networking is to begin to link your on-site network connections with your global ones. The global executive is not content with one network in the United Kingdom, one in Japan, and one in Zimbabwe. He or she is concerned to see that these networks begin to intersect, not just through the individual person of the global executive but through other connections deliberately created to make a global network work.

It is our impression that global networks are becoming better established among some of the not-for-profit development agencies, associations, and their professionals than among businesspersons. For this reason, it might not be a bad idea for the global executive to cultivate connections in those areas to learn how to broaden business networks into global networks.

The global network is a goal because business is becoming global. Separate national networks make sense for doing business in those separate countries, but they need to be linked together if the company is to enjoy the opportunities that globalization offers. Networks provide information quickly and allow for rapid communication to key persons. A global network allows for greater flexibility in marketing and in operations if it has been consciously knitted together out of connections in many different countries.

It's a whole new phenomenon in the business world, so there aren't many rules. The principal rule that is obvious, however, is to respect the nationality and person of each member of the network. That means not trying to turn it into an *American* network. Equal respect and equal enjoyment must underlie all relationships in a global network.

SUMMARY

Finding out how cultures identify and define their decision makers must come before identifying any specific person or persons. Once identified, decision makers must be taken on their terms, not on American terms, and they must be used carefully as ways of penetrating into power and information networks that will make it possible to do business in those countries. Yet national networks alone will not be enough, they must be tied together for the future into global networks.

THE GLOBAL EXECUTIVE AS GLOBAL NEGOTIATOR

An Inventory of Skills and Attitudes

- Skill to negotiate for long-term results.
- Skill to relate to persons whose negotiating styles and values are fundamentally different.
- Skill to use preliminaries to negotiation as an essential part of successful negotiation.
- Skill to recruit, train, and manage a team of negotiators for negotiations in an unfamiliar and uncomfortable setting.
- Skill to use strategic planning, involving, rewarding, timing, communicating, research, and networking in offshore negotiations.
- Skill in maintaining intimate personal relations with customers, clients, financiers, suppliers, managers, and employees through long periods of time.
- Skill in maintaining open-ended negotiations, sensing the difference between a covenant relationship and a legally-binding contract.
- Skill in handling conflict where value-systems are not identical.

The Global Negotiator

Many American companies have allowed overseas negotiations to become their Achilles heel. The list of miscues in negotiating strategy and tactics would fill volumes. From starting off too quickly and setting too low a price to blunders of a social sort that turned off the prospective customer, the chronicle is long and anguished.

This chapter is designed for both the executive who supervises offshore operations and the executive who actually negotiates. The supervising executive will need to be familiar with every step of the process, especially to assure home office support before, during, and after the negotiations. The negotiator will want to prepare carefully for offshore negotiations and for the expectations of visiting foreign delegations. Cross-national negotiating is so different that we suggest putting aside the cassette albums and how-to negotiating books before entering offshore negotiations. Of all aspects of management, negotiating practices appear to be among the most culture-bound.

The problem is familiar: Americans tend to think that the way Americans conduct negotiations is the way everyone else conducts them. There may be signs that the nationalities of the world are moving closer together, but we are still generations apart, especially on negotiating practices. The Japanese, for example, are now willing to sign a contract with an American company (Graham, 1984), and we heard just the other day of an Arab requesting a signed contract (albeit with a trader unknown to him personally). Both view contracts skeptically.

Should Americans change their negotiating style when negotia-

FIGURE 10-1
Three Faces of Offshore Negotiation

Stages of Negotiation	Approaches to Negotiation (After Roger Fisher, 1981)	Personal: The Negotiator
Plans and preps	Interests, not positions	Listens well
Selection and training	Problems, not people	Open-minded
Corporate strategy	Mutual gain, not advantage	Tolerant
Authority from HQ	Objective, not passionate	Relates well to other people
Team and teamwork		Adaptable
Language proficiency		Adjusts quickly
Corporate patience		High self-esteem, an artist
Reasonable goals and objectives		High aspirations for self in the company
Prep for non-task prelude		Personal attractiveness
Conducts and confers		Influence at headquarters
Information needed on:		Team player
Competition		Patient
Government involvement		Previous experience offshore
Hidden concerns		Language proficiency
Decision-making process		
Their agenda		
Answers to their questions		
Questions to their questions		
Silence		
Walk out/break off points		
Closes and agrees		
Linear vs. holistic		
Carries out, gets feedback, changes		

tions take place in America? Shouldn't the foreign delegation adapt to our ways of negotiating?

There is no simple and incontrovertible answer. In general, because ours is a solidly market-based approach, we would suggest that any adaptation that will affect the company's purpose is in order. If that means negotiating Japanese-style in Schenectady, then that should be in order. On the other hand, there may be messages your company wants to send to its foreign counterpart, messages that can be effectively sent by reflecting a certain style in negotiation. We do believe that foreign firms seeking to sell in U.S. markets ought to adapt their negotiating to our style—but there is clear evidence that such sophisticated marketing nations as Japan, Korea, and Taiwan are already doing that effectively. It seems to be the Americans who are hidebound to their way of conducting business.

One more generalization. Consider negotiations as a process that has only a vague beginning (in some casual correspondence or a chance meeting perhaps), a period of intensive activity during actual talks between counterparts, and then an unending continuation of relations during which fine tuning and adjustments are made to agreements, contracts, and relationships.

A new breed of negotiator is needed, along with a new management approach to negotiations. The negotiator should be more an artist than a player of games, a person with endless patience and a keen eye for the unexpected. Above the negotiator, the executive in charge of the negotiating process, overseeing the team, thus must be more the impresario than the by-the-rules business administrator.

Among all the differences in offshore negotiations and the peculiarities of negotiations in different countries, the one common denominator in most of the rest of the world is that the other party is generally looking for a relationship. The purpose of negotiation is to establish a relationship rather than make a deal, conclude some hard bargain, or bring success to a single project. This is true even in Europe. In Asia in particular, the long-term *personal* relationship between the executives and managers of one company and their overseas partners is of fundamental importance. Moran says that even the Koreans—who can come at you like a buzzsaw—respond to the long-term personal approach that splits off the persons from the issues (Moran, 1982).

The American tendency to concentrate on problems and issues tends to draw in the worst aspects of personalities and persons. Rather, we should sit back and develop a personal relationship that then permits us to separate people from problems. Roger Fisher's Harvard project on negotiation is particularly relevant to negotiation across national boundaries (Fisher, 1981). Fisher may look like a softy in the United States, but his principles appear to pay off in spades overseas.

Even if the negotiators come at you hard and ruthlessly, the global executive keeps in mind the injunction that most of the world's businesspersons are after a result which is mutually favorable, not one that humiliates the opposition. We believe that Fisher's book, *Getting to Yes* (1981) is superbly applicable to the actual negotiations. Summarized and rephrased in our words, his four major points are:

- Concentrate on *interests*, not on positions.
- Focus on *problems*, not on persons.
- Seek *mutual gain*, not advantage.
- Be *objective*, not passionate.

A few examples may illustrate the importance of understanding the relevance of negotiating styles to business effectiveness:

One American businessman buying in Japan thought that when the Japanese hesitated they were objecting to his offer, so he raised it and continued to raise it. He later learned that he had raised it three times after he had hit the offer they would accept. (Ricks, 1983, 111)

One of my own first negotiating blunders was with a major Indian publisher who took advantage of the fact that I was alone. He filled the room with senior associates, all of whom backed him up and confirmed his every point until I was reeling. I accepted a deal I had promised myself in advance never to accept, and I lost money on it as I expected I would if I accepted such terms.

In Japan, I got the American distribution rights, but at terms hardly more favorable than in India. It was because I was positively at fault in negotiations, not that they were smarter or more aggressive. The Japanese were so eager to export that they forgave my egregious errors: first, as mentioned earlier, I didn't bring any gift for the Japanese princess who directed the company; second, I talked business over dinner at a fancy restaurant; third, I asked to be taken to the company's place of business; fourth, I didn't understand the use of silence and therefore rushed in whenever conversation came to a halt; and fifth, I hastened to a decision when I should have waited. I got the distribution rights all right, but at terms that made me very little money. We both eventually lost on that one, but the relationship established did allow us to ride over some stormy seas together.

As we argued earlier, there should be a premium placed on knowing the limits to the loyalties of suppliers, customers, offshore bankers, managers, and employees. Put more positively, the global executive should take a people-oriented approach to negotiation, one that will be guided by a desire to achieve results favorable to both parties, the so-called Win-Win outcome. When dealing with individuals from another country, the influence of their value system must be considered as a significant factor to business success.

Any negotiations, the world around and irrespective of national differences, follow the same general pattern: advance preparations, agenda-building, opening, dialog, closing, and follow-up. The differences emerge within each of these steps and will affect how each stage is handled by both sides. Those differences are often deep and sometimes unbridgeable, requiring a fair trade-off that hadn't been on the agenda. In any event, they require some careful adjustment of the American pattern and approach to negotiations. The suggestions given here fit into a general pattern, but imply both some changes in the strategy usually followed by American businesspersons and some new skills and attitudes not usually required in domestic dealings.

ADVANCE PREPARATIONS

To a much larger extent than in domestic negotiation, advance preparation is critical. It is in this stage that the American team needs to prepare for the attitudinal aspects its counterparts bring to the negotiations as well as the purely business matters. It is here, in fact, that most American problems originate. We simply are not very good at doing our homework—or we fail to recognize that the homework must be much more comprehensive than when we are dealing with fellow Americans. Reflect back on the suggestion in Chapter Seven that the executive has to expand the unshaded area in the diagram of overlapping expectations.

The Team.   Always send a team. As our own personal experience demonstrates, the single negotiator usually gets slaughtered by people who have grown up negotiating daily for the price of whatever they have to purchase. American personal and private negotiating generally is restricted to buying a house or a car, or perhaps negotiating with a romantic partner. Big as these matters may loom, they are rare in our lives. For the most part, we Americans move lock-step through a fixed-price economy and work in Theory X-managed occupations. We simply don't have the day-to-day bargaining experience that many of our counterparts have had. American executives' broadest negotiating experience is usually in business situations with American peers, where a single person can survive without too much difficulty.

> I sat next to a college classmate of mine at a luncheon recently. It came up that he had been in China on business. Interested in negotiations, I asked him some questions about his experience. "How large was your team?" I asked.
> "Oh, I went alone," he replied, "I'm an engineer, so I could handle all the technical details, and I've been marketing manager for the division so long, I know all the financial details, too."
> He got slaughtered when he faced a team of six to eight Chinese bureaucrats for eight hours a day six days a week, not including entertainment. Across the table he faced a full-time, experienced Chinese who was a professional negotiator, a man who was expected to return to the office with scalps hung around his waist—or else. On either side of the pro negotiator sat a technical expert and a financial expert. Poor John.

Any negotiating team entering serious offshore negotiations ought to have a clearly designated chief, but should include, at the very least, separate financial and technical advisers. Going alone would be akin to the Miami Dolphins sending Don Schula in alone against the Bears, without either line or running ends or backs.

A team of at least three is recommended. Send a much larger delegation than you think you need, and then don't change it unless you have no alternative. At a minimum, the team should include a vice president, accompanied by a technical adviser and a fiscal adviser. One of the latter two or an additional member of the team should be young (but probably with a title of some kind) and able to move casually among the lower-ranking members of the other side's team. He may be your team's eyes and ears, and he may pave the way for the final terms to be worked out.

Sex does matter. Proud as we Americans are of the advances made in women's participation in business, most of the rest of the world has not caught up with us. In Korea and Japan, for example, the woman's role is in the home, and is one of self-effacing obscurity. Participation of women on an American team sent to those parts of the world, therefore, is not only going to appear odd, but make the Koreans or Japanese feel most uncomfortable. It is up to the executive to work out a way for a woman to participate, but in the late-1980s, it is best that a woman not be a part of the team that goes to offshore meetings with the other side. Perhaps the best way to handle this over the long run is to always include a woman on the team when the negotiating is conducted on American soil, a way of teaching others that we now include women without question in decision making. After a woman has been included here, it may be possible to use her effectively in subsequent negotiations with the same counterparts when negotiating overseas.

Chief Negotiator. Give the chief negotiator a rank your counterparts respect: usually vice president or higher. Most other nations of the world lack the American revolutionary tradition in which we abolished aristocratic ranks. Most non-Americans take rank seriously, some very seriously indeed. Not that America is free of rank, but we are not as sensitive to its pertinence in negotiations as other cultures are. Rank-consciousness is especially true in China (in spite of its egalitarian revolution) and in Japan where your business just won't float unless gold braid is a visible sign of your seriousness of purpose.

There is the key: the seniority of the chief negotiator's rank is a signal to your seriousness of purpose. It sometimes may be wise to shelve the seniormost person for actual negotiations, letting the operating executives do that job. But his high rank waves a flag that says: "Take us seriously."

> General Electric asked a young researcher (my son-in-law) to see if he could find out why it had lost a big Chinese deal to Westinghouse. The researcher reported that the only significant difference he could find in their approaches was that the Westinghouse team, right from the first scouting expedition in Beijing to the final signing of the deal, had

been headed by a vice president. GE, by contrast, had left the scouting and early negotiations to lower-ranking managers.

Chevron apparently followed an even more expensive policy. From company literature it looks as if most of the negotiations for drilling rights in Chinese waters were conducted by a delegation headed by the CEO himself.

Circumstances may dictate the CEO's personal participation, but, in general, the presence of CEO of an American company in actual negotiations creates two real problems. First, timing gets tied up in the CEO's availability, meaning that delay is almost inevitable, sometimes at critical junctures. Negotiations, second, are invariably influenced by everything the CEO says, including innocent, off-the-cuff remarks.

The association executive of one major professional association, who shared the platform with me recently, told the audience that the volunteer heads of associations should never be put in a position where they had to serve as spokespersons. Their casual, well-intended comments often result in unfortunate commitments for the association.

So head for the vice presidential level for your chief of delegation until you really need the CEO to seal the deal or for the formal signing.

Names and Titles. Where the Roman alphabet is not used, it is wise to print up business cards in the local language on the opposite side from the English. Put some care into the titles for each member of the team, for title is often more important than name, especially in Korea. Take many more cards than you need, then use them freely.

Timing. Allocate sufficient time for negotiations: it will take longer than you think. American impatience has a direct impact on negotiations. It often leads U.S. business negotiators to put all their marbles on the table too early, suggest prices and terms right at the beginning, rather than working up to them gradually. Because we are able to negotiate fast in the United States doesn't mean we can take that practice abroad with us. In almost every other part of the world, negotiations take more time. Relax and enjoy the pace.

If in the United States you would plan a three-day visit to another city for negotiations, a good rule-of-thumb is to allow three weeks abroad. There is plenty else to do other than actual talking with the other side's team: sensing business practices and protocols there, sniffing out the market, sending out intermediaries, socializing, and growing to know each other.

Anticipate Changes.   Consider negotiations not as an event, but as a continuing process. This attitude will bring you closer to your counterparts' expectations. Thus, plan for changes to occur in your own negotiating strength. Changes within your company or theirs, and in the persons involved will affect the course of negotiations. If the negotiations are especially important to your company, then any anticipated personnel changes might well be made before you start negotiating, so your team will not be unnecessarily upset by them while engaged with their counterparts. There should be no big surprises for the other side when a change has to be made. In general, however, don't change your team unless you absolutely have to.

Changes in government, economy, and world events will also affect negotiations. While specific changes and disasters may not always be predictable, the negotiating team's planning should include ways of responding to unexpected changes. Such anticipatory planning must be done in advance, so that you don't find yourself caught in prolonged negotiations without solid alternatives.

> My daughter and her husband negotiated a contract in Venezuela with another company that was in good standing with the government. When the government changed, the other company simply went out of business and they were left in precarious shape. Had they anticipated the results of the election, keeping other irons warm, they might have had an easier time of it when the fire went out.

Home Office Involvement.   Protect against interference from your penthouse suite. Although a global strategy should call for offshore relationships and contracts to become central factors in corporate planning and for exports to become recognized as a company-wide priority, there are occasions when the CEO may grow impatient or, as already suggested, make an off-the-cuff remark or give an interview that upsets the applecart 10,000 miles away.

One American company ran into serious labor, public relations, and political trouble when an interview with the CEO appeared in a prominent U.S. business publication. The CEO was interpreted as implying that Spaniards had to be shown how to manage. (Ricks, 1983, 123).

An American company's negotiating team in China never could live down the remarks made by the CEO when he spoke with the Chinese casually on his first, exploratory visit. The Chinese took him quite literally and nothing could shake their judgment that the CEO spoke the truth and the negotiators did not.

Allow time for planning internal communications and decision making within your own company. Before you hop on the 747 to wing off to Korea, for instance, be absolutely sure that you and the people at home know how to process your urgent communications and get you the information or the decisions that you need—fast. To go without this elementary precaution is like walking the plank blindfolded. To be able to communicate and get decisions fast is a further sign of your company's seriousness of purpose. In particular, if you haven't worked out these procedures in advance, and it takes time for answers from the home office, your counterparts will think you don't count in the company and will wait for someone more important to come out as your replacement.

The negotiator should enjoy latitude for accommodating opposing views within the company at home—and time to do it. Again, this has to be arranged before the team even sets out. Be certain that there is consensus on the terms that are negotiable and clear identification of what is not negotiable. In particular, be certain that marketing, technical, and financial executives have agreed in advance on what it is that you are negotiating so that their own turf issues will not rob the negotiators of their achievements even before the team get back home. Further, if the negotiating team sent out includes—as it should—marketing, technical, and financial personnel, be certain that the pecking order is fully comprehended by all involved and that each one does not feel he or she "represents" a department and reports directly back to that department, over the head or behind the back of the chief of the team.

The negotiating team, or at least its chief, should know the limits to the authority given by headquarters. This is to be certain that a position taken in negotiations overseas is not undercut from the Home Office.

Training.   The negotiating art differs from country to country and the negotiator who is an artist has that special sixth sense that picks up the key differences and is able to build them into his negotiations. Such a person can help with training the rest of the delegation.

For example, in Asia, where the establishment of a personal relationship with the other side is generally an indispensable part of the negotiations, a lot of entertaining and socializing is required at which it is virtually taboo to talk business. You may go through weeks or months of such rapport-building in the Arab lands before you are even permitted to raise the issues for which you came all that way. To learn these differences requires the sensitivity of an artist, the tact of a diplomat, and the patience of Job—and a lot of very sophisticated, dedicated, and time-consuming training and office preparation.

Before departing, be certain that the negotiating patterns of the country you're going to are fully understood. If that means calling in experts, then do so. Trainers specific to offshore negotiations are few and far between, but general cross-cultural trainers are readily available. Among the special features of your team's training should be rehearsal in such varying practices as these:

- Use of title: practice calling each other by title rather than first name.
- Touching: learn what practices of touching are followed in your target country. For instance, no touching is expected in Korea or Japan. Learn bowing instead.
- Flattery: Americans are lousy with flattery, so practice up on how to flatter someone in the target country. Try it on your secretary, your boss.
- Silence: Americans are notorious for their distaste for silence, so practice holding out in silence so you know how to do it when it really counts.
- Sequence of speaking: Practice the order in which your team members will speak, for your pecking order does transmit messages to the other side—and be sure you know what message you want to transmit.
- Special training for the youngest member: Because of the informal ties that the youngest member of the team may be

able to develop in social situations with his age peers, special training on listening and reporting ought to be given to him.

Negotiating Objectives. Objectives should be clear in advance, together with the fallback positions that go with each one. Never try to negotiate a "deal" outside the United States or Canada, for it detracts from your seriousness of purpose. You can expect complications later on if all you are looking for is a quick sale. Favor long-term and close relationships.

Make certain that what you are planning to negotiate is, in fact, negotiable on the other side. No sense wasting time if it isn't. Make certain that your opening bid or asking sales price is neither too high nor too low. American opening sales quotations tend to be too low, their opening purchasing bids too high, thus putting them at a disadvantage.

Know what *not* "winning" will mean to your company and to you professionally. Then define your objectives so that both sides have a fair chance of winning. Win-win is a better international negotiating goal than the traditional American goal of overwhelming the opposition. Think of the team you are negotiating with as "counterparts" rather than as opponents or adversaries. It should be an analogue relationship, not an adversarial one.

Strategy. Get your facts straight. Get more facts than you need, for it shows that you care about the outcomes if you can supply your counterparts information that didn't seem germane.

Don't assume that your counterparts want what you want. Be prepared for their goals to change, in some countries more so than in others. In Japan, don't expect many changes, for the practice of corporate consensus makes achieving change of position difficult.

Linear negotiation, like linear thinking and linear time, is an American practice that doesn't work well in many other countries. Linear negotiation is our tendency to go point-by-point through the whole agenda, getting each point settled before proceeding to the next. Especially in the East, the entire package is discussed without resolution of any issues. Japanese and Koreans, especially, want to see the whole before they negotiate the parts. The Chinese are experts at turning the American style against them, nibbling away point-by-point at the whole fabric until not much advantage is left to the Americans.

FIGURE 10–2 _____
Negotiation Non-Task Preliminaries (some sample questions)

_____

Identification
  Who's on their team?
  Who's the power hitter?
  Who makes the *real* decisions?
  Who's the designated informal communicator?

Travel Plans
  How long do we stay?
  When do we decide length of stay?
  How do we keep HQ happy while we stay longer?
  How do we keep our travel plans secret?

Gifts
  What gifts do they expect?
  What gifts should we expect to get?
  What do we say/how do we act when we give a gift?
  What do we say/how do we act when we receive a gift?

Entertainment
  Who entertains first?
  Where do we expect to be entertained?
    Any special preparations?
  Should we plan to be on time to their entertainment?
  Where do we entertain them?
  How do we entertain them?
    Is liquor permitted?
  When do we entertain?
  When should we expect them to arrive?
  Are their spouses included?
  Are our spouses included? Are they expected to speak/participate?
  If we are playing a game, say golf, should we play to win or lose?
  What seating arrangements are appropriate?
  How late do we stay?
  When can we first talk business? Is business *taboo* at meals?
  What other subjects are *taboo* in conversation?

Positioning at First Negotiations
  Where do we meet?
  Can we change the meeting place after first meeting?
  Who sets the layout of the room?
  Can we change it if we don't like it? How do we do that?
  Who sits where?
  Can we change the temperature of the room?
  Can we change the lighting in the room?
  When do we break for refreshment, toilet, meals?
    Do we expect to break/eat with them or separately?
  What is the protocol for interpreters?
  Do we state our agenda first or does it come out later?
  How do we agree on agenda?
  How do we proceed through the agenda: linear or holistic?
  At what stage and how do we state our goals?

_____

ON-SITE PRELIMINARIES

On Arrival. When the negotiating team gets to its destination, it should devote some time to (1) resting up from jet lag and becoming acclimated, (2) close-up research and informal information gathering, and (3) getting into your counterparts' frame of mind.

First, Americans underestimate jet lag's effects. We fly in and out of meetings with our minds lagging 2,000 miles astern. This is potentially very dangerous. The old pros at international negotiations will take at least a full day, preferably a weekend or more, to rest up and get food and sleep schedules back in rhythm with the day's light. Americans also underestimate the effects on body, mind, and soul of dramatic changes in climate or altitude. Don't ever underestimate them, rather be prepared to spend a few extra days getting your body and mind in tune with local conditions. A bad case of Delhi-belly will wreak havoc with negotiations. Be careful what you eat, avoiding cold or uncooked foods.

Second, on-site research should be pursued before even the first negotiating session is scheduled (see Chapters Eight and Nine). Find out who makes their decisions and how, whether they have had bad experiences with Americans before and what was the nature of the bad show, what they have budgeted for your project, how badly they want this negotiation to result in certain outcomes, who will comprise their team, and where those people are coming from.

At this point, it is possible to put together the whole picture, for you will have information on the locale, the people involved, something of their objectives, and a feel for the culture. It is important to develop this sense of the whole negotiation in order to avoid the difficulties that emerge from linear thinking in a society that thinks holistically.

By this time, too, you have a chance to see your proposal from your counterparts' point of view. Price alone will never seem as important as it did back home, and price alone will not be as important as benefits to both parties.

By now, you will have a sense of where your walk point should be. While the point at which you will pick up your marbles and walk will depend on what happens in actual face-to-face encounter, a feeling for what should trigger walking should be discernible now.

Preliminaries—Entertainment. North Americans are likely the only businesspeople in the world who barge right in and start negotiating. In most other countries, there are some social preliminaries. Some American businessmen have dismissed these preliminaries as nonessential time-wasters.

On the contrary, the social preliminaries to negotiations are every bit as important as the actual sessions themselves, establishing the desired relationship of mutual trust and confidence. We'll say something more about contracts later, but here it is necessary to point out the obvious, that we Americans rely much more heavily on written agreements and the possibility of legal sanctions to enforce them than do any other people. Our recourse is to sue. Your counterparts may not be familiar with this practice (which is, after all, relatively recent in the United States), preferring to know the people they are going to deal with and be certain that they can trust them as persons and trust their companies as corporations. Social preliminaries are therefore an indispensable part of actual negotiations, the proper place for establishing rapport and for establishing the relative seniority and precedence among your counterparts.

One rule of thumb that seems safe to give Americans is to avoid jocularity. We Americans love to tell jokes, but jokes are usually told *on* someone, a practice that will seem very strange and awkward to your foreign hosts. Even stranger to many foreigners is to tell jokes on oneself, which makes you end up looking very silly in their eyes. By all means, have a sense of humor, but restrict it to things that happen while you are together and, above all, be certain that no one loses face from the humor, even the youngest member of your staff. If you do have a woman with your team, be absolutely certain no jocularity reflects unfairly on the status of women.

We mentioned in the last chapter that the rules for bearing gifts and receiving gifts, and the protocols for being entertained and entertaining vary widely between countries. The only generalization that is valid is: be certain you check out the gift-giving and entertainment practices before you leave home and go prepared to give the right gift, receive with appropriate graciousness a gift from your counterparts, accept entertainment and offer entertainment in the spirit and style of the host country. Do not throw a steak barbeque in India. Entertain at tea the way they do. And be certain you know the rules for women in the country you are going to.

Because negotiation preliminaries so often relate to the actual negotiations, the wisest advice to male American executives is to leave their wives at home. Sure, a nice trip to a distant country where you only have to pay for one ticket is a plus, but it is generally frightfully awkward to handle the wife's needs and the negotiating patterns without conflict. If you want a vacation, take it later, having your wife come along when the business is well in hand. If she does accompany you, prepare her for the necessity to stay in the hotel while you are out roistering on the Ginza, for she will *not* be welcome in that activity.

OPENING

Always put yourself in your counterpart's shoes. The opening posturing is a given part of any negotiation at home or abroad. The posturing is important, whether it is done over dinner, at someone's home, or at the negotiating table. Watch for clues in that posturing and start then trying to crawl inside the other's mind, seeing your team from their perspective. This may mean that you have to change your clothes or your body language or your strategies or tactics, but is essential for the construction of an enduring relationship on which the business will be built.

Expect a different way of thinking: wait before you react until you are sure you know what your counterpart meant. A good practice is to ask questions. Even repeating the same question over and over until you are satisfied that you know what the other side means is an accepted practice in negotiations across cultures. In Asia, such repetition will be taken as a sign of your seriousness and determination to build an understanding for an enduring relationship.

It is here that your younger member can be most useful. If something has happened at the negotiations during the day that the chief negotiator on your side doesn't fully understand, it would be highly inappropriate for him to actually say so. In Japan and Korea, such a statement would reflect poorly on your side and at the same time would cause the other side to lose face, for it would look as if they weren't making their position clear. The young person can go out on the town in the evening with the younger members of the other side and, with youthful naïveté, ask what was all that about today. They know he's asking for his boss, perhaps, but it is asked at the appropriate level.

In many countries, the American executive and the American negotiating team will find red carpets thrown out for them everywhere. Beware of the too-cozy feeling red carpets may create. In some other countries, businessmen and lawyers are of very low status and the red carpets will be conspicuous by their absence. In India and Pakistan, a businessperson will almost always rank below a civil servant, a bureaucrat, in social functions. Be able to work comfortably within the relatively low status assigned to business and businesspersons in those countries. When your negotiations involve government, or your engagement takes you outside the business community, be prepared to be looked down on, find obstacles thrown in your path, be kept waiting endlessly. To throw your weight around usually does not work. So be prepared for some demeaning experiences—and do your best to establish intermediaries between you and those you have to deal with outside of business so that your plans can go forward.

Personal Relationships. Help save face for your counterpart: he may save yours. This is especially true in Asia, but true to some degree anywhere in the world. Working for the benefit of your negotiating counterpart with respect to the rest of the world will make you his friend for life. And that is where business success is apt to reside, in friendship.

Be especially sensitive to personal relations and personalities in decision making: value long-term associations. This point underlies much of what we've said earlier, but deserves special emphasis. Get to know them and maintain that association as long as you are working for the same company.

CONTRACTS

Generally, non-Americans are not looking toward a contract as the principal outcome of negotiations. That's American. Korean tradition, for example, views change as the only reality in the world, so a contract that presumes permanence is a patent absurdity. Koreans will therefore seem very casual or cavalier in their attitude toward an American contract, holding no sense of wrongdoing if they break it. In Arab tradition, a man's word should be his bond. Thus, an Arab may be offended by the suggestion of a contract, for it implies that he is not as good as his word. The Mexican's seemingly cavalier disregard of contracts emerges from a perception of contracts as expressions of ideals, not realities (See Copeland, 1985, 93–94).

The Japanese tend to regard a contract as a statement of general intention, and they assume that changes will be made in it as circumstances change. The Japanese, from some years of experience with Americans, are now more willing to enter into contracts, but that doesn't mean much more than it did in the days when they resisted contracts. In Japan, you'll find it hard to enforce a contract if you should feel you have to. Japanese lawyers, who are not very highly regarded in Japanese society, are experts in serving their fellow nationals' interests and are well practiced in using the delays the law allows. And in Japan you'd better expect plenty of requests for changes as time changes economic, political, and even personal conditions (Graham, 1984).

Because of the resistance to contracts, the global executive must work harder on the personal and corporate relationships that are more important than pieces of legal-sized paper. Think of it this way: "What is my foreign associate going to think of me, when is he going to think of me, and why is he going to think of me when I am back home?" Those what, when, and why questions should generate a personal strategy for sealing the deal, whatever it may be. But remember that the goal is a long-term relationship, not a transitory deal.

LANGUAGE—AGAIN!

The negotiating team should always have its own person who is fluent in the language of the other side. If such a person cannot be a member of the team, then hire an interpreter for the purpose, but be certain that that person has had extensive training in both the technical details of the industry and on the linguistic nuances that sometimes emerge in negotiations in that industry. And then use the same persons, rather than rely on new ones each time out in Italy or Thailand. Using the other side's interpreters is giving the other side an unfair advantage over you. Take your own, but train them first, as recommended in Chapter Seven.

THE COMPETITION

Recognize the strength of other, foreign competitors. This may seem obvious, but when you change the social, political, and economic context, you may find that what gave a competitor a disadvantage in one market may yield exceptional benefits in another. For example, a French company may have a hidden advantage in some parts of the world where there is a neutrality toward France but a strong suspicion of American intentions. Look for those unexpected, hidden advantages.

Americans tend to deprecate indigenous competitors, especially in the developing countries. They may be using old technologies and be run by creaky corporate bureaucracies, but they may possess advantages you cannot match, such as close friends or relatives in the ruling party or an "in" with the government. There are also local feelings toward indigenous companies that are roused when they see the big American corporation intruding onto home turf.

The nature of the competition in any country will make a big difference in how your negotiations work out for you.

GOVERNMENT IN NEGOTIATIONS

Sense government's hand in business. While this is particularly true for centrally planned economies, as any American businessperson knows, it's true even in the hearth of free enterprise, the United States. Outside the United States, government's hand tends to be much closer to actually stirring the pot. In fact in some economies that don't initially appear to be centrally planned, the government's approval of any arrangements with a foreign firm is essential, as is much the case in the United Kingdom. The power of MITI in Japan is a clear example, for, however much its power is being eroded, it is a mighty presence in any negotiations. In India, you simply cannot do business without calling on the senior civil servants in the appropriate ministries, especially the Reserve Bank of India and the Ministry of Finance.

> I was having some difficulty negotiating with an American consultant over the future of a film he had shot with our office's money. That was trouble enough, but on top of it I had some unexpected difficulty with government. My official liaison officer with the Government of India

told me she was refusing to let me export the film our American consultant had shot at such great expense. As I knew I had already exported the film, I didn't take her very seriously. But when she managed to get the film off-loaded in Athens (violating, by the bye, Greek sovereignty) and had it hand-delivered back to India by the Air India pilot, I knew I was in trouble. I had not calculated on direct government intervention.

The way the problem was resolved was for my Indian second-in-command to go over to the Ministry of Finance, speak the the Number Two officer in that Ministry and suggest to him that an officer in another Ministry had preempted the role of the Ministry of Finance. The Ministry of Finance was upset by a challenge to its preeminence, so I was given authority to export my film. At the same time, a reprimand was placed in the liaison officer's file, and shortly thereafter I was assigned a new liaison officer.

Discover any *hidden* role the host government may have in the negotiations. This is more difficult and more subtle sometimes. The case in India mentioned in Chapter Nine, where import was held up because the proper Ministry had not been involved, should have been pretty obvious, but regard the case of the Swedish pharmaceutical firm that discovered too late that the government operated the black market that its plant would have squeezed (Ricks, 135).

Account also for the fact that your negotiating counterparts will usually be looking to see what the U.S. government role may be. What Washington is thinking or will do becomes an essential ingredient in your counterparts' thinking before they decide. In most cases, this should be fairly obvious, but remember that the expectations of your foreign associates will lack the perspective of your years of observing the machinations and monkeyshines on Capitol Hill and in the U.S. bureaucracy. Their interpretations are bound to differ from yours and you should be prepared to meet them. Not only should you meet their misconceptions as expressed in their first questions of you, but you should be able to handle the follow-up questions about American policies, too. And that is considerably harder.

Value the different weight given to economic and political criteria in the host country. Our tendency to think that all people have been trained in the same methodologies as we have distorts our approach to offshore research. In fact, economic and political traditions color negotiations, too. Don't just expect the numbers and ratios to be appraised the same; expect facts to be interpreted in curiously different ways.

Ascertain the difference between approvals at the negotiating and the implementing levels in both the company you are proposing to do business with and in the national government. While this goes back to identifying the decision makers, it is a broader question, for it raises the issue of how involved the government is going to be *after* you have struck the deal at the negotiating level, or how involved a parent company or a major shareholder may be in the company. Many American businessmen have gone home with contracts in their pockets only to see them unravel through some utterly unexpected governmental consent requirement or because some power in the counterpart's company had not been appropriately consulted at the right time.

THE MEETING

We hear a lot from experts on negotiation that every detail of the meeting, including its setting, is crucial to success in hard bargaining. Even though the global executive may be seeking a relationship rather than to best his opponent in a duel to the end, much the same considerations apply overseas as in American negotiations. If you can, be sure the room arrangement is not deliberately set to intimidate you, and be certain that, if it is, there is a way to change it the next time you meet. Heat and cold, sunlight in the eyes, and other tricks are commonly played by certain nationals against their negotiating counterparts—even where the long-term interest is in a close personal relationship. In many cases, it will be necessary to suffer these indignities, in the hope that, if and when the negotiations resume at your place, you will be able to show them better hospitality.

SUMMARY

The global executive brings to negotiations a capacity to follow Roger Fisher's strategy. In addition, he or she listens well—in the language of the customer if that is germane—and is also an inveterate, persistent, and intelligent questioner. The global executive relates well to other people, and is a good team player. The global executive, as mentioned earlier, uses high self-esteem to sustain himself or herself through sometimes frustrating, sometimes demeaning situations during negotiations. With high aspirations, temporary setbacks can be taken in stride. He or she is always personally attractive and appropriately attired during any business or business-related entertainment functions. The global executive has and retains influence at headquarters, but does not show it brazenly. He or she is patient, but knows both how to use silence as a weapon and when to walk out without offense or recrimination.

Many of these qualities, especially using silence and walking out without recrimination, are not highly developed skills among American executives. It's time to begin training in them, then putting them together in selecting effective teams for offshore negotiations of whatever purpose.

CHAPTER ELEVEN

The Global Executive: At Home In The World

What a challenge! The global executive has to defy conventional wisdom at home and plunge into a sea of unknowns in the expectation that his or her corporation will reap even greater profits. The global executive has to entice board of directors, senior management, middle management, line and staff employees into a global strategy and thence into offshore operations. The global executive has to communicate effectively at home and abroad—sometimes not even in English. The global executive has to manage different scales of time, conduct research in unfamiliar territories, and plug into alien networks. The global executive has to master all of these challenges, then negotiate with the *panache* of a dancer, the verve of a gymnast, and the production skills of an impressario.

All of these skills must be complemented with attitudes that his or her American countrymen and women rarely share: an open, expansive, inquisitive, and nonjudgmental, yet wholly American perspective.

To this formidable assignment must be added a moral component, not just because it is required by U.S. law—which it is—but because business morality makes corporate culture whole.

Why bother? Just the other day, one American trade association executive gave his view in about these words: "There's still enough domestic market to keep us content for generations to come. Uncle Sam will protect us from the worst assaults of those unfair foreign competitors. The deficit will shrink and trade will go back in our favor." Americans need to worry about attitudes such as his.

Rather, we should welcome the new, global competition. We should welcome the new world of global interdependence. Although, in a world of change, every familiar image seems reflected from the crazy house mirror with the mirror spinning out of control, it is the world we have to live in. It is this world in which the global executive has to succeed.

WHY BOTHER?

There are at least three reasons for bothering. First, a faltering American position in the world economy needs the global executive—now. Second, there is nothing so alluring as a real professional and personal challenge and the challenge over the next decades will certainly be in international or global management. Third, the whole world needs the American creative inspiration now, the reassertion of American practical ingenuity. Our contributions have been tremendous in the last century, enriching life around the world. The world economy has gained and people's lives improved when American inventiveness, practical ingenuity, and organizing talents have been most flourishing. The world lacks much when economic activity is not informed by the American genius, or that genius is misallocated.

Lately, the United States has been backing into a corner. Surely, in part, we have been forced back by pressures beyond our control. But in part we have been stepping back because we have higher priorities than competing in global markets and, in part, because our vision has become ingrown and we have feared the unknown. Today, the United States is saddled with heavy international debt, an adverse balance of trade, and a currency that won't behave itself. Critics looking around for flaws in the underlying structure have been able to identify many contributing factors. They see declining—or at least not robustly growing—productivity, managerial malaise, financial demands for quick returns, lack of coherence in the workforce, pervasive structural unemployment especially of minority youth, an aging physical plant, too much capital goods production for nonproductive military purposes, and a lack of application to new, productive research. And those are just some of our problems—we haven't mentioned the federal budget deficit. Under these circumstances Americans quite naturally find themselves alternating between bemoaning their situation and seeking scapegoats.

Anger and despair are wasted energy; scapegoats are a way of deluding oneself into sloughing off blame. It is too simple by far to blame our situation on foreign competition, foreign capital, the Arabs, the debt-hungry but unstable developing nations, the Russians, the Japanese, the Germans, the Koreans, the Taiwanese, and assorted competitors and political rivals. It is too easy to blame massive deficits and government profligacy.

The onus should be more accurately placed on the forces that have created an interdependent world and that are propelling us toward a globalized marketplace. Neither protectionist legislation in the United States nor international agreements limiting trade offer appropriate long-run solutions to our predicament because there is always someone out there who's going to find a way around them and find the way to reach a buyer who doesn't care whether or not it is patriotic to buy a foreign car or VCR.

Evidence of the new world is all around us.

A *New York Times* article, September 25, 1986, entitled "Glum News for U.S. Apparel," reported on the "Bobbin Show," the annual textile and garment trade show in Atlanta. The American Apparel Manufacturers Association, implied the report, was prepared to warn its members that there was no possible way to reverse the growing American trend toward importing what it wanted. Therefore, the recommendation would go, the industry should find ways to survive in other ways than by manufacturing, such as providing service, especially rapid delivery and product quality.

As in the apparel industry, the gauntlet has been thrown to many American industries, not all in manufacturing but in service, too. We must pick it up and accept the challenge presented to us by a world we neither created nor whose course we can reverse. The apparel manufacturers weren't about to abandon their lobbying for fairer trade with United States and other governments. They wanted to keep their options open. But they had come to recognize that competition from imports was inevitable and were preparing to meet it. It seems to us that this attitude represents the maturing of the concept of the global executive.

The *Times* article did not expand on the implication that some manufacturers in the U.S. apparel industry are themselves making garments in Singapore, Hong Kong, India, and elsewhere. Those manufacturers and such footwear manufacturers as Nike have taken up the gauntlet: while remaining U.S. companies and contributing to our national economic health, they have turned to offshore sourcing and manufacturing. In the case of Nike, manufacture of sneakers is carried on in Korea and, with great difficulties, in mainland China.

To shrink back into our shells is not only unworthy of our pioneer tradition, but is equal to penning our own suicide note. While one recent issue of *Business Week* deplored the "hollow corporation" that did all of its manufacturing offshore and an increasing part of its marketing as well, another issue pointed out that at the same time U.S. employment has never been higher. Things have changed: heavy imports used to be directly related to loss of jobs, but here we are with the most mountainous load of imports ever, yet more people have jobs than ever before.

At the same time, we should never minimize the trauma of individual steelworkers, shoe workers, and others who are laid off directly because of import pressures. We must labor within the business community and in concert with government to find solutions to those problems that develop as we go through the convulsions of moving from national market economies to a global one. What we must *not* do is to assume that these convulsions are like the ones that hit us in the 1920s and early 30s that led to the Smoot-Hawley protective tariff legislation which, in turn, contributed to the Great Depression.

What is lagging behind world changes is our attitude toward business. Events have turned against our expectations. The good old days have disappeared when national strength was measured in terms of inexhaustibly rich natural resources, a talented labor pool, the world's most advanced technologies, and unsatisfied domestic markets.

The way we measure national strength or define national pride must change. Our attitudes toward foreign producers and competitors must change. Our attitudes toward the American corporation must change, seeing "hollowness" not as something anti-American but as a new stage of American economic growth in a global economy.

But our spirit must not change. We must reassert our role as the world's leaders in business, production, marketing, and technology.

There is a place for the global executive.

LEADERSHIP

We have in this book taken the word "management" to mean overall corporate direction, not supervision of employees. We have been discussing *management* through these pages while quite considerably expanding its definition. Before we close, we owe a justification for using *management* this way and an explanation of what we see as the difference between *leadership* and the conventional meaning of *management*. After all, what we have been talking about demands leadership: U.S. leadership in a globalized marketplace and individual business leadership by the global executive.

To us, traditional U.S. management has been *transactional*. Managers historically have been persons assigned to see to it that things get done according to principles and regulations worked out in advance and confirmed by superiors in the establishment. Managers see to it that transactions take place at the appropriate time, place, and price, that the proceeds are properly accounted for, and profits are maintained. Managers oversee processes that use individual humans to achieve results, so they manage human time and activity. The best American managers are like the famous Navy Seabees of World War II: today we do the improbable, tomorrow we do the impossible. (James MacGregor Burns, *Leadership*, 1978, spells out the distinction between management and leadership.)

For all of the very essential qualities that such American management traditions have brought to business, the real heart of management lies in something more. That is *leadership*, the quality that—with a creative spirit and an ability to take risks—turns a manager into an entrepreneur. Leadership is not merely transactional, it is *transformational*. Leaders transform the people, the processes, and the corporations for which they work into something new and different, dynamic and influential, changing other people and processes and corporations. Leadership moves people, creates new directions, invents new processes, undertakes new responsibilities, and seeks new opportunities.

The global executive is a leader, an agent for transformation, but has full control over the transactional aspects of the business. It must be patent by now that the global executive has a full agenda, and that it is going to take good management to get all those things accomplished. Thus, the global executive will be drawn from among today's most forward-looking in-service managers and from among the most talented of the next generation's stars. Creativity, imagination, diplomacy, artistry, intellect, and sensitivity must be combined with the ability to manipulate processes and manage transactions among people.

The global executive must be a leader, not a mere manager of processes and people. But the global executive's transformational activities must be informed by a new perspective of the world, of the people in it, and of the values that should govern human behavior.

VALUES

"It is only as one human community that we have any hope to enter the next century in dignity, harmony, and civility." Those are my notes of Soedjatmoko's speech in Washington, May 27, 1984. Soedjatmoko, president of the United Nations University, went on to speak of compassion, a value in generally short supply in the business world. It seems to us, however, that an understanding of compassion and its place in a competitive world begins to give some focus to the notion of global interdependence and informs our concept of management. *Management becomes creatively transformational while remaining inflexibly people-oriented.* Here is where we merge MacGregor's Theory Y with our own Theory Q. Global management means orientation to people who are very different from us, whether they are customers, employees, managers, officials, or investors. The merger of Theory Y with Theory Q must relate to marketing as well as to managing people.

Marketing to people who are not like us requires, of course, a large measure of understanding their needs and their wants—often dramatically unlike ours. Trying to sell goods in other world markets, goods that impose values not fully comprehended by the customer, has led to marketing failures and, indeed, to political confrontation. Take the Americanization of consumer goods in France through *le drug store*. Take some of the leftist regimes that have tried to ban American products because they "corrupted" the population. Take the strong anti-Americanism found behind the palms on exotic Caribbean Islands where a curious resentment festers at the "unloading" of unsold American goods on those who didn't "need" them. The global executive will be sensitive to such issues because the goal is a long-term commitment with profits spanning a number of years.

Managing people in other lands also requires the compassion that accompanies people-centered management. The manager has to see the world through their eyes, but then has to adapt production lines, products, motivation, time management, work systems, supervision, and delegation to fit into their comprehension. Those two ominous syllables, Bhopal, will be heard for years to come, reminding the executive that compassion involves responsiveness to the environment within which one does business: The export of corporate culture implies its adaptation to its new environment.

Morality is a nice thing to practice, but for those who operate offshore, a particular kind of American morality is a statutory requirement of the United States.

Responding to the discovery that some 400 U.S. corporations, mostly large ones, had made questionable payments to officials of foreign governments, the Congress enacted and President Carter signed the Foreign Corrupt Practices Act of 1977. The act does not provide a specific moral code for American businesses operating overseas, but it implies a certain moral tone that is quintessentially American.

The law makes it a crime for corporations to bribe officials of foreign governments or political parties to obtain or maintain business in their countries. The law is full of clout for the U.S. government, but also full of ambiguities that, even 10 years later, neither lawyers nor accountants are entirely comfortable with. The law provides fines for both corporations and their officers as well as up to five-year jail terms for the latter.

Among the principal provisions is that the Securities and Exchange Commission is empowered to require specific bookkeeping of all transactions. Auditors—and the SEC—began looking for "red flags" of foreign corrupt practices, such as currency dealings, checks drawn to "cash," or checks payable to accounts of noncooperating companies, institutions, or agencies in secretive nations, unusual bonuses paid to employees, or unusual credits granted customers. Probing even deeper, they could evaluate the entire cycle of various kinds of transactions from recording of the sales order to shipping of the goods to collection of the payment. The law applies to all companies whose shares are publicly sold.

This provision of the law, curiously enforced jointly by the Department of Justice and the SEC, applies to domestic activities of corporations, not just foreign (*The Wall Street Journal*, July 28, 1978).

It was Title II of this law, of course, that required reporting of the nationality and other details of any one shareholder holding more than 5 percent of the shares.

Sales commissions to independent foreign representatives are illegal if all or part of the commission is conveyed to a government official with the company's knowledge, but what "knowledge" is remains muddy. Activities of foreign subsidiaries, while not specifically controlled by the act would become known through the bookkeeping regulations. Both of these affect how American companies deal with their foreign distributors and partners.

One loophole is that payments to foreign official employees who are in clerical positions are not prohibited, making it possible to expedite shipments through customs or obtain permits and licenses more expeditiously. This is the so-called greasing of foreign transactions (*Business Week*, April 17, 1978).

When the law was enacted, SEC refused to give any advisory opinions, but more recently the Department of Justice has agreed to review confidential materials of a contemplated transaction and say if it will take action if the deal takes place. Since the law was enacted, the very small quantity of case law that has developed suggests that the draconian enforcement expected has not been imposed. Further, as we have distanced ourselves from the Carter administration's moral crusade, a more normal cynicism has crept back into such dealings. Nonetheless, experts suggest that there are cross-national problems of a major kind, as did lawyer William T. Coleman in *Financial Executive* (September 1980) who warned that enforcement of this law would have to respect cultural and national differences. As no common morality exists, perhaps an artificial, *ad hoc* shared morality could be invoked to govern international transactions.

No other industrialized country has followed our lead and the international codes have not yet evolved. Estimates in 1980 were that up to $1 billion of annual sales were lost because of the act, not so much because of its provisions, but because of its ambiguities that made companies want to appear squeaky-clean.

What then if you are doing business in West Africa and find that *dash* is a way of life, that gratuitous payments are an expected cost of doing business, just as they are an expected remuneration for services performed? What then when you find the outstretched palm in India where the senior official is asking for *pradhan*—a gracious gift of the person who has met God and wishes to express thanks to God—or *baksheesh*, Persian word for "present?" What of the absolute necessity to carry gifts to Japan, to China? What of the expectation that the American business in Saudi Arabia must somehow be eased by payments to official or quasi-official individuals?

Clearly, the FCPA runs head-on into the value systems of other nations. In Arab lands, in India, and in Africa payments of the kind prohibited are expected by certain levels of officials. That is an accepted way of life. Some years ago, a leading U.S. political scientist opined that the question the American should face is: Are the services rendered worth the size of the payment?

Ethics in business have been a recurring theme in American life. The "Great Electrical Conspiracy" of the 1950s ended with a plea by one of those convicted that he should be shown clemency because he was an outstanding civic leader, vice president of an electrical giant, and had an impressionable young daughter at Smith College, concluding that he should not be treated as a common criminal. The judge peered down at him and reminded him that he had been convicted by a jury of his peers and that he was a criminal. A study of the case concluded that the conspirators had maintained two value systems, the one prevailing in the community and a totally separate one in the office. When these executives entered their offices, the ethics of the community ceased to be relevant. (Our late colleague, Harold Larrabee, conducted his study in 1966, but we have been unable to locate a copy of it. This report is from memory.)

To a very real extent, that ethical dilemma is a fact of life when moving around the globe. There are different ethical systems and different moral constraints that affect decision-making and human relations in different countries. It places an enormous burden on the global executive. Is he or she to maintain that all morals are matters of cultural relevance, where situations alone determine how one should behave? Or should the executive steadfastly uphold the American version of Judeo-Christian ethics?

There are simply no answers to this question. Morals are matters that the executive will have to deal with on a day-to-day basis, trying to strike a balance between what our culture has taught us are universal moral principles and the values upheld by the people he or she is dealing with. The Foreign Corrupt Practices Act presumes to impose U.S. morals on the rest of the world. It is possible the rest of the world isn't ready for U.S. morality.

Because of the ambiguities of the law, one can live with its provisions. Baksheesh and dash are apparently all right if paid to employees of other companies and even to lower-level government employees. Gifts of any size to high officials of government appear to be totally forbidden. But as a whole, federal law prohibits the adaptation of the American corporate culture to the culture in which gifts and "bribes" are expected. At the lowest level, because wages are so low, gratuities can be built into the cost of personal service without trouble with the U.S. government.

It's when you get to the larger gifts and the generous cash payments to *government* officials that the executive simply has to say: "This practice is not permitted in my country." If that means losing a sale to foreign competitors unrestrained by such laws, so be it. Two things to remember: first, oddly, the act does not apply to business-to-business transactions, only to those affecting foreign governments, so presumably kickbacks from a private purchaser are legitimate. Second, remember Chapter Ten and the continuing nature of negotiations and the enduring nature of your relationship with your offshore counterparts. A bribe may win government approval of a quick deal or the winning of a government contract, but it is not likely to buy a long-term relationship. Thus, the American should use other methods of meeting the competition over an extended period of years, especially the cultivation of government officials who value the personal relationship over the gains from venality.

Morality, too, implies meeting the values of the people whom one is managing or selling to. It means adjusting work to recognize family obligations and worship rituals. It means putting aside some aspects of our moral system in order to meet the moral system of those people who make your process work. Morality in this respect merges with compassion and empathy to inform the quality of the global executive's work.

THE NEW WORLD

As we pass through the global crossroads, American business must be alert to the opportunities, ready to assume the attitudes, values, skills, and knowledge necessary to succeed in an unfamiliar world. The global executive is more than a person who copes with the unexpected. The global executive is a person who turns the unexpected into a profitable opportunity by being ready to adapt and adjust the corporate culture to any operating environment.

America's economic strength lies in the recruitment, training, and encouragement of global executives, not in quick-fixes, ersatz panaceas, or political intrusion. Let's tell our colleagues and our government that's how we feel.

There are many books in print that analyze trade, some decent how-to books on exporting, and even more textbooks on international marketing. The books on global strategic planning relate primarily to the multinational corporation rather than to the medium-sized or small company. The periodic checklists issued by Business International, although aimed at a narrow group of giant, multinational corporations, can be extremely useful, as is its periodical, *Business International*. (These are available at most good research or reference libraries.) There are virtually no worthy books on networking, even though some of the cross-cultural guides do touch on networking problems. The books on cross-cultural negotiating are still too few; the better ones are aimed specifically at negotiating in one country.

The problem we have with the international marketing books is that they try to transport U.S. marketing culture into cultural contexts where it does not fit very well—and therefore doesn't always work very well. They work well in the markets where U.S. business has always focused, namely Northern and Western Europe. They are incompatible with the Soviet bloc, China, and many of the less developed countries (LDCs), newly industrialized countries (NICs), and rapidly industrializing countries (RICs). They are misfits with respect to that other great market, Japan. In particular, we believe, they are too numbers-driven and not sufficiently sensitive to cultural differences (although each of them does take a pass at the cultural problem). Of the lot, Terpstra's is the most culturally well-informed, Cateora's the most practical.

The list that follows includes works we have specifically referred to in the text and a few others that might be useful to the reader. The list, therefore, is representative rather than comprehensive.

David Ricks' wonderful collection of horror stories should be on everyone's reading list because, I believe, it will alert the entrepreneur to some of the pitfalls, amuse one with stories about how sophisticated companies also can bomb out, but in the end will suggest that international enterprise is not so terrifying. With proper attitude, armed with appropriate skills, and knowing where to get information and what information to get, the global executive will use Ricks as an encouraging guidebook for an exciting and always interesting voyage of discovery.

Roger E. Axtell, ed. (1985). *Do's and Taboos Around the World: A Guide to International Behavior*. New York: John Wiley & Sons. Compiled by the Parker Pen Company.

Robert Ballance and Stuart Sinclair. (1983). *Collapse and Survival: Industry Strategies in a Changing World*. London: George Allen & Unwin.

Gunnar Beeth. (1973). *International Management Practice: An Insider's View*. New York: AMACOM, American Management Association. Humorous and still very much apropos.

Robert H. Bellah et al. (1985). *Habits of the Heart: Individualism and Commitment in American Life*. Berkeley: University of California Press.

Ronald E. Berenbeim. (1982). *Managing the International Company*. New York: Conference Board.

Ronald E. Berenbeim. (1983). *Operating Foreign Subsidiaries*. New York: Conference Board.

Paul-Howard Berent. (1975). "International Research Is Different," *Marketing in Turbulent Times*, E. M. Maze, ed., pp. 293–97. Chicago: American Marketing Association.

Frank E. Blair, ed. (1985). *International Marketing Handbook*, 3 v. Detroit: Gale Research.

Bottin International. (1986). Bottin International. Société Didot-Bottin, 28 rue du Doctery Finlay, 75 738 Paris Cedex 15, France. Annual.

Richard W. Brislin et al. (1986). *Intercultural Interactions: A Practical Guide*. Beverly Hills, CA: Sage Publications.

James McGregor Burns. (1978). *Leadership*. New York: Harper & Row.

Business International. (1967). *Planning for Profits: How to Organize and Implement a Global Corporate Plan*. New York: Business International.

Business International. (1974). *151 Checklists: Decision-Making in International Operations*. New York: Business International.

Business International. (1975). *Corporate External Affairs: Blueprint for Survival*. New York: Business International.

Business International. (1985). *Export Financing: A Handbook of Sources and Techniques*. Morristown, NJ: Financial Executives Foundation.

Business International. (1985–2). *161 More Checklists: Decision-Making in International Operations*. New York: Business International.

British Overseas Trade Board. (1982). *International Research Directory of Market Research Organizations*, 6th ed. London: British Overseas Trade Board.

Arthur Elliott Carlisle. (1967). *Cultures in Collision: U.S. Corporate Policy and Canadian Subsidiaries*. Ann Arbor, MI: University of Michigan Press.

Pierre Casse and Surinder Deol. (1985). *Managing Intercultural Negotiations; Guidelines for Trainers and Negotiators*. Washington: Sietar International.

Philip R. Cateora. (1985). *Strategic International Marketing*. Homewood. IL: Dow Jones-Irwin.

S. T. Cavusgil & John R. Nevin, eds. (1983). *International Marketing: An Annotated Bibliography*. Chicago: American Marketing Association.

Marvin Cetron. (1985). *The Future of American Business; The U.S. in World Competition*. New York: McGraw-Hill.

Neil Chesanow. (1985). *The World-Class Executive; Everything You Need to Know to Do Business Around The World*. New York: Bantam Books. First published by Rawson in 1985.

Pat Choate and Juyne Linger. (1986). *The High Flex Society: Shaping America's Economic Future*. New York: Alfred A. Knopf.

Robert C. Christopher. (1986). *Second to None; American Companies in Japan*. New York: Crown Publishers.

Benjamin J. Cohen. (1986). *In Whose Interest? International Banking and American Foreign Policy*. New Haven, CT: Yale University Press. A Council on Foreign Relations Book.

Virgil D. Collins. (1935). *World Marketing,* ed. Henry Assael. Salem, NH: Ayer & Co. A reprint of the original 1935 ed. Times have changed, many things haven't.

Companion, (1986). *Multinational Executive Travel Companion.* Cambridge: Multinational Executive. Annual.

Lennie Copeland and Lewis Griggs. (1985). *Going International: How to Make Friends and Deal Effectively in the Global Marketplace.* New York: Random House. Helpful once you have global strategy.

John M. Culbertson. (1986). "The Folly of Free Trade," *Harvard Business Review,* 86, 5, September–October 1986, 122–128.

E. E. Cument, ed. (1984). *Exporter's Encyclopaedia, 1985-86.* Washington: Brookings Institution.

Edward W. Cundiff and Marye Tharp Hilger. (1984). *Marketing in the International Environment.* Englewood Cliffs, NJ: Prentice-Hall.

Michael R. Czinkota, ed. (1982). *Export Management.* New York: Praeger Publishers.

Michael R. Czinkota. (1982–2). *Export Policy: A Global Assessment.* New York: Praeger Publishers.

Gary Davies. (1985). *Managing Export Distribution.* N. Pomfret, VT: David and Charles.

Stanley M. Davis. (1985). *Managing Corporate Culture.* Cambridge: Ballinger, Harper & Row.

Terrence E. Deal & Allen A. Kennedy. (1982). *Corporate Cultures: The Rites and Rituals of Corporate Life.* Reading, MA: Addison-Wesley Publishing.

Deloitte, Haskins and Sells. (1985). *Expanding Your Business Overseas.* New York: Deloitte, Haskins and Sells.

Howard F. Didsbury, Jr., ed. (1985). *Global Economy: Today, Tomorrow and the Transition.* Bethesda, MD: World Future Society.

Susan P. Douglas and C. Samuel Craig. (1983). *International Marketing Research.* Englewood Cliffs, NJ: Prentice-Hall.

Peter F. Drucker. (1986). "The Changing Multinational." *The Wall Street Journal,* January 15, 1986.

Dun and Bradstreet. (1986). *Exporters Encyclopaedia*. New York: Dun & Bradstreet. Annual.

Dun's Marketing. (1986). *Export Documentation Handbook*. New York: Dun's Marketing.

Linda Edwards. (1978). "Present Shock, and How to Avoid It Abroad," *Across the Board*. New York: Conference Board.

Richard E. Ellsworth. (1985). "Capital Markets and Competitive Decline," *Harvard Business Review,* 63, 5, September–October 1985, pp. 171–83. Japanese and German capital is invested long term.

Euromonitor Publications. (1986-7). *International Marketing Data and Statistics*. London: Euromonitor Publications. 1986–87 edition.

John Fayerweather. (1978). *International Business Strategy and Administration*. Cambridge: Ballinger, Harper & Row.

Henry Ferguson. (1985). "Global Strategy: What's That?" *Intercom*. International Business Council Mid-America, November 1985.

Henry Ferguson. (1987). *Manual for Multicultural Education*, 2nd rev. ed., Yarmouth, ME: Intercultural Press.

Henry Ferguson. (1987–2). "A Checklist for Foreign Trade," *Association Management,* 39, 5, May 1987, pp. 65–66.

Glen Fisher. (1980). *International Negotiation; A Cross-Cultural Perspective*. Yarmouth, ME: Intercultural Press.

Roger Fisher & William Ury. (1981). *Getting to Yes: Negotiating without Giving In*. Boston: Houghton Mifflin. Also available in paper from Penguin.

Gale Research. (1986). *Countries of the World and Their Leaders*. Detroit: Gale Research.

Colin Gilligan and Martin Hird. (1986). *International Marketing: Strategy and Management*. Dover, NH: Croom Helm.

William P. Glade, et al. (1970). *Marketing in a Developing Nation: The Competitive Behavior of Peruvian Industry*. Lexington, MA: D. C. Heath.

John L. Graham & Yoshihiro Sano. (1984). *Smart Bargaining: Doing Business with the Japanese*. Cambridge: Ballinger, Harper & Row.

William B. Gudykunst. (1984). *Communicating with Strangers: An Approach to Intercultural Communication.* Reading, MA: Addison-Wesley Publishing.

H. Hakansson. (1982). *International Marketing and Purchasing of Industrial Goods: An Interaction Approach.* New York: John Wiley & Sons.

David Halberstam (1986). *The Reckoning.* New York: William Morrow.

Edward T. Hall. (1959). *The Silent Language.* Garden City, NY: Doubleday.

Edward T. Hall. (1969). *The Hidden Dimension.* Garden City, NY: Doubleday.

Edward T. Hall. (1976). *Beyond Culture.* Garden City, NY: Doubleday.

F. T. Haner. (1980). *Global Business Strategy for the 1980s.* New York: Praeger Publishers. Academic and numbers-driven. Useful.

Philip R. Harris & Robert T. Moran. (1979). *Managing Cultural Differences.* Houston: Gulf Publishing. A second edition appearing in 1987.

Samuel L. Hayden. (1979). Background paper on business employment, *President's Commission on Foreign Language and International Studies.* Washington: Superintendent of Documents.

Samuel L. Hayden. (1980). "Foreign Languages, International Studies, and Business," Annals of American Academy of Political and Social Science. Philadelphia: American Academy.

Steven R. Hendryx. (1986). "The China Trade: Making a Deal Work," *Harvard Business Review,* 64, 4, July–August 1986, pp. 75–84.

Richard J. Herring, ed. (1986). *Managing Foreign Exchange Risk.* Cambridge: Cambridge University Press.

Craig R. Hickman & Michael A. Silva. (1986). *Creating Excellence: Managing Corporate Culture, Strategy and Change in the New Age.* New York: New American Library.

Tyler G. Hicks. (1987). *How to Prepare and Process Export-Im-*

port Documents. A Fully Illustrated Guide, 3rd. ed. Rockville Center, NY: International Wealth Success.

Geert Hofstede. (1984). *Culture's Consequences: International Differences in Work-Related Values.* Beverly Hills, CA: Sage Publications.

David S. Hoopes. (1983). *Global Guide to International Business.* New York: Facts on File. Global executive's principal reference book.

Graham Jackson et al. (1981). *Effective Patterns of International Marketing.* New York: State Mutual.

Subhash C. Jain and Lewis R. Tucker. (1986). *International Marketing: Managerial Perspectives.* Boston: Kent Publishing.

Japan Directory. (1986). *Japan Directory.* Japan Directory Div., Japan Press, Ltd., CPO, Box 6, Tokyo. Annual. $140. Tokyo: Japan Press.

Somkid Jatusripitak. (1985). *Exporting Behavior of Manufacturing Firms.* Ann Arbor, MI: UMI Research Press.

Ruel C. Kahler. (1983). *International Marketing.* Houston: Southwestern Publishing Co.

Ashok Kapoor. (1970). *International Business Negotiations: A Study in India.* New York: New York University Press.

Ashok Kapoor. (1975). *Planning for International Business Negotiation.* Cambridge: Ballinger, Harper & Row.

Robert E. Karp and Allan Gorlick. (1974). *Cross-Cultural Considerations of Marketing and Consumer Behavior.* New York: Irvington Press.

Erdener Kaynak. (1982). *Marketing in the Third World.* New York: Praeger Publishers.

Erdener Kaynak, ed. (1985). *Global Perspectives in Marketing.* New York: Praeger Publishers.

Warren J. Keegan. (1984). *Multinational Marketing Management.* Englewood Cliffs, NJ: Prentice-Hall.

Kelly's. (1986). *Kelly's Manufacturers and Merchants Directory.* Annual. E. Grimstead: U.K. Kelly's Directory. UK directory.

Stephen J. Kobrin. (1984). *International Expertise in American*

Business: How to Learn and Play with the Kids on the Street. New York: Institute of International Education.

Kompass Directories. *Kompass Directories* (for 15 nations). Croner Publications, 211-03 Jamaica Av, Queens Village, NY 11428. Queens Village, NY: Croner Publications.

Philip Kotler et al. (1985). *The New Competition: What Theory Z Didn't Tell You about Marketing.* Englewood Cliffs, NJ: Prentice-Hall.

V. H. Kripilani. (1984). *International Marketing.* New York: Random House.

Joseph G. LaPolombara. (1977). *Multinational Corporations.* New York: Conference Board.

Theodore Levitt. (1986). *The Marketing Imagination.* New York: Free Press. Contains "Globalization of Markets." New, expanded ed.

John R. Liebman and Robert L. Johnson. (1985). *Export Controls in the United States.* New York: Harcourt Brace Jovanovich.

Abraham H. Maslow. (1970). *Motivation and Personality,* 2nd ed. New York: Harper & Row.

J. B. McCall and M. B. Warrington. (1984). *Marketing by Agreement: A Cross-Cultural Approach to Business Negotiations.* New York: John Wiley & Sons.

Douglas McGregor. (1960). *The Human Side of Enterprise.* New York: McGraw-Hill. Theory Y is outlined here.

Foseco Minsep, comp. (1982). *Business Traveller's Handbook: How to Get Along with People in 100 Countries.* Englewood Cliffs, NJ: Prentice-Hall.

John H. Mitchell. (1984). *Ceremonial Time: Fifteen Thousand Years on One Square Mile.* Garden City, NY: Doubleday. A beautiful book with new sense of time.

Robert T. Moran and Philip R. Harris. (1982). *Managing Cultural Synergy.* Houston: Gulf Publishing. v. 2 of Harris, 1979. Important, useful.

Robert T. Moran. (1984). *Getting Your Yen's Worth.* Houston: Gulf Publishing.

Gerald David Newbould. (1978). *Going International: The Experiences of Smaller Companies Overseas*. New York: John Wiley & Sons.

Nordisk (1986). *Key to Scandanavia/Nordisk Handelskalendar*. Scan-Report A/S, 49 Sydvestvej, DK-2600 Glostrup, Denmark. Annual. $60. Glostrup, Denmark: Scan-Report.

Ardan J. O'Reilly. (1985). *International Marketing*. Brookfield, VT: Brookfield.

Official Export Guide. (1986). Philadelphia: North American Publishing Co. Annual.

Kenichi Ohmae. (1985). *Triad Power; The Coming Shape of Global Competition*. New York: Free Press.

Organization for Economic Cooperation & Development. (1984). *Competition and Trade Policies: Their Interaction*. Washington, DC: OECD.

S. P. Padolecchia. (1979). *Marketing in the Developing World*. New York: Advent.

Stanley Paliwoda. (1981). *Joint East-West Marketing and Production Ventures*. Aldershot, U.K.: Gower.

Jacques L. Picard. (1978). *Marketing Decisions for European Operations in the United States*, ed. Gunter Dufey. Ann Arbor, MI: UMI Research Press.

Michael E. Porter. (1986). *Competition in Global Industries*. Boston: Harvard Business School.

Price Waterhouse. (1985). *Expanding into Exports*. New York: Price Waterhouse and Company.

Lucian W. Pye. (1986). "The China Trade: Making the Deal," *Harvard Business Review,* 64, 4, July–August 1986, pp. 74–80.

J. A. Quelch and E. J. Hoff. (1986). "Customizing Global Marketing," *Harvard Business Review,* 64, 3, May–June 1986, pp. 59–68.

Reference Book. *Reference Book for World Traders: A Guide for Exporters and Importers*. Queens Village, NY: Croner Publications.

David A. Ricks. (1983). *Big Business Blunders: Mistakes in*

Multinational Marketing. Homewood, IL: Dow Jones-Irwin. A "must" for the budding global executive.

Franklin R. Root. (1987). *Entry Strategies for International Markets.* Lexington, MA: D. C. Heath.

Marlene L. Rossman. (1986). *The International Businesswoman: A Guide to Success in the Global Marketplace.* New York: Praeger Publishers.

Roy Rowan. (1985). *The Intuitive Manager.* Boston: Little, Brown.

Diana Rowland. (1986). *Japanese Business Etiquette: A Practical Guide to Success with the Japanese.* New York: Warner Books.

Pat Ryan, ed. (1982). *International Directory of Marketing Research Houses and Services,* 20th ed. New York: American Marketing Association. (Called "The Green Book.")

Dietrich L. Schaup. (1978). *A Cross-Cultural Study of a Multinational Company.* New York: Praeger Publishers.

Edgar H. Schein. (1985). *Organizational Culture and Leadership.* San Francisco: Jossey-Bass. An academic study of management culture.

George J. Schultz, ed. (1977). *Foreign Trade Marketplace.* Detroit: Gale Research.

S. Prakash Sethi and Hamid Etemad. (1986). *International Context of Marketing Strategy: Designing and Implementing Strategies for Competition at Home and Abroad.* Cambridge: Ballinger, Harper & Row.

Mitsuaki Shimaguchi. (1978). *Marketing Channels in Japan.* Ann Arbor, MI: UMI Research Press.

Allan J. Siposs. (1985). *Exporting: Practical Guidelines for Entrepreneurs and Managers.* Irvine, CA: International Commercial Service. Updated ed.

Robert D. Smither. (1984). *Competitors and Comrades: Culture, Economics and Personality.* New York: Praeger Publishers.

Sondra Snowdon. (1986). *The Global Edge; How Your Company Can Win in the International Marketplace.* New York: Simon & Schuster.

Edward C. Stewart. (1972). *American Cultural Patterns: A Cross-cultural Perspective.* Yarmouth, ME: Intercultural Press.

Telex Directory. (1986). *International Telex Directory.* New York: International Publishing Service. Annual. $140. International Publishing Service, 114 E. 32nd St., New York, NY 10016.

Vern Terpstra. (1982). *International Dimensions of Marketing,* ed. David A. Ricks. Boston: Kent Publishing Co.

Vern Terpstra. (1983). *International Marketing,* 3rd. ed. Hinsdale, IL: Dryden Press. A rare textbook that regards culture.

Hans Thorelli et al. (1975). *The Information Seekers: An International Study of Consumer Information and Advertising Image.* Cambridge: Ballinger, Harper & Row.

Hans Thorelli and Helmut Becker, eds. (1980). *International Marketing Strategy,* rev. ed. Elmsford, NY: Pergamon Press.

United Kingdom Marketing Handbook, 1982–83. New York: International Publications. Among many regional directories.

United Nations. (1985). *Yearbook of International Trade Statistics,* 2 v. New York: United Nations.

U.S. Department of Commerce. (1975). *Directory of Export Management Companies.* Washington: U.S. Department of Commerce. Updated periodically.

U.S. Department of Commerce, ITA. *Trade Opportunities Program.* Washington: International Trade Administration. Bulletin issued weekly; special selections available on request.

Martin van Mesdag. (1987). "Winging It in Foreign Markets," *Harvard Business Review,* 65, 1, January–February 1987, pp. 71–74.

Harry M. Venedikian and Gerald Warfield. (1986). *Export-Import Financing,* 2nd ed. New York: John Wiley & Sons.

Raymond Vernon and Louis T. Wells, Jr. (1986). *The Manager in the International Economy.* Englewood Cliffs, NJ: Prentice-Hall.

Pompiliu Verzariu. (1985). *Countertrade, Barter, and Offsets: New Strategies for Profit in International Trade.* New York: McGraw-Hill.

Ingo Walker and Trade Murray, eds. (1982). *Handbook of International Business*. New York: John Wiley & Sons.

Washington Researchers. (1979). *Sources of Aid and Information for U.S. Exporters,* ed. Donna M. Jablonski. Washington: Washington Researchers.

Ross A. Webber, comp. (1969). *Culture and Management*. Homewood, IL: Richard D. Irwin.

Rolf H. Wild. (1986). *Strategy for Export: Foreign Business Development for Small Companies*. Asheville, NC: Thurau Press.

M. Y. Yoshino. (1971). *Japanese Marketing System: Adaptations and Innovations*. Cambridge: MIT Press.

RESOURCE ORGANIZATIONS

There are many organizations offering resources for both the novice and the experienced global executive. We have listed a few of them here. Some are associations or public agencies that offer free information, the most important of which is the United States Department of Commerce, International Trade Administration. (Remember, if you want ITA/DOC help, start by going to your *regional* office where you will be referred to the trade representative for your area.) Some of the resources listed provide database services or published reports, for which there are charges.

In dozens of countries, there are American chambers of commerce. By all means check in with them, get their membership lists, and start networking, but don't expect them to provide either market research or firm trade leads.

Two items in the Reference section should be used: Hoopes' *Global Guide to International Business* and Washington Researcher's *Sources of Aid and Information.*

Africa
Continental Africa Chamber of Commerce
Box 33144
Washington, DC 20033
(202) 722-4575

ADP Network
ADP Network Services
175 Jackson Pl.
Ann Arbor, MI 48106
(313) 769-6800
International time sharing data.

BI/Data
BI/Data. Business International Corp.
1 Dag Hammarskjold Pl.
New York, NY 10017.
Reports on 35 major economies, 131 nations.

BI/Washington
Business International Corp.
1625 Eye St., NW
Washington, DC 20006
(202) 833-8600
Many seminars, publications.

BIZ-DEK
BIZ-DEK, Chase Manhattan Bank
1 Chase Manhattan Plaza
New York, NY 10081
Monthly abstracts on international business subjects.

Chamber of Commerce
Chamber of Commerce of the United States
1615 H St., NW
Washington, DC 20062
(202) 463-5427
Publications from International Division.

Commerce
International Trade Administration
U.S. Department of Commerce
Washington, DC 20230
Contact your Regional DOC office first.

Conference Board
The Conference Board
845 3rd Ave.
New York, NY 10022
(212) 759-0900
Global investment flows.

Countertrade
National Association of Trade Exchanges
27801 Euclid Ave., #440
Euclid, OH 44132
(216) 731-1094
For referrals to countertrade exchanges.

Data Resources
Data Resources, Inc.
24 Hartwell Ave.
Lexington, MA 02173
(617) 861-0165
Much economic data from around the globe.

Dun & Bradstreet
Dun & Bradstreet International
1 World Trade Center, #9069
New York, NY 10048
(212) 938-8578
Marketing information of rich variety.

Economist
The Economist Intelligence Unit
75 Rockefeller Plaza
New York, NY 10019

Export Companies
National Export Company
65 Liberty St.
New York, NY 10005
(212) 766-1343
EMC trade association: leads to EMCs.

Japan
Japan Economic Institute of America
1000 Connecticut Ave. NW, #211
Washington, DC 20036
(202) 296-5633
Official agency with much information.

Latin America
Chamber of Commerce of Latin America
1 World Trade Center, #2343
New York, NY 10048
(212) 432-9313
Inter-American Foreign Trade (monthly)

National Affairs
Bureau of National Affairs, Inc.
1231 25th St., NW
Washington, DC 20037
(202) 452-4200
Export Shipping Manual, weeklies.

NTIS
National Technical Information Service
U.S. Department of Commerce
5268 Ft. Royal Rd.
Springfield, VA 22161
(703) 487-4600
Much translated technical information.

Overseas Marketing
Overseas Sales and Marketing Association
5715 N. Lincoln Ave.
Chicago, IL 60659
(312) 334-1502
Association of export management companies.

Predicasts
Predicasts, Inc.
11001 Cedar Ave.
Cleveland, OH 44106
(216) 795-3000
Subject index to international business.

Sharp, I.P.
I. P. Sharp Associates
Suite 1900, 2 First Canadian Pl.
Toronto, ON M5X 1E3
(416) 364-5361
Provides database for World Trade Councils.

System Development
System Development Corp.
Information Services
2500 Colorado Ave.
Santa Monica, CA 90406
On-line international business data.

Tourism
U.S. Travel & Tourism Administration
U.S. Department of Commerce
Washington, DC 20230
(202) 377-0140
Helpful for marketing travel or tourism.

U.S. Council
U.S. Council for International Business
1212 Avenue of the Americas
New York, NY 10036
(212) 354-4480
U.S. affiliate of International Chamber of Commerce

Washington Research
Washington Researchers
918 16th St., NW
Washington, DC 20006
(202) 828-4800
Important published resources for export.

World Trade
World Trade Institute, Export Development Group
1 World Trade Center, 55th floor
New York, NY 10048
(212) 466-3068
Port Authority has marketing data.

Worldcasts
Worldcasts
200 University Cr. Res. Ctr.
11001 Cedar Ave.
Cleveland, OH 44106
International version of Predicasts.

INDEX

Joseph H. Lauder Institute of Management and International Studies, 136
Just-in-time inventory control, 101

K

Kaynak, Erdener, 155, 161, 163
Keegan, Warren J., 28
Kelley's Directory, 170
Kennedy, Allen A., 10, 52
Kentucky Fried Chicken, 158
Kiam, Victor, 125–26
Kidder Peabody, 38
Kobrin, Stephen J., 138
Kompass, 170
Kotler, Philip, 21
Kpelle society of Africa, 93–94

L

Labor force information, 158–59; *see also* Non-American employees
Language
   and acculturation, 142–43
   blunders, 14, 149
   of business, 136–38
   cultural and social aspects, 141–43
   educational failure, 139
   learning guides, 146–47
   myth of universal English, 136
   need for translation, 137
   need to learn, 138–40
   role in culture, 135–36
   training, 149–50
   use of interpreters and translators, 147–49
   varieties of English, 137
Larrabee, Harold, 234
Latin America, 191
Lauder, Leonard A., 136
Leadership (Burns), 230
Leadership in management, 230–31
Letters of credit, 107, 115–16
Levitt, Theodore, 6–7, 10, 12, 97–98, 104
Libraries
   company, 166
   overseas, 157
Licensing, 30
Linear negotiation, 215
Loyalty of employees, 71–73

M

McCall, J. B., 87
MacGregor, Douglas, 231
Macro economic market research, 168
Management; *see also* Global executives
   advantages of generalists, 44
   authority, 89–90
   commitment to globalization, 49–50
   dangers of offshore specialization, 78–80
   of details, 114–16
   drawn into overseas operations, 76–80
   ethical standards, 234–35
   fundamental shifts in, 40
   impact of investment attitudes on, 130–32
   incentives and rewards, 132–33
   intuition as a tool, 175–76
   and leadership, 230–31
   morality and corruption, 232–34
   need to change perspective, 50
   of non-American employees, 87–97
   overseas motivation, 112–14
   people-centered, 231–32
   planned redundancy, 74–75
   predeparture orientation, 62
   recruitment, 69–70
   role of on-site executive, 173–75
   specific globalization concerns, 52–53
   tasks and alternatives, 88–89
   transactional, 230
   understanding offshore markets, 42–43
   values, 231–35
   women in, 70, 94–96
Manipulation of people, 44–45
Manufactures, captive, 7
Marketing
   adjustments for globalization, 83
   credit policies, 106–8
   delivery of products, 101–102
   keys to success, 98
   pricing policies, 104–6
   product quality, 97–99
   replies to overseas inquiries, 102–4
   service dependability, 99–100

LUIS